DENIS MACSHANE was a Labour MP serving in Tony Blair's government as Minister for Europe. He was first elected as MP for Rotherham in 1994 and served until his resignation in 2012. MacShane studied at Oxford and London Universities and has four children. He is a prominent commentator on European issues.

———————————————

The UK's Brexit vote in 2016 and the inconclusive general election just 12 months later have unleashed a wave of chaos and uncertainty – on the eve of formal negotiations with the EU.

Denis MacShane – former MP and Europe minister under Tony Blair – has a unique insider perspective on the events that led to the Brexit vote and ultimately to Theresa May's ill-fated election gamble of June 2017.

He argues that Brexit will not mean full rupture with Europe and that British business will overcome the rightwing forces of the Conservative back-benches and UKIP, which have already been weakened by the latest election. Although negotiations with the EU may prove excruciating, Britain cannot and will not divorce itself from the continent of Europe. Indeed, the European question will remain the defining political issue of our time.

D0108140

'As a multi-lingual citizen of the EU with unique access to key Brexit negotiators, Denis MacShane is an acute observer of post-referendum politics. He predicted the Leave vote back in January 2015. His superbly argued case against the fatalism of defeated Remainers, and the cynical financial interests behind the Leave campaign demands the widest possible readership.'

Ian McEwan

'Denis MacShane, the former Minister of Europe, is almost unique among British commentators on the EU in spending more time in European capitals than in London. He therefore enjoys an extraordinarily rich network of European political contacts, which allows him great insight into how the EU and its member-states are changing. In January 2015 MacShane correctly predicted that Brexit would happen, and anyone interested in the next stages of the Brexit saga would be well advised to read this book.'

Charles Grant, Centre for European Reform

'Britain has been involved in European affairs for centuries to ensure the UK's security and economic health. Now Britain is set to leave the European Union. But is the narrow vote in the referendum on June 2016 the last and only word on Britain's future relationship with the continent and what does it mean for the future of the unity of the United Kingdom? Denis MacShane was a UK politician with one of the widest network of friends and contacts in many EU capitals. Remarkably, he predicted the referendum outcome in his book *Brexit: How Britain Will Leave Europe* in January 2015. Now he argues that Britain can and must remain part of Europe. Everyone involved in the Europe debate, whether or not they agree with the author, will find plenty of facts and arguments in this book relevant to this next chapter in our island's history.'

Brendan Simms, Director of the Forum on Geopolitics, Cambridge and co-author of *Donald Trump: The Making of a World View*

'The question of Brexit is set to dominate British political life for the foreseeable future. There has never been anything like it before. A closely fought referendum with a narrow outcome leading to a decision to leave the European Union, as well as the end of a prime minister's career and the arrival of the second female prime minister in British history. Now the fraught and difficult negotiations are under way. Denis MacShane has been one of the most passionate pro-Europeans in Parliament and Government and today still networks across Europe, speaking and writing in more than one language on the future of the EU and about Brexit. Leavers and Remainers will find plenty in his new book to agree and disagree with. It reflects the pro-European commitment of Denis MacShane but adds facts and arguments, especially from across the Channel and Irish Sea, that will interest anyone following this new chapter in our national life.'

Adam Boulton

'All is not lost. That's the important message of hope from one of the very few who forecast the referendum result correctly. Brexit is the biggest challenge for Britain in a generation as a hard UKIP-style Brexit would align Britain with Donald Trump and Vladimir Putin, rather than with progressive forces and friends in Europe such as Emmanuel Macron and Angela Merkel. Denis MacShane has the deepest knowledge of Europe, having spent much of his life working with European political and civil society. He has been the most prominent pro-European voice as an MP and Minister. This book exposes the dark forces that won the Brexit vote and how it may be possible to take them on and ensure that British citizens do not lose all rights to trade, work or live in Europe. This is a must-read for those who need encouragement to fight on for Britain's close relationship with the EU.'

Polly Toynbee

BREXIT, NO EXIT

Why (in the End) Britain Won't Leave Europe

DENIS MACSHANE

I.B. TAURIS
LONDON · NEW YORK

Published in 2017 by
I.B.Tauris & Co. Ltd
London • New York
www.ibtauris.com

Copyright © 2017 Denis MacShane

The right of Denis MacShane to be identified as the author of
this work has been asserted by the author in accordance with the
Copyright, Designs and Patents Act 1988.

All rights reserved. Except for brief quotations in a review, this book,
or any part there of, may not be reproduced, stored in or introduced into
a retrieval system, or transmitted, in any form or by any means, electronic,
mechanical, photocopying, recording or otherwise, without
the prior written permission of the publisher.

References to websites were correct at the time of writing.

ISBN: 978 1 78453 878 1
eISBN: 978 1 78672 257 7
ePDF: 978 1 78673 257 6

A full CIP record for this book is available from the British Library

A full CIP record is available from the Library of Congress
Library of Congress Catalog Card Number: available

Printed and bound by CPI Group (UK) Ltd, Croydon, CR0 4YY

MIX
Paper from
responsible sources
FSC® C020471
FSC
www.fsc.org

CONTENTS

PREFACE   vii

PART ONE: THE IMPACT OF BREXIT

1   THE BREXIT REVOLUTION   1

2   BREXIT AND TRUMP: TOWARDS A NEW WORLD

    DISORDER?   17

3   BREXIT: A NEVER-ENDING SAGA   24

4   NATIONALIST IDENTITARIANISM   42

5   CLOSING FRONTIERS   53

6   THERESA MAY: HOW MUCH BREXIT DOES SHE REALLY

    WANT?   62

7   EUROPE REACTS   69

PART TWO: WHY BREXIT HAPPENED

8   THE ESTABLISHMENT WAS WARNED BREXIT WOULD

    HAPPEN BUT BURIED ITS HEAD IN THE SAND   89

9   THE BREXIT GENERATION   **98**

10   THE LEAVERS   **106**

11   THE CAMPAIGN   **117**

12   LABOUR FAILS TO MAKE AN IMPACT BEFORE, DURING

     AND AFTER   **129**

13   THE BBC'S DISDAIN FOR EUROPE WON IT FOR BREXIT   **145**

PART THREE: BREXIT IN THE CHANNEL: BRITAIN

    CUT OFF

14   BUSINESS HATES BREXIT BUT STAYS SILENT   **157**

15   FIXING AN EXIT: TRADE   **167**

16   EUROPEANS *CHEZ NOUS* AND BRIT EXPATS IN EUROPE   **188**

17   DIVORCE AND A NEW PARTNERSHIP   **203**

18   BREXIT SPELLS DANGER FOR IRELAND AND CONCERN

     IN SCOTLAND   **214**

PART FOUR: WHY BREXIT WILL CHANGE EUROPE

19   HOW EUROPE CAN SURVIVE BREXIT   **225**

20   WHAT IS TO BE DONE?   **240**

21   WHY THE EURO WILL SURVIVE   **250**

22   NEW POLITICS ARE NEEDED IN EUROPE   **261**

23   THE EU AFTER 2019 MUST BE DIFFERENT OR IT WILL DIE   **270**

AFTERWORD   **281**

24   HOW THE UK STAYS IN EUROPE   **281**

    INDEX   **294**

PREFACE

This book explains the main reasons why Brexit came about and why the populist plebiscite of 23 June 2016 and the election of 8 June 2017, which saw a major defeat for the pro-Brexit forces in Britain, are not the last word on Britain's place in Europe. Indeed, already by spring 2017 opinion polls were showing that a majority of voters now thought the decision to leave Europe was a mistake.

The election of June 2017 was when the 48 per cent of the voters in the country who said No to Brexit twelve months previously, and were then treated with contempt by the Conservative government, took their revenge.

Particularly in London, the candidates who opposed Brexit from Labour and the Liberal Democrats did very well. Remain voters kicked out the pro-Brexit Conservative MP in Kensington and Chelsea, the wealthiest constituency in the country, and previously a sure-fire Conservative seat.

After Emmanuel Macron in France, it was the turn of British voters to astonish themselves and the world with an election result that was unthinkable six months previously.

In 2016 David Cameron believed that his cynical plebiscite on Europe could not be lost. In 2017 Theresa May believed her opportunistic early election would result in Labour being crushed. Never have two British prime ministers shown such lack of judgement in just twelve months.

Theresa May, whose election manifesto was almost a UKIP document in its repudiation of Europe, suffered a humiliating defeat after less than a year in office. Although she did not resign on the spot as David Cameron did after his Brexit referendum defeat the year before, few could see Mrs May staying long in office after voters rejected her policy and her decision to call an opportunistic election.

Mrs May had opted for a hardline on Brexit but she no longer has a majority in the House of Commons for this policy. The Northern Irish Democratic Unionist Party is very right-wing on issues like gay and women's rights or climate change but its voters base is in Northern Ireland's farming community which depends on there being no border or customs clearing between Northern Ireland in the UK and Ireland in the EU.

Jeremy Corbyn, the leftist Labour leader, has saved his honour and his focus on domestic issues like austerity, cuts to public services like health care and the police found an echo especially among young voters.

Mrs May and the pro-Brexit press in Britain tried to portray Corbyn as a friend of terrorists, a leftwing extremist living in an imagined left-wing 1970s past. But voters saw an elderly man with a white beard talking about injustice and inequality at home and abroad and young voters in particular liked the message and gave Corbyn their support.

But the Labour leader only added 32 MPs and the party is still far short of a majority in the Commons. In London, where many Labour candidates defied Corbyn's support for leaving the Single Market and imposing immigration controls on fellow Europeans and campaigned to stay in Europe, Labour did very well.

The losers of the election were English and Scottish nationalisms. The UKIP vote disappeared and pro-European Liberal Democrats won seats from the Conservatives in London even if the party's former leader, Nick Clegg, was defeated by Labour in Sheffield.

In Scotland, Scottish nationalism suffered major blows as Scottish Nationalist Party seats fell to Conservatives, Labour and the Liberal Democrats. The party's leader in the House of Commons and the former Scottish Nationalist leader, Alex Salmond, were both defeated as Scottish voters rejected calls for independence and separation from the rest of the United Kingdom.

Many assumptions about British politics have turned out to be false. Mrs May was an accidental prime minister who arrived in Downing Street after the Brexit plebisicite because all the main anti-European Tory MPs who expected to take over after David Cameron resigned had stabbed each other in the back, front, top and bottom so that she was the only senior Tory minister left standing as her colleagues destroyed each other.

She had no clear programme for government. She made a powerful pro-European speech in April 2016 but then adopted UKIP policy on Europe. She refused to explain to the public what the costs and consequence of a hard Brexit would be. In exchange, the public refused to endorse her when she asked for a personal mandate in the general election many saw as cynical.

The assumption that Corbyn's leftism would destroy Labour has been shown to be false. The assumption that the mass circulation British press, with its daily fake news propaganda attacks on the European Union, spoke for Britain is also untrue.

Since 2014 Britain has had two major referendums – on Scottish independence and Brexit – and two general elections. But nothing has been finally decided. Anti-European Conservatives were hoping to be joined by dozens of pro-Brexit candidates but the reverse has happened. A clear majority of British MPs want Britain to stay as fully in Europe as possible. The cause of Europe was lost in Britain in the referendum in June 2016 but won in the election of June 2017.

When Mrs May met President Trump as the first European leader to go and pay homage to the new US president she was seen holding his hand. Now Trump's best friend in Europe has been mortally wounded.

As in Austria when the extreme nationalist candidate was defeated in presidential elections at the end of 2016, in the Netherlands where the anti-immigrant racist Geert Wilders failed in the March 2017 election and then in France where the anti-European Marine Le Pen was rejected in the May 2017 presidential election, Europe has emerged as the winner in the British election.

Important new polling published in the general election for the Best of Britain campaign shows that 50 per cent of British people believe the UK should stay inside the Single Market, against 21 per cent who follow the UKIP–Tory–Labour manifesto acceptance that the UK has to quit the Single Market.

Another question asked: 'Do you think our government should offer EU citizens the right to travel, work, study or retire in Britain, in exchange for EU countries giving British citizens the same rights?' Sixty-two per cent agreed that keeping EU travel, work and retirement rights for British citizens should be a negotiating priority against 17 per cent in favour of immigration controls applied to all EU citizens, including British passport holders, with 21 per cent 'don't knows'.

A final question combining the issue of the Single Market and free movement asked: 'Do you think our government should or should not allow free movement of people between Britain and EU countries in exchange for the EU allowing British businesses full access to the European Single Market?' Forty-three per cent supported such a deal, 31 per cent rejected it and 26 per cent were unsure.

It is deep in the instincts of the average British citizen that we do well when markets and frontiers are open to British commerce, citizens and ideas. A group of 29 Labour MPs issued their own manifesto during the election saying that Labour should back continued full membership of the Single Market.

Organised by Chuka Umunna MP, the group said any form of trade deal other than the Single Market would make working people worse off and mean higher costs for business, fewer jobs and inflated prices.

Umunna told the BBC that external immigration controls which would require leaving the Single Market could be replaced by internal management of migration, which I discuss later in the book. London Labour candidates supported this line and put pictures of the pro-EU Mayor of London, Sadiq Khan, on their election leaflets.

They did much better with the unambiguously pro-EU manifesto than Labour candidates in the Midlands and the North where MPs stood on a manifesto which supported immigration controls and in some cases lost their seats.

It should not be forgotten that in June last year there was a clear majority of Remain MPs in the Commons even if the BBC and the press bigged up the loudmouthed anti-Europeans like Boris Johnson, Michael Gove, Iain Duncan Smith, Andrea Leadsom and David Davis. MPs from Scotland, Wales and Northern Ireland (other than Unionist supremacists) were all opposed to amputating Britain from Europe. So too were most Labour MPs and more than half of Conservative MPs.

In nominal terms there is no election until 2022 though given the absence of a majority for the Conservatives the possibility of an earlier election remains a likely possibility. The Labour government of 1974–79 limped on despite the absence of a clear majority thanks to the support of Nothern Irish MPs.

Today MPs can stand back and consider the wider national interest rather than looking over their shoulders at UKIP as many Tories have been doing for a decade or worrying about white working class voters in Labour heartlands.

Professor Matthew Goodwin predicted that UKIP would win 5–6 MPs in 2015 and Labour MPs Frank Field and Dan Jarvis prophesied early this year that UKIP would win Labour heartland seats in the North of England.

But the UKIP threat has run its course like the Poujadiste populist movement in France in the 1950s when the French nationalist populist movement looked as if it would displace mainstream parties. The UKIP leader, Paul Nuttall, came a poor third in the constituency he boasted he would win and resigned.

From time immemorial Britain, like all dynamic economies, has needed to import labour. The Irish and Afro-Caribbeans came in the 1950s and 1960s. The Pakistanis, Indians and Bangladeshis in the 1970s and 1980s. Europeans from ex-communist countries in the 1990s and after 2000 and up to a million Portuguese, Greek, Italian and Spanish after the financial crash of 2007/9. London has been home to 400,000 French citizens and other professionals from all European countries, many drawn to work in the financial services sector after the creation of the Single Market which allowed every bank, investment and pension fund and currency trader to operate across 27 borders under EU rules.

It is hard to see after the election how a British government can cut off British firms, especially those in the service sector, from access to European talent and willingness to work hard, often for low pay and in parts of the nation where such employment pools do not exist. Britain can revert to Cold-War era work and residence permits, or it can perhaps examine how the Swiss adapted to their referendum decision of February 2014 calling for a ban on EU immigrants. By changing internal labour market rules with the aim of controlling immigration while still avoiding discriminating against EU citizens, the Swiss maintained access to the EU economy. In any event, the majority of immigrants into the UK at any given time are from outside the EU, so there is plenty of scope to introduce new immigration controls without victimising Europeans and provoking reciprocal barriers hurting British people.

We now learn that just five very rich individuals provided 61 per cent of the funds for the Brexit campaign. Far from being a win for the powerless, Brexit was bought with the wealth of the richest of the land. Brexit is part of the new politics discussed by the geo-political writer and former editor of *The Economist* Bill Emmott in his book *The Fate of the West: The Battle to Save the World's Most Successful Political Idea*. Emmott argues that the fate of the West is in 'the hands of our ability [...] as citizens of Western countries [...] to resist attempts to close doors, borders and minds'. The Brexit–Trump–Putin (BTP) world of post-truth, propaganda politics does indeed need to be challenged. If the BTP axis wins we are at the beginning of the end of the long decades of peace, prosperity and liberal freedoms that a uniting Europe put in place after 1945. Over the last 70 years, working in a broader Euro-Atlantic community of partnership with North America, Europe turned its back on the idea of a Europe of the 'nation *über alles*' that came into being in the nineteenth century and reached its apogee of violence, hate and extermination in the first half of the twentieth century.

Brexit was a victory for a wealthy, powerful elite with the enthusiastic, and unprecedented, backing of newspapers and tacit endorsement from broadcasters, as well as the bottomless purses they have had since the 1990s to achieve their ends.

The anti-European isolationists won a narrow victory in June 2016. Just 37 per cent of the electorate was persuaded by a 20-year political project to undo Britain's agreement to international treaties linking us to Europe. But the vote is not the last word. As David Davis, the Brexit minister, has stated: 'If a democracy cannot change its mind, it ceases to be a democracy.' Although some try to turn the vote of 23 June 2016 into a holy sacrament, and mark the date as a sacred day whose significance will live for a thousand years, in truth it was just a vote.

One vote, once, for ever and ever is a concept that belongs in the Robert Mugabe or Vladimir Putin political playbook. In British democracy, we lose a vote, pick ourselves up and keep campaigning for what we believe. I have talked to many Conservative MPs, especially younger ones who entered the House of Commons in 2010 or 2015 and held their seats in 2017. They dislike Brexit intensely and know the damage cutting us apart from Europe will do to Britain. Before the 2017 election their natural loyalty to their prime minister and Mrs May's sense that the Tory government must be seen to give effect to the plebiscite result left Conservative parliamentarians silent and not ready to oppose a course of action they know is disastrous for Britain.

Now the election is over and they are secure in their seats for five years (unless yet one more election is called) their patriotic voices will sound out and provide a counterweight to the extreme anti-EU figures and UKIP fellow-travellers Mrs May put in her first cabinet and those ageing anti-European Tory voices in the unelected House of Lords. The Tories have not survived three centuries as Europe's most enduring and successful party of government by taking fundamentalist positions. Under weak anti-European leaders like William Hague, Iain Duncan Smith, Michael Howard and David Cameron the Conservatives refused to tackle the xenophobia and demagogy of UKIP. The 2017 election has exposed UKIP as a hollow political force. Assuming a minimal resiling from the EU treaties there will be no UKIP MEPs elected in 2019 and they will lose their European Parliament funding for staff, offices, travel and campaigning resources.

UKIP will have served its purpose in frightening David Cameron, with his fusion of upper-class cockiness and political insecurity, into appeasing xenophobic anti-European ideology much as Tory prime ministers in the 1930s were unwilling to challenge xenophobic nationalism. Can the Conservative Party now close the chapter of appeasing anti-European prejudices in Tory Party history, 1997–2017.

The narrow victory for Brexit in the 2016 plebiscite was won on the basis of the most monstrous lies ever told before a key national vote. These lies were never challenged by the BBC, once the guardian of balance and fairness and the champion of hard questioning of politicians telling clear falsehoods. All politicians make dubious promises or forecast a dreadful future if their side does not win. But the Brexit vote was won by telling the biggest lies, repeated incessantly and added to with fresh lies to make an Everest of untruth to persuade people to vote to isolate Britain from its partners and allies.

There are plenty of reasonable and rational objections to how the European Union is structured and run. Euroscepticism is normal. We should all be sceptical of any source of power over what we do. But

Brexit was also won by a foul campaign of hate and xenophobia against Europeans who came to Britain at the invitation of employers to work within a specific labour market based on high employment and low pay. A few days after the vote laminated cards were delivered to the Polish community in Huntingdon. They read, 'Leave the EU – no more Polish vermin.' No British citizen living and working in Europe has had to face the denigration and sneers over many years of mass-circulation newspapers that Poles or Romanians or Slovakians have faced from politicians in UKIP and, sadly, too many others in mainstream parties.

A vote won by such dishonest means cannot stand without challenge. This book seeks to explain why and how it should be challenged. There is not one Brexit but many. In 1950, an exhausted Labour government decided not to participate in European cooperation and integration. Now it is a Conservative minority government which has to decide the extent of our separation from Europe. The 1950s and 1960s were wasted years for Britain, which was not present in shaping our global region's direction of travel on key economic and geo-political issues.

For hardline Brexit supporters, the EU is on the brink of collapse. The need for anti-Europeans to assert that Europe is rotting from within is summed up in the title of Douglas Murray's *The Strange Death of Europe: Immigration, Identity, Islam*, published as the 2017 general election got under way. The book looks at the question of Europe's rejection of 1930s monoculturalism or the concept that Europe's essence lies only in Judeo-Christian ideologies. A decade ago I wrote a book on European anti-Semitism and the threat of Islamist ideology, so I share part of Murray's concern over the negative, indeed dangerous aspects of monotheistic ideologies. Unlike Murray, however, I believe it is by asserting core European values of eighteenth-century rationality and post-1945 humanist social liberalism that we tackle the threat he outlines. Isolating Britain from the working majority in Europe that wants to tackle hate crime and faith-inspired practices that demean women or gay men seems perverse. Finding a solution to the mass movement of refugees fleeing from the US-, UK- and French-initiated wars and conflicts in Arab countries (Iraq, Libya, Syria) in the twenty-first century is indeed a major strategic challenge. It can be met by more intra-European cooperation, not by pulling up drawbridges.

In fact it has been a core argument of Brexit anti-Europeans that a British rupture with the EU would be the first move in the collapse of European integration, such as has been in place since 1945 and given effect by a succession of sovereignty-sharing treaties with their common rule book and enforcement mechanisms. This was put with startling arrogance by Boris Johnson in a speech just before the referendum when he said English nationalist Brexit demagogues and populists were 'speaking for hundreds of millions across Europe who agree with us but who currently have no voice'. This is 'nonsense on stilts', to paraphrase Jeremy Bentham. Anti-Europeanism politics is strong and has been so since the 1950s, fuelled by extremist ideologues of both left and right. Anti-Brexit commentators in London predicted and continue to predict a wave of Brexit-style wins for anti-EU nationalist populism across Europe. It did not happen. First in Austria, then in the Netherlands, then in France, such European fans of Brexit as Geert Wilders and Marine Le Pen failed to win support in national votes. That there is a rise in, as well as a solid base for, nationalist, xenophobic and anti-immigrant politics or anti-Brussels demagogy, including in governments in Poland and Hungary, is not in doubt. But if anything Brexit has been a warning to the rest of Europe that new leadership and a new reforming energy has to be found to avoid a Brexit-style Balkanisation of Europe.

In addition, as the UK economy slowed markedly in 2017 even though exporters were able to take advantage of the Brexit-devalued pound sterling by increasing exports to the EU, the member states of the EU all posted positive growth rates and increases in employment. What's more, the eurozone grew faster in 2016 than the US economy. To be sure, there are regions in Europe which are weak, but so too are there regions in the UK which perform poorly. No one can travel to the main cities of France, Germany, northern Italy, to Scandinavian cities within the EU or the bright new cities in Eastern Europe and say the EU is broken or bankrupt. It has been a long, hard decade since the crash of 2007/9, imported from the US financial system as fashioned by Americans like 'Sir' Alan Greenspan. But compared to the similar crash of 1929–31 that led to the lost decade of the 1930s and the emergence of extreme nation-first politics, the EU has now weathered the storm of global financial meltdown. Europe faces difficulties, but only in Britain is the solution seen as leaving the EU and becoming isolated from sister nations in Europe. Is it now Britain's fate to be fully marginalised for 10–20 years until a new generation arises and makes the self-evident point that eluded tired Labour ministers in 1950, namely that Britain cut off from our common continent is always weaker than when we play a leading and active role within it?

Theresa May was never a leader but a prisoner of the politics her predecessor unleashed, with his folly of imposing a populist, immigration-obsessed plebiscite on a representative parliamentary democracy. Mrs May carefully avoided explaining the extent and scope of the Brexit she wished for during the first six months of 2017, including during the six weeks of election campaigning. The incessant repetition of her preferred sound-bites 'Brexit means Brexit' or 'strong and stable leadership' was not a policy, still less coming clean with the British people about what a full Brexit of leaving the Single Market and Customs Union would entail as well as the termination of the right of British citizens to work, live, retire and travel in the EU with extensive rights shared with citizens of other countries including health care and access to education for children.

It may be that she does not understand fully what Brexit entails. She speaks no European language, cannot read a European paper, has a largely monolingual staff at Downing Street and thinks *El País*, the title of Spain's largest-circulation daily newspaper, is pronounced 'Elle Pace'. At no stage in the run-up to the Brexit plebiscite in the three years after David Cameron proposed it in 2013 or in his last 13 months as prime minister did the political class seek or claim a mandate for the economic, geo-political, social and human damage the extremist Brexit ideologues insist upon.

European heads of government and senior government officials in EU capitals responsible for preparing for Brexit negotiations confess freely to visitors their surprise at the lack of understanding in London and by Mrs May and her team of what is involved. In Brussels in June 2017 I was asked by a lead European Commission negotiator on Brexit 'Why does Mrs May sound as if she is a member of UKIP?' Accounts of a dinner in Downing Street for Mrs May and her Brexit team and the president of the European Commission, Jean-Claude Juncker, and the chief Brexit negotiator, Michel Barnier, late in April 2017 sum up this gulf of misunderstanding.

Mrs May told Juncker that Britain did not have to pay any of the UK's outstanding bills or liabilities. She insisted all negotiations should be kept secret and was surprised when Juncker said there would have to be reports to the European parliament. If the UK left the Single Market and the Customs Union, Britain would have a lower status as a 'third country' than Turkey, Juncker told the Prime Minister.

Mrs May was reminded that the EU is a legal construction, not a golf club, and she was told that given the length of time it took negotiating a deal with Canada or Croatia it would take years of talks to finalise a UK–EU trade agreement.

She said that the issue of EU citizens in the UK could be settled by June 2017. It was pointed out that this involved health care and social security issues and these were national government competences. Moreover, the UK has no list of EU citizens in Britain.

She referred to the meaningless temporary opt-outs she negotiated from EU Justice and Home Affairs measures and suggested this could be a model for Brexit, with the UK opting back in on a cherry-picking basis to bits of the Single Market she liked.

The EU team left Downing Street in a state of shock. Juncker placed a late-night call to Angela Merkel to convey his pessimism about the lack of knowledge or understanding in Downing Street about the Brexit policy of the EU27 governments – every bit as sovereign and accountable to their voters as May is in Britain.

The next day Merkel told the Bundestag that Britain suffered from 'illusions' over Brexit, which produced the predictable insults from anti-EU Tories and London's monolingual journalists writing for the off-shore-owned press.

What is surprising is that anyone is surprised. The dominant centre-right confederation of EU conservative parties, the European People's Party, published a full-page advertisement in the Brussels weekly *Politico* setting out Brexit negotiating priorities. These include 'EU citizens will not pay the bill for the British; EU citizens will not accept British blockades; The right order of the negotiations has to be respected', along with other demands.

In visits to seven EU capitals in the first half of 2017, I heard all of these points from senior ministers and officials responsible for Brexit talks. In Berlin I was told that the German government has been asking London for months for a list of EU citizens in the UK. There has been no reply. In Warsaw I was told that Britain had to meet its financial obligations to the EU before any exit deal could be agreed. In Lisbon I was told that despite friendship with England going back to a fourteenth-century treaty between the two countries, Lisbon now thought in terms of the EU27 and would stay loyal to its EU partners. In Paris I was told that the frontier would move to British territory and that customs-clearing centres would be set up in all French ports to control British lorries and cars and that there was no question that the $120-trillion City money-making machine of trading and clearing euros could stay in a non-EU or EEA country.

In Dublin the deep fear is that if the UK leaves the Customs Union, there would have to be border-crossing checks between Northern Ireland and Ireland, with cars, vans and lorries checked for any goods on which duty had not been paid. In one major EU capital, the chief Brexit negotiator at the foreign ministry told me: 'We know the UK ambassador sends accurate reports of our Brexit policy to London but does anyone read them?' 'What can we do when the British Foreign Secretary is a clown!'

The biggest 'illusion' in London that Mrs Merkel referred to is that the 27 EU member states would just roll over and accept the British plebiscite, aimed at the very core of European cooperation since the Treaty of Rome in 1957. All that had been achieved should be cast away to appease the victorious nationalist ideologues who had funded the years of anti-European campaigning and secured their nationalist victory in a populist plebiscite. In the months after the referendum there was continuing exultation in mainly Conservative newspapers about the result. Endless alarm signals came from business and those who knew the reality of foreign investment decisions, but they tended to be buried in bottom-of-the-page stories in the business sections of newspapers.

To be sure, some sort of formal political separation and treaty withdrawal may be unavoidable, short of an energetic political opposition from anti-Brexit MPs or a transformation in public opinion bringing about real leadership from the business community and economic actors in the City who have been utterly absent, supine almost, in refusing to challenge Brexit. It is perfectly possible to be outside EU treaties, and thus to have 'left' the EU, yet to remain fully connected as a cooperating nation in many areas of intra-European collaboration and not lose most economic access. The question now is whether the UK wants one Brexit or many. Whether there should be a limited, pragmatic decoupling from the political EU while we remain a full partner in all other areas.

In May 2019, a new EU cycle starts, with a new Commission, a new European Parliament and new presidents of the European Council and Eurogroup. France's new president, Emmanuel Macron, has insisted on the need for EU reform to support growth and jobs with ideas like a Buy European law that will only allow access to public tendering for contracts in the EU to firms that have half their employees working in Europe. He also wants to see single digital and single energy markets in Europe, both longstanding British demands. So the EU that Britain left in 2016 will have changed. Both the EU and national leaders who take final decisions are looking at a more flexible Europe with nation states in the driving seat. Britain is leaving the EU just at the moment when it conforms more than ever to British needs, interests and overall philosophy.

It is important to stand back a bit and see the EU not through the eyes of anti-Europe politicians and journalists but as others see it. As Princeton Professor Andrew Moravcsik wrote in *Foreign Policy* in April 2017, 'Europe is the "invisible superpower" in contemporary world politics.' Moravcsik points out that 'By the simplest measure of economic power, nominal GDP, the EU is nearly the same size as the United States and 63 per cent larger than China', and argues that:

> Europe today is a genuine superpower and will likely remain one for decades to come. By most objective measures, it either rivals or surpasses the United States and China in its ability to project a full spectrum of global military, economic, and soft power. Europe consistently deploys military troops within and beyond its immediate neighborhood. It manipulates economic power with a skill and success unmatched by any other country or region. And its ability to employ 'soft power' to persuade other countries to change their behavior is unique.'

If a political Brexit – formal withdrawal of Britain's name from all the treaties that govern the international legal base of integration and common rules between European states – is unavoidable, it should be possible to limit the rest of the many Brexits to a minimum. As Philip Hammond, named as chancellor by Mrs May after the Brexit plebiscite, rightly says, 'People did not vote to become poorer.'

Nissan workers in Sunderland did not vote to see Japanese firms disinvest. Nor did farmers vote to see hormone-injected beef or chlorine-washed chickens and other food dumped on supermarket shelves by North and South American and Asia-Pacific agro-industry global corporations. The British still expect to keep taking 42 million flights a year to European destinations without let or hindrance. We did not vote to deny ourselves the right to work or retire in Europe or lose the right to free hospital care if an accident happens.

For hardline anti-European isolationists none of this matters. But soon the dishonesty of their positions will be exposed. The 63 per cent of the population who did not endorse root and branch separation from Europe have a right to new answers. Those aged over 65 won the Brexit vote. Now Britain's next generation need to wake up and rise up to secure a future such as their parents and grandparents have enjoyed in the last 40 years. There are examples in other proud European democracies of maintaining warm win-win relations with the EU without being co-joined in treaties. Britain can no more leave Europe than planet Earth can leave the solar system. This book explains why Britain will stay part of Europe.

Churchill's motto was 'Never, never, never give in'. For those proud to be British and European, these words of resistance should guide us as others accommodate themselves to the dislike of sharing power and the future with our fellow Europeans. What happened on 23 June 2016 is not the last word in British democracy. If in January 2015 I was confident enough to write a book asserting that Britain would leave Europe, I now am willing to assert that will not happen in a full, complete sense, or if it does it will be temporary. I will explain in the course of this book why I do not believe Britain will fully leave Europe in the way those who have promoted anti-Europeanism in recent years desire. I may be wrong and they may succeed. If that is the case, Britain will be a far lesser nation than its people need and deserve.

PART ONE

THE IMPACT OF BREXIT

1

THE BREXIT REVOLUTION

Wednesday 22 June 2016 was a typical London mid-summer day – warm, but muggy, with the occasional chilly wind and a hint of the thunderstorms that later in the night led to a month's worth of rain falling in less than an hour.

The next day, Thursday 23 June, was to be one of the most momentous in British and European history. In the eighteenth century Lord North was the Tory prime minister who lost America. In the twenty-first century David Cameron became the Tory prime minister who took Britain out of Europe.

The word 'revolution' barely appears in the lexicon of British political history. The seventeenth century saw a civil war, a restoration and then an invited-in invasion by a Dutch king to ensure Protestant supremacy and parliamentary sovereignty. There were major reforms in the nineteenth century but nothing that justified the word 'revolution'. That was something that happened across the Channel or the Atlantic or, in the twentieth century, in Russia in 1917 or Iran in 1979.

Yet it is hard not to see the process of Brexit as anything short of a revolutionary moment in the placid waters of Britain's political life. In Brexit combined with the arrival of Donald Trump in the White House following a Brexit-type post-truth campaign and wild exaggerations, the two great English-speaking democracies voted to end the era that opened with the defeat of Nazi Germany in 1945. Then the United States and European democracies, including Britain, joined in the construction of the Euro-Atlantic project of peace, economic integration and liberal democracy· It lasted from the Marshall Plan of 1947 until a US president and a British prime minister held hands as they celebrated a return to nationalist protectionist populism, with some hard-working taxpayers in Britain and America now targets of choice for government action against 'immigrants'.

The new Brexit–Trump political axis was based on a contempt for truth and a rejection of all the lessons of rationality painfully learned since the Enlightenment. Hannah Arendt, who gave the world the concept of 'totalitarianism', might have been predicting the Brexit–Trump world when she wrote in 1974, during an interview with the French writer Roger Errera:

> If everybody always lies to you, the consequence is not that you believe the lies, but rather that nobody believes anything any longer. […] On the receiving end you get not only one lie – a lie which you could go on for the rest of your days – but you get a great number of lies, depending on how the political wind blows. And a people that no longer can believe anything cannot make up its mind. It is deprived not only of its capacity to act but also of its capacity to think and to judge. And with such a people you can then do what you please.

The modish term 'post-truth' came into play as analysts tried to grapple with a new politics in which provable facts and rational argument were regarded as old-fashioned forms of communication irrelevant to the era of social media and fake news. The BBC in particular gave up discharging its duty to truth, instead allowing endless lies about the EU to be broadcast without challenge. To be fair to President Trump, as his first months in office went by he did seem to leave behind some of the surreal tweeted policy pronouncements that helped him win the White House. NATO was no longer 'obsolete' but essential to US global interests. He would work with Angela Merkel on a US–EU trade agreement and Britain would have to wait. Vladimir Putin's support for the Syrian president after he used gas to kill young children was unacceptable. Trump's America would now work inside the US–Mexico–Canada North American Free Trade Agreement (NAFTA), which Trump had scorned much as UK Tories attacked the EU. In contrast to Mrs May's line on Europe, President Trump said he wanted to work to reform NAFTA, not walk out of it. Trump's campaigning ideology appeared to be giving way to a more measured realist assessment of US core interests. Might this also happen across the Atlantic, as the excitements of the Brexit plebiscite and general election gave way to the realities of what a full rupture with Europe entailed?

The Brexit plebiscite vote opened up divisions in Britain. The young voted for Europe. The old voted against Europe. Scotland voted for a European future. England voted to cut links with the EU. London voted to remain a giant European global city, but many smaller cities and towns in England voted to stop Europeans coming to live and work freely in their community.

The Conservative Party was convulsed as a successful Tory prime minister and chancellor left office just a year after winning a majority in a general election. Tory MPs who had been excluded from power for years on the grounds of unreliability and political eccentricity now held high office because they had secured an exit from the EU. The Labour Party was depressed and divided as its leader ordered his MPs to vote in the same lobby as the Conservatives and UKIP rather than vote with and in the name of the 63 per cent of the population that did not vote for Brexit.

As part of the Brexit-engendered hate campaign against any kind of foreign entrant in Britain, a small amendment was added to the Article 50 vote in the Commons to stop the arrival in Britain of 2,500 child refugees from the wars that British policy in the Middle East had helped ferment. There had already been agreement to let the children into homes waiting for them in this, our generous country, just as the *Kindertransport*s had brought Jewish children and adolescents to safety from 1930s Europe. But as Jonathan Freedland wrote, post-Brexit Britain felt able to break 'a promise to give shelter to 3,000 of the most desperate people on Earth, children fleeing war and devastation? What kind of government sneaks out an announcement that the 3,000 places it had reserved for child refugees will be shrunk to 350 and, after that, the doors to this peaceful and prosperous country will be slammed shut?'

It is not that Mrs May or Tory ministers are cruel, but anti-Europeanism has coarsened and degraded the quality of public and press discourse in Britain. Thus today's Conservative ministers were confident they could act more harshly than their predecessors in the 1930s. So void of coherence and confidence or even plain political courage was the Labour Party that they offered neither hope and a voice to the old values of the British people nor any policy for healing the wounds of the 20-year Brexit campaign.

Scotland and Ireland were transformed by Brexit. The ruling nationalist separatist party in Scotland invoked the possibility of an independence referendum to secure Scotland's future as a European nation. In Ireland, there were great fears in both the Irish Republic and the six counties of Northern Ireland that are part of the UK that the full-scale rupture with all European institutions demanded by Prime Minister May's Brexit ministers would mean customs posts to check on all goods crossing to and from the European Customs Union, to which Ireland belongs, and the six counties of Northern Ireland, which would now have different tariffs and duties. There would be different rules about farming subsidies which would encourage smuggling across the UK–Ireland borders. Many Irish firms export from the north and south as a single economic entity. Outside the (EU)

Single Market and Customs Union that would stop. They feared a range of new tensions along the border, which before England's vote to leave Europe was completely free, open and tranquil.

There were worries in Gibraltar and Britain around leaving the EU treaties which obliged Britain and Spain to cooperate. As Gibraltarians lost EU rights thanks to Brexit, they could be exposed to new pressures from Spain. There would be a hard border between Spain and the territory now outside the EU. The Rock's airport could lose the right to receive flights once the UK left all the aviation bodies that policed EU airspace.

The immediate aftermath of the Brexit–Trump victory was a reversion to scapegoating and finger-pointing on the basis of nationality or religion. European citizens long based in Britain, with British spouses and British-born children, were told they did not qualify for residence in Britain. In streets and workplaces, hard-working, tax-paying Europeans were told to their face 'Go home!' Five days after the referendum, a 20-year-old man, Robert Molloy, appeared in court in Manchester after shouting at an American who had lived in the UK for 18 years, 'Don't chat shit when you are not even from England, you little fucking immigrant. Get back to Africa.' The defence lawyer explained to the judge that 'Leading up to the referendum those in positions of great responsibility employed divisive rhetoric that clearly has had an impact.' The lawyer sensibly added, 'That's not an excuse.' No, it isn't, but as the Brexit-induced hate against all foreigners in Britain increased as a result of the referendum, those who attacked the presence of Europeans in Britain refused to accept any responsibility for the tensions their demagogic rhetoric unleashed.

British Muslims who had some connection to a country President Trump did not like, including Sir Mo Farah, the Olympic Gold medallist, who was born in Somalia, were told not to try and travel to President Trump's America. But other Muslims were being hauled off planes from Europe, as they would not be allowed entry into the new world that arose after the Brexit–Trump vote.

Prime Minister Theresa May announced that Britain would leave the world's biggest open trade market, the EU's Single Market. A thousand Japanese firms, including global names like Nissan, Toyota, Honda, Mitsubishi and Hitachi, and scores of banks and financial firms in Japan had set up business and opened factories in Britain to export to Europe after Mrs May's predecessor, Margaret Thatcher, abolished national vetoes in Europe, when she forced through the Single European Act creating the EU's Single Market. She enticed the Japanese to make Britain their gateway to Europe and helped bring back to life the UK automobile industry and renew jobs in depressed regions with the promise they would be able to trade anywhere in the European market of 500 million consumers. That pledge was reaffirmed by all of Mrs Thatcher's successors until Mrs May arrived.

Many economists and objective think-tanks and consultancies believed that unless Britain agreed to stay in the Single Market the nation could see a significant decline in its GDP and loss of growth. To be fair, other economists hostile to the EU argued the opposite. In truth, no one will know until well into the 2020s, when Brexit fully happens, and much of the frantic writing in the press is little better than forecasting next year's weather or announcing the Premiership League Champion in a decade's time. If the UK limits itself to a political Brexit, and sustains, like other non-EU governments in Europe, relations with Europe based on open trade, respect for common European rules and laws, free movement of goods, capital, services and people – then perhaps the outcomes of the more apocalyptic fears and prophecies will be avoided.

Brexit was voted in 2016. It will be some years until it is fully effected, and its exact form depends on the decision of the Prime Minister and the ruling Conservative Party. The worries over the impact of UKIP on the Conservative vote that many believe impelled David Cameron to hold the 2016 plebiscite have disappeared, as has any serious parliamentary political challenge to

Mrs May. Can she rise above party passions and see the wider national interest?

A massively complicated set of negotiations lies ahead to extricate Britain from dozens of tightly interwoven agreements with other EU nations, covering everything from aviation landing rights for low-cost airlines to agricultural subsidies or involvement in European-wide policing and anti-terrorism measures and common climate change agreements. Enda Kenny, the Irish prime minister, declared it was impossible for all these complex negotiations to be successfully terminated in the space of two years before the next European Parliament elections in May 2019 – the deadline desired by Theresa May.

Jean-Claude Piris, widely accepted as Europe's best legal expert on EU negotiations, reckoned British withdrawal would take a full decade after the UK left the EU following the start of the negotiations (which under the EU treaty were meant to be concluded in two years). Piris told me further that:

All legal and budgetary commitments, accepted by the UK before day D of withdrawal, shall remain legally obligatory for the UK and remain subject to the jurisdiction of the EUCJ after the UK's withdrawal.

The UK shall remain bound to fulfil its budgetary obligations created by regulations, directives and decisions adopted by the EU's institutions when the UK was still an EU Member State.

This obligation is valid both in classic public international law and in EU law.

So even after the withdrawal treaty has been negotiated, there will be continuing UK financial obligations to other EU member states that cannot be avoided unless Britain wants to break all its traditions and norms of respecting international law.

Political leaders and senior officials in national governments as well as the EU institutions have been clear that Britain would leave the EU treaty framework and cease to elect British Members of the European Parliament, no longer have an EU Commissioner and no longer send ministers and officials to take part in the meetings that decided EU policy and laws. The substantive negotiations could take place only once the UK was no longer bound by the common treaty obligations that other European nation states agreed to live by.

There was considerable confusion about the length of time it would take to negotiate Brexit. The two years stipulated in Article 50 of the EU treaty which allows for a member state to withdraw from the EU has to include time for consultations with member states about the withdrawal agreement or treaty agreed with the leaving country – in this case the United Kingdom. The talks over what future relationship Britain would have with Europe will only begin in detail once we have left, even if some exploratory talks could happen before formal withdrawal. The notification that Britain would invoke Article 50 was sent in March 2017 but then had to be examined by 27 EU member states, with effective negotiations not starting until after the formation of a new German government late in 2017.

Then there has to be a six-month period at the end of the negotiations for the 27 member states to agree the final terms negotiated in Brussels to allow Britain to secure a political exit from the EU before the new EU Commission, Parliament and Council President begin their five-year term of work in May 2019. So in effect there would be about nine months between the end of 2017 and autumn 2018 to negotiate a withdrawal treaty with the full authority of the new government in Germany. Few in Brussels or Brexit specialists in the 27 EU member states believed that the relatively short time frame for Article 50 talks could cover big issues like trade and market access, still less the question of the Customs Union. The EU selected three priorities for the withdrawal negotiations. First, the UK would have to pay, and the EU would have to agree on how much, to discharge its obligations and liabilities to the EU. Second, the rights of EU citizens living and working in Britain and British citizens in Europe should be clarified and guaranteed. Third, the status of Ireland and especially the Peace Process in Northern Ireland underwritten by the EU should be agreed. If all these points could be agreed then the EU would offer Britain the possibility of maintaining tariff-free trade in goods that respected the EU's rule-of-origin obligations for a number of years pending a final settlement.

According to researchers in Brussels, there were more than 20,000 EU laws and regulations that Britain had helped promote or had accepted which would no longer apply unless negotiators agreed otherwise. There are 350,000 so-called Single Market 'passports' awarded to financial service firms in the UK (British and foreign) that allow a firm based in Britain to buy and sell financial products or offer advice and consultancy services without further controls to 27 EU member states. Several references to the UK are included in EU treaties and would have to be removed.

One of the trickiest issues is paying for the pensions and redundancy payments of all the British citizens who were EU employees. There are 1,800 British citizens who are currently working and being paid by the EU and 2,000 former employees who enjoy EU pensions which Britain will be asked to take responsibility for. UKIP has its quota of parliamentary aides who are on the EU payroll and some will not reach pension age until 2064, when they will expect to be paid some pension on the basis of their EU employment.

One of the paradoxes of Brexit is that having fulminated against the 'corruption' and excessive costs of British membership of the EU, no UKIP or pro-Brexit Tory MEP followed the wishes of voters and stood down following the referendum result. Instead they and an army of pro-Brexit British political aides paid for by the European taxpayer want to extract the maximum amount of salary and expenses right up to the last moment of membership and for years afterwards in terms of pensions.

British citizens make 42 million trips to EU member states every year. As EU citizens they are covered for free hospital care if they have an accident or fall ill. Now they will have to take out travel insurance, adding to the cost of holidays and other visits. Aviation industry experts believe that low-cost airlines based in Britain may face difficulties, as the whole basis of low-cost flying is based on the Single Market rules which Mrs May now rejects. Indeed all flying within the EU is governed by EU-wide rules and supervised by agencies and safety bodies ultimately under the overall authority of the European Court of Justice (ECJ). British Airways flies its planes back for maintenance in Britain. If these planes no longer have an EU certificate of airworthiness because a Brexit Britain refuses to work under common EU laws and rules and the European Court of Justice, then BA may have to relocate its maintenance hangars and workshops to somewhere within the EU in order to be able to keep flying to EU destinations.

A major problem will be how to deal with the EU citizens living in Britain and the British citizens living and working in EU countries. Until May 2019, the rights conferred by virtue of being EU citizens allow Brits to travel, live, work and retire freely wherever they want. No one has an accurate figure for how many there are, but estimates go up to 2 million. There are an estimated 3.3 million EU citizens in Britain, including up to 400,000 French citizens working in London. 'Estimated' is the correct term, as there has never been an official national register for EU citizens living or working in Britain, and the non-stop movement around Europe that has developed in recent years thanks to the end of border controls on every road that crosses from one European nation into another, means that it is genuinely hard to produce reliable statistics.

It will be a massive bureaucratic undertaking for the UK government to track down, list and work out when millions of EU citizens entered the UK, how long they have lived here and how often they go back home for short or longer visits. The status of both British citizens in Europe and EU citizens in Britain will change, be diminished. Britain has never required people to carry identity cards or register with a local council or police station, which can be the norm in many European countries. No one has any reliable list of foreign EU citizens, including Irish citizens, living or working in Britain.

There were calls for the British government to confirm the residence rights of EU citizens here, as many did not know if they could continue living and working after May 2019, even if they had spouses, partners or children who were British citizens. But Mrs May insisted that she would make no such concession until there were reciprocal guarantees for the status of British citizens living elsewhere in Europe. Ministers referred to European citizens in Britain as a 'bargaining chip', with the implication that London could demand Brexit concessions from other EU governments, who would otherwise see their citizens denied the right to live and work in Britain. To apply for residence in Britain it is necessary to fill in an 85-page form with details of every trip in and out of the UK over the past five years. Home Office bureaucrats took pleasure in rejecting applications. European spouses of British citizens who had lived in Britain for years, raised a family and felt at home were suddenly made to feel unwanted and rejected by their adopted country.

At a British–Spanish political seminar held in Seville in December 2016 attended by senior Spanish cabinet ministers as well by the UK's Brexit minister, David Davis, the latter said he hoped a quick deal between the UK and the EU could be reached before the start of Article 50 negotiations. Spanish ministers looked at him in amazement. Beyond the broad rights contained in successive European treaties since the 1950s permitting movement of workers across borders and then the concept of EU citizenship, which allows all citizens of EU member states to live or retire where they wish, the specific rules governing the obligation to declare residency are national regulations and in some countries even provincial laws and rules which the EU Commission could not override. These are slow bureaucratic processes requiring much form filling. According to the Oxford University Migration Observatory, at the current rate of granting residency rights to foreign residents in the UK, it would take 140 years to issue such permits to the up to 3.5 million European citizens living amongst us.

The government hasn't the faintest idea who they are, when they arrived or where they live. So for David Davis to suggest it was a just quick negotiation, over in a matter of weeks, was baffling. In any case, for Spanish ministers this was a bilateral matter, not one that could be decided by the EU's Brexit negotiating team. And in the case of Spain, any bilateral issue with Britain always seems to involve Gibraltar! The fate of the up to 700,000 – possibly up to 1 million, according to British embassy officials in Madrid – British expatriates who own a property in Spain or the estimated 160,000 Spaniards in the UK was an issue to be settled between London and Madrid, as a European Parliamentary Committee report published early in 2017 made clear.

Now Mrs May and Brexit ministers say the status of EU citizens in the UK and Brits in Europe can be settled in the Article 50 negotiations, but as MEPs and most national ministers in other countries make clear, this is a matter for national governments. Britain could, if it wished, be unilaterally generous and state that all EU nationals currently in Britain can stay, but there is no indication that such generosity is part of the Prime Minister's mental make-up. In any event, the point about free movement is that it is about movement. Trying to freeze and stratify numbers when people expect that family members can come and visit or that there can be movement involving more than one country is possible in theory but will be unpleasant to police and enforce, with considerable human distress in practice. For the xenophobes of UKIP and some anti-European Tories, of course, the chance to be unpleasant to foreigners, especially Europeans, is part of the pleasure they derive from political action, but it is far from clear that the broad mass of British people, usually held up as models of a tolerant, welcoming people, were that keen on deporting European men, women and children.

In the spring of 2017 I travelled to Berlin, Paris, Madrid, Lisbon and Warsaw to meet officials and politicians in foreign and finance ministries who would be negotiating Brexit. I met other European politicians at conferences and seminars in different cities in Europe to talk about Brexit. They were all well prepared, with a thorough, professional approach. There was no desire to punish Britain. But equally there was no willingness to allow the EU to be broken up and its rule book thrown away just to suit the Tory–UKIP–*Daily Mail/Telegraph* victors after their years of campaigns against Europe. The EU in the eyes of today's Berlin is seen as a *Rechtsgemeinschaft* – a community of laws. Germany more than any other nation of Europe knows what it means to exist on the basis of rejecting agreed laws and reciprocal obligations.

Representatives of the 27 EU member states accept of course that Britain has every right to leave a treaty organisation, one based on international law, which is what the EU is despite all the talk of a 'federal' super-state or some nebulous 'European project' which means anything and nothing at one and the same time. The EU flag of 12 yellow stars on a blue background was actually designed for the Council of Europe in the 1950s and taken over later by the European Community. Beethoven's 'Ode to Joy' is just lovely music and a poem, and the idea that the Union Flag or *tricolore* or 'God Save the Queen' and the *Marseillaise* have been replaced by a blue and yellow flag or an extract from a symphony is just silly, but something still heard. On BBC Radio 4's *Today*, a presenter like John Humphries will announce that a European super-state with flag and anthem has been created behind British backs. No one suggests that with or without a plebiscite a British parliament and government cannot withdraw from any international treaty it has signed. But equally, I was told, no one in Britain should expect the remaining 27 member states of the European Union to give up their common rule book, which permits unfettered access to the market of 450 million mainly middle-class consumers.

This access is protected by the ultimate guardians and referees of the EU's common rule book, the judges sitting in the European Court of Justice. Prime Minister May's rejection that common EU trade and other elements refereed by the ECJ should ever apply to Britain will make arriving at any kind of serious agreement protecting the interests of British-based firms as well as British citizens who want to live, work or retire in Europe extremely problematic. The new term was 'Third Country'. Britain would become a third country in relationship to the rest of Europe, no longer as John Donne wrote, in 'No Man is an Island',

> a piece of the continent,
> A part of the main.

'Europe is the less', to use Donne's words, as a result of Brexit – until the politics of rejoining our nation to Europe can be brought to life. Once the formal process of withdrawing from EU treaties is accomplished – in March 2019 – Britain then is a Third Country like any other in the world in terms of its relationship with the EU, assuming Prime Minister Theresa May sticks to her plan of repudiating the Single Market and the Customs Unions. Alternatively, as I argue, if Britain adopts a pragmatic pro-economy approach to Brexit after the Article 50 negotiations are finished, it may be possible to avoid years and years of negotiations, with every economic actor in Britain uncertain what the future will hold and every British citizen losing rights that in recent times we have got used to and rather enjoyed.

Third countries can do business in Europe under the rules of the World Trade Organization (WTO). But the WTO does not cover trade in services like banking, investment, insurance, consultancy, creative industries or education. Service industries account for 80 per cent of the UK economy and our exports to the EU of UK-produced services are hugely profitable. In 2015 Britain imported €27 billion of services from the EU but we exported four times as much – €104 billion. Thus the UK runs a massive balance of trade surplus in our main export industry with the EU. These exports cannot be protected by WTO rules but require Britain to be in compliance with EU laws, directives or regulatory authorities, and if there is a dispute it means Britain accepting the authority of the ECJ, just as American and Russian firms have done. Yet Prime Minister May has insisted that Britain will not be subject to the ECJ. Moreover, joining the WTO and using its rules is not automatic. There are 164 WTO members and any one of them can ask for trade concessions from Britain as a price for voting for British membership of the WTO.

After the Brexit plebiscite and Theresa May's decision to interpret it as requiring the hardest possible amputation from the rest of Europe by quitting the Single Market and the Customs Union, which allow business to be done without mountains of customs clearing paperwork, paying duties or publishing rules of origin on every product, the Eurosceptic campaigner and writer Christopher Booker declared that such economic isolationism was folly.

Booker cited the UK chemical industry and pharmaceutical exports. Outside the Single Market and Customs Union these products lose their 'authorisations' which allow access to firms in the EU27. Negotiating replacements 'would be so complex that it could take years'. The same is true, he argued, for food exports and flying low-cost airlines – and even the UK's £3.5 billion horseracing industry which relies on freedom movement of horses to EU countries such as Ireland and France.

Mrs May's threat to walk out of talks is 'terrifying because, by bringing our trade with Europe crashing to a halt, this would be as catastrophic an act of national self-harm as the world has ever seen', wrote Booker. The question remains: is Mrs May's language of threat and walk-out and no deal a negotiating tactic or has she bought in fully to the maximalist ideology of UKIP and other anti-EU extremists? No one knows. Does the Prime Minister?

2

BREXIT AND TRUMP: TOWARDS A NEW WORLD DISORDER?

Donald Trump is Brexit writ large across the Atlantic. When the American president declares 'The only important thing is the unification of the people, because the other people don't mean anything', he, like the politicians and press who campaigned for a quarter of a century for Brexit, is excluding all those who do not identify with him or with a narrow, limited idea of the nation.

Across Europe every populist and xenophobe nationalist who wants to undo the degree of cooperation and integration that generations of Europeans, including British giants like Winston Churchill and Margaret Thatcher, have painfully created since 1945 felt enthused by Brexit and then re-enthused by the Americans who followed the same nationalist-populist appeals which traded on emotions, not facts.

It places a giant question mark over Europe's future. Already rising economic and military powers in Asia are challenging the domination of the Euro-Atlantic economic, trading, military weight and the liberal rule-of-law values that since the Reformation and the Renaissance have allowed European peoples to become rich and since 1945 live the best years that any Europeans, including British Europeans, have enjoyed in their total sum of existence. Brexit was not just a British vote, but a plebiscite that will transform Europe.

The fate of America's new president and Brexit became symbolically intertwined when the Prime Minister went to the White House and President Trump said the UK could negotiate a trade agreement with the US. Although he grabbed Mrs May's hand as they left the White House, it was far from certain if the openly protectionist Trump was serious in offering many trade openings just to the Brits. It is the US Congress that decides US trade treaties, not the White House.

US medical industry firms would want to take over parts of the National Health Service. US media giants would demand that the BBC licence fee be reduced. The US food industry would demand free access into Britain for its genetically modified food or for meat and chickens processed in ways illegal in Britain and the EU. The US was not about to abolish its protectionist legislation and its states were not going to allow British professionals to practise without first passing state-mandated professional examinations. None of this would happen before the 2020 elections in America. The uncertainty would grow.

The Brexit-devalued pound put up the price of imports, and shoppers noticed all sorts of price rises in supermarkets once the Christmas/New Year sales rush was over early in 2017. Investment in the UK car industry was down 33.6 per cent in 2016. Many banks, from Barclays to HSBC, announced they would have to relocate employees to EU capitals and open branch offices there in order to secure full access to the Single Market. Another bank, Lloyds, announced it was looking to move one of its key London divisions to Berlin in order to stay within the EU.

Some had hoped that Britain might opt for agreements such as those negotiated by the Swiss or Norwegians, who were not part of the EU but maintained Single Market access. Mrs May, however, having filled her cabinet with anti-European ministers, appeared to be insisting on a full amputation. She talked of Britain leaving Europe to become a global trading power, even though countries like Germany and France had greater levels of exports to America and elsewhere in the world than Britain. Leaving the Single Market and the Customs Union was alarming news for Ireland, where experts forecast a drop of 30 per cent in exports to the UK. One Tory MP pointed out that Ireland had made the mistake of leaving the union with Britain in 1922 and perhaps should once again accept British suzerainty.

The EU negotiating team would be led by Michel Barnier, the former French foreign minister and EU commissioner, who would represent the European Commission, along with Didier Seeuws of the European Council, acting on behalf of the 27 nations still in the EU. Barnier is going to be polite, friendly and without any *aggressivité*, to use his word in French. 'My job is to defend the interests of the 27 member states of the EU', he told me.

As the months passed following the Brexit vote, the debate got ever more heated in Britain. There were debates and votes in the Commons and Lords. Almost every day there were press headlines or interviews on Radio 4's *Today* about Brexit. Each day seemed to bring contradictory news. Following Brexit, the pound suffered its biggest devaluation in a century. But the London Stock Exchange rose in value. Xavier Rolet, chief executive of the London Stock Exchange, said the City would lose 200,000 jobs as trades and clearing in euros and derivatives transferred back to the EU. But other economists said the EU needed the UK more than Britain needed access to the Single Market. It was not clear where such 'facts' came from. Spain, for example, exports US$14.2 billion to the UK annually but over seven times as much – US$106.5 billion – to France, Germany, Portugal, Italy and Benelux countries.

Yet far from being happy about their victory, the pro-Brexit politicians and journalists became ever more agitated in their denunciations of Europe, as if Brexit had to be a permanent, unending political process rather like Trotsky's 'permanent revolution'.

Instead of celebrating their victory, the isolationists felt uncertain. As more and more people began to reflect on the level of lies told to win the vote, the clear evidence of economic damage, and the vanity and attention-seeking of the main pro-Brexit ministers, the inflated claims of what would follow a Brexit vote seemed more and more risible.

A visible sense of panic set in. In the first four months after the vote the *Daily Express* published no fewer than 74 front pages attacking Europe or making claims about the threat of immigrants. After Theresa May's Conservative Party conference speech announcing the start date for the Article 50 negotiations, the *Daily Mail* ran 14 comment articles attacking those who were unsure about Brexit. 'OUT OF TOUCH ELITE WILL DO ANYTHING TO KEEP US IN THE EU' was typical of *Mail* headlines.

The *Sun*'s former political editor, Trevor Kavanagh, who had been denouncing Europe since the 1990s, attacked Chancellor Philip Hammond for pointing out that Brexit meant turbulence and volatility. For Kavanagh, these were 'scary warnings' and 'Mr Hammond is now at war with his own party.' About the same time, the *Sun*'s circulation fell below 2 million. In his eighty-fifth year, its proprietor, Rupert Murdoch, looked sadly on at the slow decline of his favourite paper. But both he and the *Sun* had achieved their main objective since the early 1990s – helping take Britain out of Europe.

One exuberant pro-Brexit Conservative MP, Chris Roycroft-Davis, used a column in the *Daily Express* to attack MPs – as much in his own as in other parties – who suggested that the House of Commons might be allowed to debate and vote on Brexit. This 'rabble of MPs demanding a Commons vote' were guilty of 'snake-like treachery that cannot go unpunished', he proclaimed and added, 'Clap them in the Tower of London. They want to imprison us against our will in the EU so we should give them 28 days against their will to reflect on the true meaning of democracy.'

This feverish tone was caught by Allister Heath, who was one of the most effective journalist crusaders for Brexit as editor of London's important *CityAM* morning paper before becoming deputy editor of the *Daily Telegraph* and now editor of the anti-European *Sunday Telegraph*. He felt obliged to write a column under the headline 'WHY IT'S TIME FOR A NEW CAMPAIGN FOR BREXIT' four months after his camp's victory. He urged his fellow EUphobes to keep up the struggle and not assume the vote on 23 June 2016 was the end of the story. 'There is no such thing as permanent victory in politics. History never ends: triumphs are fleeting; majorities can turn into minorities; and orthodoxies are inevitably built on foundations of sand', he wrote.

Heath is right. The Article 50 negotiations are just a prelude to what will be years of hard Brexit reality. Goldman Sachs estimates the pound will fall in value by 40 per cent compared to its value before 23 June 2016. It is not so much a divorce as a sequence of parallel Siamese twin separation operations without anaesthetic and carried out using chain-saws and axes, not the precise words of surgical diplomacy. Every national government and voters in 27 EU nation states will want their say – including difficult parliamentary votes – on the terms of Britain leaving Europe and then the terms on which Britain re-engages as a commercial partner with Europe, as well as working in cooperation with EU member states across a range of issues from arrest warrants to airline landing rights.

It is possible that Britain will simply walk away from the negotiating table and like Ian Smith's Rhodesia in the 1960s make a unilateral declaration of denunciation of EU laws and renounce all its obligations and legal relations under EU treaties going back to the 1950s. This might happen if Britain places a unilateral demand in front of other governments in Europe – for example, stipulating that their citizens must henceforth have a written job offer before boarding a plane or train or driving to Britain. This has been suggested by Daniel Hannan, the leading Tory Brexit MEP. Labour MPs had earlier discovered the virtues of imposing complicated work permit and quota systems for Europeans working in the UK, even though according to the Office of National Statistics the majority (about 5 million) of the 8.3 million immigrants in Britain are not EU citizens. In fact, following the Brexit vote the rate of entry into the UK of EU citizens declined as the devalued pound made working in Britain less attractive.

Such an unnegotiated diktat would produce a backlash in most EU member states, especially those who have welcomed British citizens as workers, retirees or just those desirous of living under the common rights all citizens of EU member states have enjoyed for a quarter of a century.

If such unilateral action was initiated by the British government between 2017 and 2019 – the period of the formal exit negotiations – then the chaos and lack of legal certainty would be immense.

On the whole this does not seem likely, as Britain is a very old state in which the Latin phrase *pacta sunt servanda* (treaties must be obeyed) has been an article of faith for centuries. So Britain, if it interprets the result of 23 June 2016 as permitting the state to rip up any existing obligation without writing into its own and international law satisfactory replacement arrangements, will be embarking on a kind of Leninist road of repudiation of all its existing commitment and obligations.

That might appeal to some Brexit zealots, who have all the fervour of 1640s Cromwellian Puritans in their desire to chop off the king's head – in the second decade of the twenty-first century read that as cutting off anything that implies a cooperative sharing of power with nation states in Europe – but is it the British way of doing things?

Unlike the Trump vote, which can be tempered in mid-term elections in 2018 and reversed in 2020, the Brexit vote cannot be undone. Equally it cannot be converted overnight into Britain becoming a nation which is not part of European geography, part of European economic and social relations and part of a Europe with all its muddled and muddy history. Brexit does not allow Britain to become New

Zealand or Vancouver or an island close to Florida. The Brexit vote cannot alter geography, history, economics or modern society. Daniel Hannan was lyrical about Brexit, and rhapsodised in his 2016 book *What Next? How to Get the Best from Brexit* about a Britain finally cut loose from the rest of Europe. 'A rectangle of light dazzles us and, as our eyes adjust, we see a summer meadow. Swallows swoop against the blue sky. We hear the gurgling of a little brook.' Theresa May does not have the luxury of handling Brexit in such poetical terms.

3

BREXIT: A NEVER-ENDING SAGA

The question of Brexit will dominate British politics and economics for years to come. The UK has been trying for eight years to negotiate a trade agreement with India that would get the Indians to drop their 150 per cent tariff on Scotch whisky. So far no agreement has been possible. Leaving the common trade area of the EU and negotiating specific new arrangements with Britain's neighbours will not be easy. For more than 40 years British laws, trade regulations, environmental rules, criminal justice laws covering arrests and extradition, cooperation on foreign policy, joint funding for universities and student scholarships, laws covering employers and employees and innumerable rights that British citizens enjoyed as citizens of the EU were intricately intermingled with treaty obligations under different supranational laws agreed by the House of Commons since 1973.

Brexit should be seen not in the singular, but as a plural concept. Not one Brexit, but dozens. Just three aspects of Brexit will be discussed in the short period before October 2018 when a withdrawal agreement has to be submitted to 27 national governments (and the House of Commons and European Parliament). These include the money Britain owes as existing obligations, the status of EU and British citizens currently residing in the UK or in the EU – not the question of freedom of movement and the status of Northern Ireland, the latter depending on what Theresa May wants to walk out of the Customs Union. All the other Brexits as set out below will be discussed and negotiated once Britain becomes what is called a 'third country', that is, a nation with the same legal relationship to the EU as Brazil or Russia. In mandatory guidelines agreed by the European Council in May 2017 it was made clear that 'Preserving the integrity of the Single Market excludes participation on a sector-by-sector basis' and that 'nothing is agreed until everything is agreed, individual items cannot be settled separately'. The hopes of some sectors of the economy – for example financial services in the City – that the EU would accommodate their wish to keep trading in Europe are not possible given this decision and language. The different types of Brexit include:

Political Brexit. This the end of the UK's formal participation in the EU. The UK will have no more Commissioners, no more MEPS, no automatic transmission into UK law of EU directives. Only the House of Commons deciding how Britain is governed. British ministers and officials will be unable to influence EU policy. Short of a revolutionary change in public and political opinion before spring 2019, it is hard to see how a political Brexit can be avoided. But when British citizens contemplate all the other Brexits that hardline anti-Europeans want to achieve, there will be second and third thoughts.

Single Market Brexit. This is the end of full, unfettered access to the EU's Single Market of 450 million customers. It will erect the biggest barriers to trade between the UK and its partners ever seen in British history. It is possible to be outside the political EU but have access to the Single Market, such as Norway and Switzerland enjoy. But this means accepting common rules and the authority of the European Court of Justice whenever a dispute arises that requires some body to arbitrate differences or make a ruling. Having secured a political Brexit it is possible to envision a compromise that allows open trade to continue, even if in her first period in office, looking over her shoulder at anti-EU Conservative Party activists, Mrs May had to rule it out.

Customs Union Brexit. Leaving the Customs Union would require every good or component in goods destined for sale in Europe to be customs cleared. It will be a massive problem in Ireland. There are 10,000 lorry journeys a year between Dublin and Belfast carrying Guinness made in Dublin to be packed in Belfast and then returned to Dublin for onward shipment to supermarkets and other outlets. But outside the Customs Union different duties and tariffs would apply. Ireland makes 90,000 tons of strong cheddar each year mainly sold to Britain, without much demand for it outside the UK. Currently there is an EU tariff of €1,671 per ton of cheddar, which of course does not apply to products made within the Customs Union. Cheese makers in every other EU member state will shed no tears if life becomes more awkward for Irish dairy farmers. Some Brexit ministers have promised to get rid of EU regulations but in the food industry they are mainly about safety and quality. If the UK, outside the Customs Union, refuses to abide by EU food quality and safety regulations then British food exports – the most important segments of the Northern Irish economy – will be badly hit. And ultimately the final court of appeal for a dispute over the interpretation of EU regulations is the European Court of Justice, which Mrs May has denounced in extreme terms. Michel Barnier told me he had already warned the French government it would have to set up customs-clearance depots and facilities at all the ports along the French Atlantic coastline where currently lorries, vans and cars from Britain arrive and are waved through. The same is true for Belgium, the Netherlands, Spain and other European ports where up to now British and Irish lorries or vans have faced few formalities because the UK has been inside the Customs Union. The UK's road haulage industry reckons their firms will have to fill in 60 million forms every year with costs of £50 added to every lorryload of goods coming into the UK and with waits of up to two to four days at ports and terminals for every lorry and van to be checked. Car boots will also need to be inspected to ensure that anything bought on the continent has proper customs clearance. Turkey is not in the political EU but is in the Customs Union. The UK will lose the right to use the Customs Union consumer kite mark which tells customers all over the world that a product – especially food products – meets the highest safety standards.

Foreign and Security Policy Brexit. The EU agreed economic sanctions against Russia to deter Putin's military aggression following his intervention in East Ukraine and annexation of Crimea. The EU took a lead in defanging Iran's nuclear ambitions and in seeking to secure Europe's external borders. If President Trump carries out his threat to impose protectionist taxes on imports into America, the EU, acting on behalf of all 28 member states, including, up to 2019, the UK, has said it will mount a massive case against the US at the World Trade Organization. Soldiers from EU states are fighting or standing guard in the struggle against Islamist terror or to send messages to Kremlin aggressivity. EU units are guarding Europe's external borders or patrolling the Mediterranean to discourage people trafficking. This is the EU at work as a global power, not in the sense of a giant military machine but as a unified voice representing the world's largest economic region and one that is not run by a communist party, as in China. Britain outside the EU will be a geo-political and foreign policy player in the same way that Brazil or Mexico are vis-à-vis the United States or Japan and South Korea are vis-à-vis China. Some have already questioned whether the UK can retain its seat as a permanent member of the United Nations Security Council. The Foreign Office will have an embassy in Brussels, but that is not the same as taking part as of right in all the discussions and decisions that determine Europe's foreign policy. A British prime minister will cool heels in the same waiting-room as a president from, say, Nigeria or Brazil – both representing a medium-sized power with much history and a professional military but not weighing in the global geo-political balance. Until now the UK's security has depended on a combination of soft power delivered by the EU and hard power delivered by NATO. Outside the EU, the UK will remain in NATO but lose the daily cooperation and operational contacts with EU foreign policy players. Margaret Thatcher first called for a common foreign and security policy for Europe at a speech in Fontainebleau in 1984. The first EU foreign policy supremo, called the High Representative, was Britain's Cathy Ashton. In many remote countries, the British diplomatic presence is reduced to a minimum given Whitehall budget difficulties. Working with an EU mission, especially on consular issues, has benefited British citizens far from home. For the first time in centuries Britain will voluntarily renounce the right to shape European foreign and geo-political policy and purpose. Like Venice and Austria-Hungary, the years of Britain as a major power will dwindle. Yes, the UK will keep a seat as a permanent member of the UN Security Council, but as London no longer has an influence over Europe's foreign policy decisions, there will be increasing pressure from rising powers like India, Nigeria or Brazil or indeed Germany to take over Britain's seat on the UN Security Council if we opt for a twenty-first century isolated from Europe.

Frontier with France Brexit. The new president of France, Emmanuel Macron, along with other candidates hoping to become president of France in 2017 insisted that the French frontier be moved to British soil. Assuming Britain starts to impose visas and residence permits on French citizens living and working in Britain, it is hard to see how the present friendly arrangements, which were agreed at a UK–France summit in Le Touquet in 2004 where I represented Britain as Europe minister, can be maintained. France disliked the massing of people – immigrants, refugees and others – at Calais seeking to join families or friends in Britain or just get a job lost in the UK's ultra-flexible unofficial labour market. Both Nicolas Sarkozy as French interior minister and then President François Hollande dismantled the camps and moved or dispersed people elsewhere in France. But human nature cannot be dispersed and there will always be those who want to enter Britain one way or another. Having passport controls and the official UK frontier on the French side for entry into Britain has been very convenient for anyone taking a lorry or car from France into Britain. So too has having passports checked at the Gare du Nord in Paris rather than queuing when the Eurostar arrives in St Pancras. But when Brexit Britain begins to make life awkward for France and for French European citizens to come to work or live in Britain, there will be a political backlash and the chances of maintaining the Le Touquet arrangements are slim.

Free Movement Brexit. UKIP and the Conservatives have made the number of EU citizens in the UK a number-one domestic political issue this century. Theresa May's entire ministerial career was dominated by the issue. The number of Europeans in Britain was the core issue of the Brexit campaign, with the plebiscite being as much about immigration as the EU. Imposing a cumbersome bureaucracy of quotas, seasonal work permits, travel visas or regional work permits like a passport stamp for the City will be expensive and alienate all other governments in Europe, who will resent such discrimination against their voters. There are major sectors of the economy – health, catering, agricultural work, old-age care, transport and construction – that depend on workers from Poland, Ireland, Romania and other EU countries. Financial services, the creative industries, sport and universities will shrivel if

denied access to talented Europeans. As discussed later, there are
many ways of controlling immigration and supporting the right to
work of many more British citizens as well as helping communities
who feel challenged by new arrivals, but successive British governments have refused to implement such policies. It is not too late. In
any event, the majority of immigrants into the UK have come from
outside the EU and the numbers of EU citizens coming to work in
Britain fluctuate wildly. As the boss of the restaurant chain Pret A
Manger told the Commons in 2017, only 1 in 50 applicants for a
job with the firm, which pays fair wages, is British. EU and other
immigrant workers come to Britain to do work British citizens do
not take up.

Expat Brexit. It will be harder for British citizens to automatically live
or retire in warmer regions of southern Europe without let or hindrance and they may be required to take out expensive insurance
policies for health, old-age and social care. For example in Spain,
there are 300,000 British citizens who are *empadronados* – officially
registered on the electoral rolls as full-time residents in Spain. But
according to British embassy officials in Madrid there are up to 1
million British expatriates who have bought or rented a home or
do business on the Spanish islands and costas and pass much of
the year in the country. Their status once they lose the automatic
right under EU law to live unmolested in Spain is far from clear
and will be hard to define. A non-EU citizen, for example, resident
permanently in Spain, who wants to drive his or her car has to sit a
driving test, both practical and written. The latter has to be done in
Spanish, and many British expats living on the costas of Spain have
not really sufficiently mastered written or spoken Spanish to pass a
driving test examination in it.

Geo-Political Brexit. For the Kremlin, seeing Europe revert to disu-
nited nation states is a longstanding strategic goal. Speaking to his
campaign supporters in Florida some weeks after his inauguration,

President Trump hailed Brexit as part of a worldwide movement. Britain can seek to become a minor helper in a global Brexit–Trump movement, but other world powers are aghast at the protectionist and Islamophobe rhetoric of the US president. In France, supporters of the rightwing anti-EU Front National said they had to win, because if they do not, France would see the arrival of 'Sadiq Khans' running major French cities as a FN leader told the BBC. On the whole the UK has integrated Muslim immigrants well, as the presence of British Muslims from immigrant families in the cabinet, city halls, the professions and journalism demonstrates. There are more prisoners in British jails than soldiers in the British Army and Serbia has more battle tanks than Britain. Can Britain retain a global role if utterly disconnected from Europe? And once parts of the British community have discovered a taste for being unpleasant to Europeans and even seeing some leaving the UK, are we sure other forms of xenophobia against recent incomers will not surface?

Policing and Security Brexit. Can the UK stay in the post-national networks of information exchange and policing once Britain has left the EU? Even Mrs May is a fan of the European Arrest Warrant used to bring back terrorists after they fled from London after the London Tube and bus bombings in July 2005. She is also said to appreciate the role of Europol – the European police coordination centre run by a British official. It is an EU agency employing 800 people, so ultimately under the control of the European Commission, and in case of a dispute the European Court of Justice has an arbitration role. If Britain says it wants to stay part of Europol, why cannot Britain agree to stay part of other EU networks and agencies? And if policing across borders is now vital for UK security, is that not true of economic and trade activity within the Single Market and Customs Union?

Environmental and Global Warming Brexit. Many pro-Brexit Eurosceptics are also climate change sceptics. Does the UK give up its leadership role in shaping environmental politics in Europe, or how can this be achieved as British ministers and elected politicians no longer play a role in EU policy making? It is the EU, often urged on by British ministers, which has taken the boldest steps at a supranational level to try and slow down global warming, set standards for protection of oceans, for clean beaches and to lessen harmful emissions from vehicles. Does Britain now go it alone or simply incorporate EU decisions and policy in this area?

Human Rights Brexit. Mrs May says that British judges must now decide all British law and the European Court of Justice – largely a commercial and administrative tribunal – should have no place in Britain. But it is the European Court of Human Rights (ECtHR), linked to the Council of Europe set up by Winston Churchill, that is the supranational court which most imposes its rulings on British judges. So after political Brexit from the EU, does a Brexit from the ECtHR not logically follow? That would leave Britain isolated, with Belarus, as the only two European nations not observing the European Convention on Human Rights as members of the Council of Europe.

Social Europe Brexit. EU directives transposed into British law have given rights to British workers protecting them from unfair or harsh treatment, especially in the case of women or workers with disabilities or the working hours and holidays of employees. European Works Councils now cover about 19 million workers in bigger British firms or US, German, French and other multinational companies operating in Britain. Again, Mrs May says worker rights will be protected, but many in her party and in business would like to see a weakening of EU directives like the Working Time Directive, the Posted Worker Directive or the Agency Workers Directive. Any bill which repeals EU legislation allows amendments to be tabled that can turn back the clock on Social Europe. And as new measures are decided at EU level, British workers will be again left behind.

Farming Brexit. Fifty-five per cent of farming income comes from transfer payments under the EU's Common Agricultural Policy. The UK food and farming sector employs 800,000 people and is worth £108 billion a year to the British economy. Eighty per cent of the sector's exports go to the rest of the EU. Finding new alternative markets for UK food and farming products will not be easy.

The CAP provides 87 per cent of farmers' income in Northern Ireland, 75 per cent in Scotland. Hill farmers and other farmers who care for the countryside and try to work with ecological and nature-friendly forms of farming receive more help from the EU than the big agro-industry monolith, even though the latter are vital in keeping the cost of what we eat at a reasonable level. To be sure, the prices for the 62 per cent of the food Britain eats which is produced in the UK are supported by common EU tariffs. If they were eliminated, cheaper food produced without the health and workers' rights safeguards in EU law could certainly arrive in the UK. The UK imports around £40 billion of food, drink and animal foodstuffs and exports about half that amount, mainly to Europe. Brexit could easily mean the end of British farming as it is today and the end of a degree of self-sufficiency in Britain's food supply. Certainly denying European workers access to employment in the British food industry would lead to the closure of many firms in the agro-food supply chain. Farmers would demand direct subsidies from the British taxpayer and there would be difficult parliamentary and government decisions to take on what level of subsidy was acceptable.

University, Scientific and Student Brexit. British universities get the lion's share of EU budget allocation for scientific research – £836 million a year. In 2014–15 the 125,000 EU students in Britain helped generate £4 billion, as well as spending on accommodation and living costs. Some 200,000 British students have benefited from the EU's Erasmus programme. Many of the new universities in Britain are now thriving educational institutions helping the regeneration of once poorer regions precisely because they are the most open to working with EU students and professors and extremely smart at accessing EU funds. With government budgets under massive domestic political pressure, particularly to provide care for an ageing population, the guaranteed EU income for universities is not likely to be replaced in full.

SatNav Brexit. Britain plays a key role in projects like the European Space Agency and the EU satellite system, now an integral part of the global navigation system. Is it possible that public funds can be found to sustain a purely national space programme? Can a British navigation satellite can be developed and paid for to compete with existing US and EU operations? This will be costly. Opting out of this aspect of post-national technology and communications will leave Britain weaker.

Euratom Brexit. The European Atomic Energy Community was set up in the 1950s along with the European Economic Community and the European Coal and Steel Community. By virtue of EU membership the UK is in Euratom, which now has the responsibility for inspecting the 15 British civil nuclear reactors that generate a fifth of UK electricity output. The UK can replicate such inspection work but only at significant cost to the taxpayer. The UK is a strong supporter of nuclear energy in the EU energy mix. Brexatom would minimise British influence on any future direction European energy policy takes. Without European regulatory authorisation, imports and exports of nuclear material, including medical isotopes, would stop until a new system was in place and agreed internationally.

Insurance and Savings Brexit. The EU regulates under its 2016 Solvency II law and under EIOPA – the European Insurance and Occupational Pensions Authority – the cross-border operations of the insurance and pensions profession in which the UK is a specialist.

This sector of the financial services industry is a major UK profit centre. Firms from all over the world based in the City of London have freedom to operate anywhere under EU rules in 27 countries. British officials and UK MEPs have been at the heart of shaping EU rules and laws. With Brexit, British firms in these sectors will not be able to operate in Europe unless they abide by the law and accept, ultimately, that the European Court of Justice is the final arbiter on a dispute. EIOPA represents British and other insurance firms at global supervisory bodies including IAIS, the International Association of Insurance Supervisors. This allows British expertise to shape world, as well as EU rules. Since the time in 1688 that Lloyds of London got going as a global insurance firm, the UK has developed one of the most profitable insurance industries in the world. Losing a role in Europe will cause the important global British insurance industry business serious damage.

Ratings Agencies Brexit. London is home to three of the most important firms that help measure and influence the world economy. These are the three rating agencies – Moody's, Fitch and Standard and Poor's. They employ 1,500 people whose job it is to award a credit rating to national governments and big companies. This determines how easy or costly it is for government and big business to raise money on the international money markets. The three rating agencies generate an annual £600 million for the UK economy. They are regulated and supervised by ESMA – the European Securities and Markets Authority, based in Paris. Outside the EU, there are doubts if a purely UK-based regulatory body would be acceptable and the firms would have to transfer their business across the Channel or the Irish Sea.

Lawyers/Professionals Brexit. The ability of lawyers, doctors, architects and other qualified professionals to practise across Europe will be thrown into chaos. It will be pointless asking expensive London lawyers to draw up contacts or represent, say, one partner in a bitter divorce case as anything drawn up in London or decided by a London court will have no legal value in Europe. The British Medical Association has carried out a survey of European doctors who work in the NHS. Most said they would like to return home because of the anti-European climate created following the Brexit vote. Many professionals from across the Channel enjoy working in Britain but expect to be able to bring families to join them, including, if necessary, ageing parents. If new anti-European immigration rules decided by Britain make this more difficult or dictate that the spouse of an EU professional paying taxes in the UK has fewer rights than a British citizen, they will not come. Training up UK-born professionals to replace all highly qualified and trained EU citizens working in the UK can indeed be done. But it will take years and be expensive

European Communities Act Brexit. Brexit propagandists claim leaving Europe is simply a question of repealing the 1972 Act which said that henceforth the UK would incorporate EU law into British legislation. In 1948, when India became independent, the Indian government simply transferred lock, stock and barrel all existing imperial law and ordinances onto the Indian statute book. The UK government is proposing to do the same under its pompously named Great Repeal Bill. But that means EU laws will still apply in Britain, and for many Conservative MPs the object of Brexit was to abolish laws on, say, social rights protecting workers and women as well as those granting trade unions a certain status. Most EU legislation is transferred into UK law by means of statutory instruments. This gets cursory scrutiny in ad-hoc Commons committees and is rarely, if ever, debated on the floor of the House. In writing out many thousands of statutory instruments going back four decades there will be endless opportunities for ministers and civil servants to add, delete or alter bits and pieces of UK law which they do not like. It is legislative work of years and impossible to accomplish before 2019. It opens the way for many new laws which will never be tested in full parliamentary debate. Far from taking back control, this aspect of Brexit hands unprecedented arbitrary power to the executive. The government has proposed it should have the executive power to legislate replacement laws for existing EU legislation – mainly regulations common across all EU member states. But each regulation touches on some aspect of how we live, do business or are told by law what should happen. For the government to arrogate to itself the right to make law without debate and decision in parliament may appear at first right convenient but it represents a major change in parliamentary democracy and accountability and control by elected MPs over what the executive does and the powers ministers have without obtaining permission from parliament.

Gibrexit. The future of Gibraltar will change as a result of Brexit. At the moment, as a UK territory Gibraltar is in the Single Market and Customs Union. Ninety-five per cent of all goods, food and other products enter Gibraltar from Spain free of customs duties and 10,000 Gibraltarians with UK passports who live in houses in neighbouring Spain cross the frontier every day. The Spanish foreign minister has said Britain should examine joint sovereignty with Spain for the future status of Gibraltar, a position rejected angrily by the Gibraltar government. But Brexit will leave the inhabitants of the Rock very exposed as they lose EU citizenship rights to live in Spain and trade or do business in any EU market.

Flying Brexit. One of the most spectacular outcomes of the reforms leading to the creation of the Single Market has been the fall in the costs of air travel and the rise of low-cost airlines like EasyJet and Ryanair, as well as many other smaller low-cost services that allow direct air links to many different cities and regions in Europe. Previously, national airlines like British Airways or

Alitalia or Air France jealously guarded their national markets to keep prices and profits as high as possible. In addition, low-cost airlines can be based in Britain, like EasyJet, but fly from different locations inside the EU, not just back and forth to the UK. Nations guard jealously their airspace and regulate who can take off and land. The EU has all but abolished those monopoly privileges. There is also a broad so-called Open Skies Agreement signed between the EU and the US in 2007 which allows airlines from Europe, including Britain, to fly to the US and Canada. The European Common Aviation Area extends to Norway and Iceland, and as a result there are some interesting low-cost carriers now offering cheap flights from the UK to North America. Britain has pushed for the creation of the 'Single European Sky' to allow airlines to choose the best, most-effective route irrespective of national borders and control system so as to save on fuel costs and speed up trips. All these arrangements are ultimately under EU law and in consequence the final arbiter in case of dispute is the European Court of Justice. Negotiating bilateral aviation agreements is notoriously tricky. The clout the EU, with hundreds of millions of passengers, has is much greater than that of any single European nation. Planes will still come and go to Britain after Brexit, but if the UK insists on walking out of all EU and EU–US agreements because of an ideological obsession with acknowledging that air travel above all requires supranational laws and a final court, then British holidaymakers may have to discover the charms of holidays in their own country and British business travellers will find themselves using trains, cars and ships as the UK insists on aviation Brexit.

Cooperation Brexit. Other than specialists, few will have any idea of the width and depth of useful value-adding cooperation that Britain has promoted as an EU member state. Here is a list of the main EU agencies in which Britain participates and helps fund. The reader can skip the titles of the organisations but they are examples of what may be lost if the full, hardline Brexit desired by politicians like Nigel Farage and Iain Duncan Smith is achieved: Agency for the Cooperation of Energy Regulators; Clean Sky Joint Undertaking; Community Plant Variety Office; European Agency for Safety and Health at Work; European Asylum Support Office; European Aviation Safety Agency; European Banking Authority; European Centre for Disease Prevention and Control; European Centre for the Development of Vocational Training; European Chemicals Agency; European Defence Agency; European Environment Agency; European Fisheries Control Agency; European Food Safety Authority; European Foundation for the Improvement of Living and Working Conditions; European Global Navigation Satellite Systems Agency; European Institute for Gender Equality; European Institute for Innovation and Technology; European Joint Undertaking for ITER and the Development of Fusion Energy; European Maritime Safety Energy; European Medicines Agency; European Monitoring Centre for Drugs and Drug Addiction; European Police College; European Police Office (EUROPOL); European Railway Agency; European Securities and Markets Authority; European Training Foundation; European Union Agency for Fundamental Rights; European Union Agency for Network and Information Security; European Union Agency for the Management of Operational Cooperation at the External Borders (FRONTEX); European Union Institute for Security Studies; European Union Satellite Centre; European Union's Judicial Cooperation Unity (EUROJUST); Fuel Cells and Hydrogen Joint Undertaking; Innovative Medicines Unit Joint Undertaking; Office for the Harmonisation in the Internal Market – Trade Marks and Design; Office of the Body of European Regulators for Electronic Communications; Translation Centre for the Bodies of the European Union.

Two of these agencies – the European Banking Authority and the European Medicines Agency – are located in London, employ key British professionals and make London the centre for regulating and dealing with the two sensitive areas of pharmaceutical authorisations and banking. Airlines flying out of London are controlled by the European Civil Aviation Safety Agency. It would be extremely expensive to duplicate these agencies as national bodies in Britain. And they would have to be in full compliance with EU norms and standards to allow British citizens, firms and institutions like universities to operate across Europe. Moreover, if there is a dispute involving any of these agencies it is often the European Court of Justice which is the final arbiter. So, much as Prime Minister Theresa May can splutter about removing any role for the ECJ, if Britain wants to do business or have a relationship with Europe, we will still be subject to the ECJ whether we like it not.

In fact it was Theresa May who set out the classic case for international cooperation and arbitration like that embodied in the EU and the ECJ. In April 2016 she argued in a speech that

> no country or empire in world history has ever been totally sovereign, completely in control of its destiny. Even at the height of their power, the Roman Empire, Imperial China, the Ottomans, the British Empire, the Soviet Union, modern-day America, were never able to have everything their own way. At different points, military rivals, economic crises, diplomatic manoeuvring, competing philosophies and emerging technologies all played their part in inflicting defeats and hardships, and necessitated compromises even for states as powerful as these.
>
> Today, those factors continue to have their effect on the sovereignty of nations large and small, rich and poor. But there is now an additional complication. International, multilateral institutions exist to try to systematise negotiations between nations,

promote trade, ensure cooperation on matters like cross-border crime, and create rules and norms that reduce the risk of conflict.

These institutions invite nation states to make a trade-off: to pool and therefore cede some sovereignty in a controlled way, to prevent a greater loss of sovereignty in an uncontrolled way, through for example military conflict or economic decline.

This defence of involvement in international treaty organisations like the EU and accepting their rules, being subject to their courts and, in two words, sharing sovereignty, is in the longstanding tradition of Britain's relations with other countries. Is the Theresa May who defended such supranational cooperation and sovereignty-sharing in April 2016 lurking somewhere under the carapace of the Brexit prime minister? Or was her speech a cynical, indeed duplicitous set of remarks designed to show the then prime minister, David Cameron, that she was on his side in opposing Brexit but she did not mean a word? On the whole, Theresa May has a reputation for being serious in what she says and writes as a politician, and indeed that was her reputation before entering the House of Commons in 1997.

There are more than 30 EU agencies in which Britain plays an important role and in which that involvement will now come to an end unless the government decides it wants to keep paying contributions to the EU budget in exchange for maintaining a presence and a role. But many of these agencies, like the Unified Patent Court that began work in London after the Brexit vote, accept the ultimate supremacy of the ECJ. All depend on the right of EU nationals to be able to travel, live and work freely without the work or residence permits that those in favour of Brexit want to see introduced in Britain.

4

NATIONALIST IDENTITARIANISM

The costs of Brexit were barely raised during the campaign. Instead, on 23 June 2016 a giant populist plebiscite saw the Enlightenment values of reason, logical argument and truth being crushed by a nationalist identitarian tsunami of lies, fear and hate. Jo Cox, a young Member of Parliament, was stabbed and shot as the campaign reached its climax. Her killer shouted 'This is for Britain', 'Keep Britain independent' and 'Britain first' as he murdered the Labour MP as she campaigned in support of Europe.

There were reports that people speaking with foreign accents were insulted and told to 'Go home!' Leaflets were put through letters-boxes showing Turkey, Iraq and Syria about to join the EU or showing an apparently endless snake of Levantine-looking men queuing, so it seemed, to invade England.

The hate unleashed by the Brexit politicians was one of the most disturbing outcomes of the campaign. A poll carried out by ICM in March 2017 reported that one in three of Britain's Black, Asian and minority ethnicity population had either experienced or witnessed abuse, with one in five – 19 per cent – witnessing or suffering racial assault. Two-fifths, 41 per cent, had witnessed racist remarks or opinions and 38 per cent had seen racist material online. More than a quarter, 27 per cent, had seen racist graffiti, posters or leaflets. Gina Miller is the businesswoman who initiated the High Court review that led to three senior judges ruling that the government should seek parliament's approval before starting a process that would remove a significant number of rights. She was subject to an avalanche of abuse on Twitter and Facebook. Pro-Brexit activists said they hoped she and her children would die of cancer. She was threatened with gang rape, while according to the *Metro*, an organisation called 'UKIP Peoples Forum 2020' stated: 'I hope she gets fucking killed', another: 'Kill her! Throw her in the garbage, dustbin, whatever.'

Ms Miller, a 51-year-old investment fund manager and philanthropist, was born in the former British Guyana in South America. The *Metro* also reported that one Twitter user wrote: 'Gina Miller is NOT even British this black immigrant bitch should be deported she is a fucking traitor to the UK.' Another tweeted 'Get the fuck out of our country deport the bitch.' The police advised her not to appear in public as pro-Brexit fury rose up in hate and threats against someone who had dared challenge their perspective.

Nigel Farage set the tone when he announced he didn't like being on a train and hearing foreign languages being spoken and he would not want a Romanian as a neighbour. His fellow UKIP MEPs, in particular, have further been exposed making misogynist statements. Joan Smith, the feminist novelist and writer, author of the best-seller *Misogynies*, wrote after the referendum: 'I have never known a time when woman-hating has been so seething or so widespread.'

In February 2017, the Community Security Trust, which monitors anti-Semitic attacks on Jews and their institutions, reported that the months after Brexit saw the biggest surge in anti-Jewish hate attacks ever seen in Britain.

Hate crimes recorded by regional police forces rose by 100 per cent in the months after the Brexit vote, according to the *Independent*. A major rise in the number of racially and religiously motivated crimes reported to police following the June referendum result, including assaults and arson, was recorded.

Community groups representing EU nationals in the UK have warned about the potential for an 'undercurrent of xenophobia' to spread as the negotiations for Brexit, with their emphasis on stopping European citizens coming into Britain, get under way. 'The 100,000 Swedish citizens living and working in Britain feel vulnerable', Sweden's Europe minister, Ann Linde, declared after a visit to London when she met Swedes living and working in Britain as EU citizens.

The chair of the Equality and Human Rights Commission, David Isaac, has also said he is 'hugely concerned' about a Brexit backlash against EU citizens living peacefully in Britain. Europeans were apparently told at work to 'go home' or asked 'Don't you know where Dover is?'

The novelist John Lanchester reported in a *London Review of Books* podcast that the language of the Leave campaign had opened the doors to permit hate against our neighbours.

All those millions of our fellow citizens who have spent the last few decades privately muttering to themselves that Enoch had a point now feel empowered, entitled, free to speak their minds at last. There is a real darkness in this country, a xenophobic, racist sickness of heart that is closer to the surface today than it has been for decades. That is a direct result of the referendum campaign. The campaign's dual legacy is the end of the idea that politics is based on rational argument, and a new permission to hate immigrants.

After Brexit, as the pressure increased to close frontiers, a Polish man, Arkadiusz Jóźwik, was punched to death by young louts in Harlow, Essex, where the hate campaigning against European immigrants was at its strongest. The Polish ambassador went to lay a wreath at the site of the victim's murder. Not even the most obdurate of those who pretend that xenophobia, especially against Poles, played no part in the Brexit decision could deny that the Pole was attacked and beaten after the proud young Brits overheard him speaking Polish on his mobile phone, as local witnesses confirmed.

Polish police officers came over to patrol the streets of Harlow with English constables. It was a clever outreach move by the Essex chief constable, but so fast had Brexit changed Britain that foreign policemen from Eastern Europe were invited to walk the streets of an English town to reassure the community! A British journalist, Stephen Bush, who is black, reported on the Harlow killing in the *New Statesman* and described how he was insulted as a 'Paki'.

The *Independent* newspaper gave other examples in the weeks that followed Brexit. These included:

- Gangs prowling the streets demanding passers-by prove they can speak English.
- Swastikas in Armagh, Sheffield, Plymouth, Leicester, London and Glasgow.
- Assaults, arson attacks and dog excrement being thrown at doors or shoved through letter-boxes.
- Toddlers being racially abused alongside their mothers, with children involved as either victims or perpetrators in 14 per cent of incidents.
- A man in Glasgow ripping off a girl's headscarf and telling her 'Trash like you better start obeying the white man.'
- A crowd striding through a London street chanting: 'First we'll get the Poles out, then the gays!'

Supporters of the campaigning against foreign people in Britain which lay at the core of Brexit populism refused to acknowledge that the surge in hate crimes that followed had anything to do with the nationalist-populism that fuelled the Brexit vote. No one ever admits to open racism, just to making the point that there are foreigners in our midst and they are not welcome. But to deny the dark side of Brexit xenophobia, like denying the fear that went through many Muslim hearts at President Trump's travel ban in his first week in the White

House is to deny reality. Brexit–Trump xenophobia is now the English-speaking world's contribution to shaping a different planet.

It would be wrong to link all the language used against immigrants in the Brexit campaign to acts of violence or physical attacks. But when it became as coarse and menacing as it did and when Europeans living in Britain were painted in such negative hues, a climate is created in which acts or words of hate followed sequentially. Well-intentioned organisations like British Future produced polls in which those surveyed all denied they were xenophobic. Who would admit to such a label? But nonetheless an atmosphere was created in which denigration and dislike of foreigners became the norm, and there were daily reports of European citizens, many long-time residents and economic actors in Britain, saying that they no longer felt welcome and comfortable in Britain as a result of the Brexit vote.

In his book *The Edge of Reason*, the philosopher Julian Baggini writes that 'The rehabilitation of reason is urgent because it is only through the proper use of reason that we can find our way out of the quagmires in which many of the big issues of our time have become stuck.' If ever there was a political quagmire in Britain which has defied reason it is the question of Europe in the twenty-first century. There have always been competing positions on the European question, both in the British Isles and across the Channel. European cooperation and integration after 1945 was an idea based on the eighteenth-century Enlightenment, not nineteenth- and early twentieth-century nationalism – even if it's a paradox of the EU that it has led to a springtime of nations without precedent in European history.

Baggini goes on to argue that:

> Without a clear sense of what it means for one point of view to
> be more reasonable than another, it seems that the position one
> adopts is ultimately based on nothing more than personal opin-
> ion or preference. People take sides in debates not on the basis

of evidence or arguments but on the basis of the side where they feel most at home.

This identitarian politics is not new. Identifying oneself as belonging to a clan, a race, a city-state, a nation, a movement, a religion, has been the main organising tool of politics since Classical Greece and Rome. Nor is it unhealthy, unless a patriotic belief in what we identify with becomes a xenophobic hatred of those who do not share our views.

I have never challenged the rights of those sceptical of or opposed to the cooperation implicit in EU membership and its common rule book to their view, but when it crosses a frontier into open contempt and dislike of fellow Europeans or when anti-Europeans have to enter a post-factual world which may do massive damage to the future prosperity and coherence of my country and my children then I believe it is necessary to enter the lists.

As Timothy Garton Ash points out in the *Guardian*, it takes time for people to see through the rise of the politics of identity and emotion and in that period what is required is 'courage, determination, consistency, the development of a new political language and new policy answers to real problems'. To solve Brexit, therefore, Europe has to change. The mere presence of those British opposed to neo-isolationism and English nationalist-populism working to explain to fellow citizens the folly of Brexit will not be sufficient.

Even the most devout of Leavers or Brexiters would not dispute that most of the emotion was on their side. Indeed, across Europe those who want to assert the supremacy of national preference certainly believe that their case is both rational and reasonable. But rational and reasonable cases do not normally have to rely on open xenophobia and demonstrable lies. This in today's modish political parlance is called 'post-truth' politics. The politics of lies rose to dominate the Brexit campaign itself, as well as creating the conditions for Brexit over many years prior to 23 June 2016.

From the brutal language of Roderigo Duterte, the president of the Philippines, through Vladimir Putin we arrive at Donald Trump, with perhaps a look at Viktor Orbán, and then pausing to examine the language of Nigel Farage and Boris Johnson about Europe, it is hard to have confidence that an age of reason can return to politics, especially in Europe.

Brexit was a triumph of unreason, but then Europe's national leaders have not been able to use reason to construct a set of policies that answer their citizens' needs this century. In 1929, the British political scientist R. H. Tawney wrote: 'An integration of Europe, whatever its precise form, has reason on its side; but the natural human egotisms of interests and emotion; of locality, class, and occupation; of regional loyalties and national pride, will rally to resist it.' In the twenty-first century Tawney's words ring more than ever true. Brexit was a triumph of emotion, locality and national pride. A few European integrationists may dwell in Brussels but national political leaders have stopped being willing to share national sovereignty in the manner of a Thatcher, Kohl or Mitterrand.

Europe watches with indifference the procession of black BMW or Mercedes limousines disgorging prime ministers and presidents at the huge, badly designed office block that houses the European Council, across the road from the European Commission's Berlaymont building at the top of the Rue de Loi in Brussels.

Close by is an even more pharaonic cluster of buildings, gigantic in scale, that provide meeting rooms for members of the European Parliament. It is matched by a giant edifice for MEPs in Strasbourg that is empty most of the year as MEPs prefer to work in Brussels. There is a perfectly serviceable parliamentary assembly chamber and linked offices at the Council of Europe. When I was an FCO minister working on EU affairs, meetings of heads of government took place in different European cities. Europe, as it were, came to its constituent nations. The European Parliament could easily sell off its bloated buildings and hold many of its sessions where the people of Europe live, not in a special Brussels bubble.

But so far this century the guardians of the European ideal have seemed to think that the more sealed off they are from the people of Europe, the wiser or better their decisions will be. I make no criticism of any individual, and many MEPs and national politicians who do EU business are friends and acquaintances and I wish them well. The EU at all levels has appalling professional communications skills and no ability to generate the instant rebuttal of the lies and propaganda of nationalist, often extreme rightwing populists.

As the passions over the campaign and outcome of the vote subsided it gradually became clear that no one in government or amongst the pro-Brexit politicians and their supporters in the think-tank, media and business world had made any plans of any sort for how to set about rewriting all the trade, commercial, legal and other rules that had linked the UK to Europe since 1973.

The UK's top EU official, Sir Ivan Rogers, the Permanent Representative of Britain to the European Commission in Brussels, resigned in frustration early in 2017 at the sheer lack of leadership and clear instructions from the government and the Prime Minister over whether she was prepared to sign an act of unilateral economic destruction by amputating Britain fully from the EU market of 500 million consumers or whether she was prepared to compromise.

Theresa May's summer holidays are spent walking in the Swiss Alps. In February 2014 the Swiss voted in a referendum to stop EU immigration into Switzerland. For three years, the Swiss chewed over the problem of whether such a ban made economic sense. With 27 per cent of the Swiss population foreign-born, nearly every sector of the Swiss economy depends on European workers and Swiss companies would shrivel if they lost access to the Single Market just across the border.

There were negotiations with Brussels, but the EU made it clear that if the Swiss took unilateral action against EU citizens then full, unfettered access to the Single Market would close. In the end the Swiss People's Party, the main rightwing nationalist party, saw economic sense and agreed with other parties to strengthen the internal labour market in favour of Swiss citizens but not to impose external controls.

Might Mrs May be inspired by the Swiss example? Does Britain have the strategic patience to wait and place some distance between 23 June 2016 and the final decision about what sort of exit from the EU we want? Can the MPs who arrived in the House of Commons in June 2017 step away from the prejudices and passion that fuelled anti-European politics and brought about Brexit? None of the costs and consequences of amputating Britain from Europe were spelt out in the years and months before the Brexit vote and were barely mentioned by the media, especially the BBC, during the campaign itself. Can British companies follow the example of their Swiss confrères and make it clear to ruling-party politicians that unilateral economic disarmament will not herald a radiant future for the UK economy?

A study by the Centre for Economic and Business Research (CEBR) released just before the Autumn Budget Statement in 2016 found that Brexit would affect every major British wealth-creating sector negatively, with manufacturing hit if the UK left the Single Market and Customs Union and British creative industries suffering a 'body blow' if there were strict controls on immigration. In January 2017, the CEBR cut its forecast for British growth by 50 per cent as Brexit impacted on investment.

The CEBR is close to mainstream business and to the Conservative Party, and its director has never been much of an EU fan. However, the CEBR report dismisses the idea of one-by-one sectoral agreements which Prime Minister May and Brexit ministers have suggested is a way forward. On the contrary, the CEBR report warns that 'all major sectors are linked to the EU and could be harmed if the UK govern-ment sought a free trade agreement which prioritised some sectors over others'. In any event, the EU27 have since ruled out any sector-by-sector separate agreements.

The Tories have survived for nearly three centuries as the main governing party of Britain on one simple premise. The Tory Party exists to preserve, protect and augment the nation's wealth. Other parties may be better at redistributing this wealth, but no Tory prime minister will survive if he or she presides over a significant reduction of British wealth and income.

To be sure, trade will continue. We like driving BMWs, drinking French wine, buying second homes in Spain or soaking up sun and history in Italy and Greece, as do others. Marmite and muffins will continue to be exported to Europe, but British food exports which are suspected of having genetically or hormone-modified elements (especially if a UK–US trade deal allows such products to be imported) will not gain easy entry to the EU. The extent in width and depth of that trade will be reduced. It remains to be seen if India, China or the United States will reward Brexit by concluding bilateral trade terms with Britain on advantageous terms.

Britain runs a trade surplus with the United States – we export more to America than we buy in return. President Trump says he wants to reduce US trade deficits with individual countries and has talked of big tariff increases on imported goods. Individual American states have their own licensing laws for service industries like banking, insurance, pension funds or the legal profession – areas where the UK hopes to win export markets. So the assumption that the UK outside the EU can massively increase exports to America may prove optimistic.

President Trump's commerce secretary, Wilbur Ross, has described Brexit as a 'God-given opportunity' to take business away from the UK as Britain was facing a 'period of confusion' following the Brexit vote and therefore it was 'inevitable' there would be 'relocations' of banks and business from the UK. Mr Ross shows the true face not so much of the Trump administration but of any country or business that seeks to maximise trade advantage. Common to the ideology of many rightwing anti-Europeans in Britain, such as Boris Johnson, Michael Howard, Nigel Farage or Michael Gove, is the belief that Britain should look to and link with the US rather than play a role as a leading European polity.

One or two other English-speaking economies like Australia or New Zealand and the English-speaking provinces of Canada are admitted into the 'Anglosphere' – the grandiose name given by rightwing London-based nationalists to their dream of a new world order at whose centre sits England. However, there is no evidence that the US and its latest commerce secretary will lift a finger to help Britain in any trade deal. On the contrary, the US loses a valuable springboard for doing business across Europe once the UK quits the EU and its Single Market.

5

CLOSING FRONTIERS

The vote was not just a British political phenomenon. The German chancellor, Angela Merkel, was surely correct in asserting: 'Brexit is not just any event. It is a deep break in the EU's history of integration[...] We must face the consequences [of Brexit] and consider the future of the EU.' Once Brexit is consummated the balance of power in Europe will change. Between them Germany and France will have 43 per cent of the EU's GDP, 44 per cent of EU exports, 33 per cent of the EU's population and 49 per cent of the EU's military spending.

The political leaders of Poland and Hungary, Jarosław Kaczyński and Viktor Orbán, hailed Brexit as a 'fantastic opportunity' for a 'cultural counter-revolution'. By this they mean the return of an illiberal Europe of braggadocio national identitarians in which the give-and-take of the Europe shaped by Christian and Social Democrats and Liberals in the decades following Winston Churchill's famous appeal for European integration in Switzerland in 1946 is replaced by a politics of modernised post-totalitarian *Führerprinzip* in which hatred of Islam and Muslims replaces pre-1939 hatred of one of the other major Abrahamic religions.

Orbán, Hungary's stridently anti-liberal prime minister, tried to cash in on the Brexit-generated hatred against immigrants by holding a referendum to change the constitution of Hungary to reject the EU suggestion that the country might take a few of the refugees fleeing tyranny and violence in the Middle East. Orbán treated with contempt the appeal from Angela Merkel and the EU for a modicum of generosity towards today's refugees. After all, Western European nations had offered refuge to 200,000 Hungarians when Soviet tanks rolled over democracy activists in Budapest in 1956. He won a Stalinesque level of support, with 98.5 per cent of voters agreeing with his proposition. But as ever, Hungarians are smarter than their political bosses. Only 39 per cent of the population turned out to vote. The referendum needed 50 per cent participation to be valid, leaving Orbán humiliated. Curiously, only 37 per cent of the British electorate voted for Brexit, but this vote has been fetishised as a sacred moment in British history.

It was hard on the new government, on opposition parties and the press. Since the seventeenth century England and then Britain had been run by parliamentary democracy. Now suddenly there was a snapshot of emotion on a day in June which allowed a little more than a third of all electors to express discontent with immigration or to vote for the promise of £350 million a week for the NHS once out of the EU – a promise that was very attractive to older voters, who voted for Brexit and who believed the NHS, which they need more than younger voters, would get a massive financial boost.

Never before had Britain taken such a major decision by means of a plebiscite. It implied the undoing of the most important treaties ever negotiated and signed in British history. It would alter every relationship Britain had with every country in the world. Leaving the agencies and institutions in which Britain has played an active part for more than 40 years, regulating trade and other inter-government relations, means setting up purely national agencies in Britain even though they would have to comply with EU rules outside Britain. Few modern problems, from air pollution, to mobile-phone pornography in school playgrounds, to terrorism, are to be tackled within national borders.

Britain's Brexit prime minister appears to have interpreted the narrow decision as a mandate to take the most extreme measures against the EU. 'We are going to be a fully independent, sovereign country, a country that is no longer part of a political union with supranational institutions that override national parliaments and courts', she declared. Her foreign secretary, Boris Johnson, kept repeating that Britain could stay fully engaged in the Single Market, trade as on today's terms and yet ignore any EU rules or mutual obligations laid down in EU treaties. Jeroen Dijsselbloem, president of the Eurogroup and finance minister of the Netherlands, rebuked him, saying that Johnson's claims are 'intellectually impossible' and 'politically unachievable'.

Global investors and global markets are also independent and in their own spheres sovereign, and they showed just what they thought of Mrs May's strident language by reducing the value of the pound sterling to below par with the euro and helping the pound sink against the dollar to its lowest value in 160 years. On 24 June 2016 the pound was worth US$1.49. Five months later it had fallen to US$1.24. Sovereign firms who have no duty to support an isolationist Britain showed their independence by announcing major withdrawals from the UK.

The European Court of Human Rights, which is entirely separate from the EU, has overridden British judges and parliament far more than the ECJ. So is Mrs May planning to Brexit from the Council of Europe and withdraw from the European Convention on Human Rights, to join Belarus as the only European nation not in membership? And what other international treaty organisations which impose supranational decisions on Britain is Mrs May proposing to Brexit from? As Janan Ganesh of the *Financial Times* correctly notes, Theresa May 'is the Brexit prime minister and nothing else'.

She will find out that rhetoric about a sovereign independent nation cuts no ice in the world outside Great Brexitannia. Decisions that impact massively on Britain are taken by men and women who have no interest in the anti-EU obsessions of many in the ruling elites of London.

'Taking back control over decisions affecting the UK' was the mantra of those supporting Brexit. Restoring parliamentary sovereignty was another. Yet until three High Court judges said taking away existing rights and privileges from British citizens needs to be initiated and approved by parliament, it was clear that the new Brexit government had no intention of handing any power to parliament to decide how the vote on 23 June should be interpreted and put into effect. It was a curious paradox that the first act of a government that was 'taking back control' from Europe was to seek to deny the House of Commons any say or control over what Britain's immediate future would be.

It was also clear that very many of the decisions that shape our lives in Britain are taken outside Britain – in Wall Street or in the boardrooms of big global corporations or by financial industry traders from Shanghai or San Francisco – and the British people have no influence over them. Indeed, in the EU Britain had a great deal of influence in deciding not just its affairs but the direction of travel of the continent which has always been determinant in our economic, political and strategic life despite the 20 miles of water that cuts the British Isles off from continental Europe. The Brexit years mean we will again have to learn the lesson that was self-evident to Mrs May's predecessors as Conservative prime minister from Winston Churchill to Margaret Thatcher.

Membership of first the European Community then the European Union gave Britain unprecedented influence over the political and economic architecture of Europe. In decades and centuries past, Britain had to expend blood and treasure to ensure Europe was run in a manner that did not threaten our interests. For a relatively small amount of money and some limited sharing of sovereignty, Britain gained influence and direction over the tide of affairs across the Channel that both the Pitts, Canning, Palmerston, Grey and Eden would have given their eye teeth for.

In addition, Brexit will turn out to be very expensive for the tax-payer. New bureaucrats had to be found to staff new ministries set up to deal with Brexit. *The Times* reported that lawyers were being hired at £5,000 a day and management consultants at £1,000 a day as no one in Westminster or Whitehall had the faintest idea what to do next. In a disturbing precedent, *The Times* noted, consultancies were offering their expertise and services for free to the Brexit ministry while simul-taneously selling advice to client companies on Brexit. The total cost of the new Brexit bureaucracy was said to be at least £5 billion. Far from the decision to leave Europe opening the way to a promised land of economic growth it seemed the winners would be expensive outsiders hired by Whitehall at mammoth cost to the taxpayer.

An estimated 30,000 new civil servants will have to be hired to manage Brexit. A former head of the civil service, Lord Butler, an octogenarian Old Harrovian, proclaimed that the civil service had risen to the challenge of organising Britain in World War II. True, but the nation was bankrupted as a result, taxes rose to astronomi-cal levels and many freedoms were suspended for the duration of the war. And in the end the war was won by America and Russia. Is that what Brexit entails? Is it what people voted for? Will giant powers save our bacon?

The weeks and months that followed Brexit were full of conflict-ing signals. The Japanese government issued a formal statement that Japanese firms could relocate to Europe if Britain no longer had the full, unfettered access to the Single Market. Citigroup began planning to move 900 jobs from London to Dublin so their employees could have full access to the Single Market. The giant Swiss bank UBS said it was looking at moving 1,500 employees out of London as the new government insisted that keeping Europeans out of Britain was more important than unfettered access to the Single Market of 500 million consumers. The British banks HSBC and Lloyds also announced moves to mainland Europe in order to keep access to the Single Market.

Little by little, the post-truth world of the Brexit blowhards who had been promising for more than two decades that isolating Britain from the EU of 28 sovereign nations would usher in a new economic and political paradise seemed more and more far-fetched.

As the pound slumped, Apple increased the price of its new iPhone7 because of the Brexit devaluation and Microsoft raised the price of its computers by up to 15 per cent. Investment funds closed their books to prevent investors pulling money out of the UK ahead of Brexit. Overseas businesses said they were not sure if they would keep investing in a UK outside the Single Market, and the governor of the Bank of England slashed interest rates hoping this would restore confidence. The result was that pensions which depend on funds assuming a certain interest rate on their invested money faced being cut as interest rates were close to being negative.

The American Chamber of Commerce in Britain said that the US$600 billion of investment in the UK would come under threat in the event of full Brexit. Using more forthright language than the Conservative-friendly British business outfits, American business leaders in the UK dismissed as 'nonsense' the argument of anti-European ministers that firms in the UK could trade normally with the EU using WTO rules and accepting the tariffs the EU applies to any good imported from outside its border.

In October 2016 Britain's finance ministry, the Treasury, warned that a full Brexit would lead to a 9.5 per cent reduction in the nation's GDP, with tax revenues of £66 billion – about twice the UK defence budget – disappearing. Even the pro-Brexit Open Europe think-tank estimated that leaving the Customs Union would reduce British GDP by at least 1.5 per cent, while other economists reckoned that leaving the Customs Union would cut 4.5 per cent from the value of the British economy. The pound sterling became a political currency of exceptional volatility. Suddenly wines, cheeses, even the delicious Spanish ham, *pata negra*, became more expensive to bring into Britain. The

British Retail Consortium warned that outside the EU the duties on imported meat products could rise 27 per cent and the duty on popular Chilean wine 14 per cent. The Japanese ambassador in London said that losing the right to trade and clear euros would have 'nightmarish' consequences for Japanese finance houses that had set up in London on the assurance that Britain would always have full access to the Single Market.

Not all the economic news was bad. Britain remained a fully functioning member of the EU and profited from its four freedoms of allowing capital, goods, services and workers to go where they could create or add the most value. The vote in June 2016 was not Brexit itself, so growth had been steady in 2016 and held up in the months after the vote. All EU member states were posting growth in 2017, so Britain enjoyed its share of that growth. The devaluation of the pound sterling following Brexit meant that foreign tourists coming to London to shop and spend money had a bonanza. The top 100 FTSE companies listed on the London Stock Exchange were able to post higher profits from overseas earnings converted into devalued sterling so their shares rose.

Pro-Brexit blowhards seized on every non-negative bit of news as proof beyond peradventure that the British economy faced no problems at all from future difficulties. Meanwhile in the Dordogne in France and other regions of southern Europe that had been colonised by British citizens taking advantage of the freedom to live and work anywhere in Europe, there were earnest conversations as British locals decided whether to put their homes on sale as they had no guarantees that once Brexit was fully consummated they would retain the right to live and travel freely. Those who depended on fixed-income pensions from the UK also found themselves poorer following the decision of their compatriots to leave Europe. The NHS sends £250 million each year to Spanish health care authorities to cover the cost of looking after ageing ex-pat Brits. It is unlikely such transfer payments to foreign governments will continue, leaving elderly British citizens with the choice of taking out expensive personal health insurance or returning to Britain to add to NHS waiting lists.

Pro-Brexit cheerleaders had the chutzpah to blame those opposed to Brexit for pointing out that the economic consequences of Brexit had so far not been positive. This the Leavers claimed was 'talking down the economy', as if the decisions of the markets were under the control of pro-Europeans in Britain. The *Daily Mail* in a hysterical front-page headline screeched 'DAMN THE UNPATRIOTIC BREMOANERS AND THEIR PLOT TO SUBVERT THE WILL OF THE BRITISH PEOPLE'. A later front-page headline screamed 'CRUSH THE SABOTEURS' – which is how the journalists on the *Daily Mail* defined British citizens uneasy about cutting off links with Europe. 'Unpatriotic', 'plot', 'subvert', 'saboteurs' – this was language from a Soviet show trial of the 1930s or the trials that followed Count von Stauffenberg's attempt on Hitler's life in 1944. When some very senior judges politely pointed out that leaving the EU meant a serious change in the conditions under which the British people lived and that therefore parliament should be consulted, the *Daily Mail* pasted their faces across its front page with the headline 'ENEMIES OF THE PEOPLE', pointing out that one of them was gay. Andrei Vyshinsky, the legendary prosecutor in the 1930s Soviet Union show-trial who used *Daily Mail* language against those Stalin considered 'enemies of the people', should be living at this hour.

Brexit, however, was about more than Britain. In every capital of Europe as well as in Brussels fresh impetus was given to the eternal debate about what the future of Europe is and whether Brexit was the first sign of a future winding-down of European integration or a spur to greater cooperation and sharing of sovereignty to lift the EU out of the economic low growth, high youth unemployment muddle in which it appeared to have got trapped in the last decade.

The German writer Thomas Schmid produced a book soon after Brexit, its title based on the famous announcement when a French king dies: *Europa ist tot, es lebe Europa!* (Europe is dead, long live Europe!). Pierre Moscovici, the French socialist pro-EU politician and EU commissioner, called his 2006 book *L'Europe est morte, vive l'Europe*. Once a decade it is necessary to pronounce the death of Europe and its miraculous rebirth!

6

THERESA MAY: HOW MUCH BREXIT DOES SHE REALLY WANT?

Every EU leader from Angela Merkel downwards has said flatly that the UK cannot have its gateau and eat it. Will Boris Johnson, who wrote of a 'Gestapo-controlled Nazi EU', really sway Angela Merkel and her ministers? Will Boris Johnson's crude anti-German insults charm the strongly pro-EU German politicians from the Social Democrat Party, who chose as their champion for the 2017 federal elections the passionately pro-EU politician Martin Schulz? Will demands from Boris Johnson and the other Germanophobe Tories persuade the pro-EU Free Democratic Party or even those in the anti-Muslim, racist Alternative für Deutschland party (AfD) that they should tear up their values and common rule book to appease UKIP and anti-Europeans in the British government?

The conservatives expelled the AfD from their group in the European Parliament in March 2016 as part of David Cameron's attempts to schmooze Angela Merkel ahead of the Brexit referendum. There is understandable bitterness that having been welcomed by conservatives as a fellow Eurosceptic party after winning seats in the 2014 European Parliament elections, the AfD should be dumped by British Tories two years later in a futile attempt to curry favour with the German Chancellor. Once they are in the German parliament after the autumn federal elections in Germany in 2017, the AfD are unlikely to want to help the British Conservative Party that first embraced them and then dumped them in a crude political manoeuvre.

German politicians, like others in Europe, are trying to come to terms with the Three Musketeers of Brexit – Boris Johnson, David Davis and Liam Fox. For Mrs May their appointment was an unmistakable signal that she embraced the anti-Europeans in the Tory Party who won the day thanks to their campaign of lies in the Brexit plebiscite. But they now have to deliver a successful Brexit and prove that outside the Single Market and with new barriers to Europeans doing business in the UK, Britain becomes a new powerhouse of global trade and economic expansion. In their world outlook, the EU is a foreign body to be expelled from Britain much as Henry VIII expelled the Catholic Church from England five centuries ago. But supposing Messrs Johnson, Davis and Fox fail to deliver?

No one any longer disputes that the 23 June 2016 vote was won on the basis of massive lies not witnessed in European politics since the 1930s. Now the men who won their plebiscite are in charge of turning their wishes into reality. They will soon confront the truth. And if they fail, will Mrs May put her hand on her heart and say, 'I tried, I tried. I let the anti-Europeans run the show. Now they haven't delivered, Britain needs a rethink'?

As home secretary, Mrs May authorised schemes in which vans drove around with large signs inviting people to send the authorities information about anyone working illegally. They were quickly dubbed 'Shop an Immigrant' vans and were widely derided. They both failed to deliver a single illegal immigrant for deportation and were like an Orwellian echo of demands in totalitarian states that citizens inform on and denounce each other. Recognising her error, Mrs May quickly abandoned the programme and the vans disappeared from public view.

In May 2016, a month before the Brexit vote, Mrs May went to talk to Goldman Sachs bankers. In a secret recording of her remarks later leaked to the *Guardian* she expressed warm enthusiasm for the EU and spelt out the dangers of leaving. 'If we were not in Europe, I think there would be firms and companies who would be looking to say, do they need to develop a mainland Europe presence rather than a UK presence? So I think there are definite benefits for us in economic terms.'

In her secret remarks she appears an enthusiastic pro-European. 'I think the economic arguments are clear. I think being part of a 500-million trading bloc is significant for us. One of the issues is that a lot of people will invest here in the UK because it is the UK in Europe.' She added, with her knowledge as the guardian of Britain domestic security and safety, that 'There are definitely things we can do as members of the European Union that I think keep us more safe.'

So is that the real Theresa May or was she just finding words that would please a global banking Moloch like Goldman Sachs? Her words were different a few months later during innumerable speeches and interviews during the Conservative Party conference in October 2016. No prime minister has made so many speeches at a party conference or spent so much time on the key political shows during the conference week.

But what did May say? The most important reference was to reject any role for the European Court of Justice. In fact, to remove UK courts from supranational accountability she would have to leave the Council of Europe and the European Court of Human Rights – set up by the Churchill government in the 1950s.

Britain does not become 'sovereign and independent' by leaving the EU. It requires leaving the ECtHR, and indeed as home secretary, Mrs May seemed to be more angry with ECtHR decisions than those of the ECJ.

Many Tory MPs are privately very worried about the economic impact on the UK when the message goes around the world that opening a factory in the regions of England or an office in London means you can only do business in the UK and any product or service destined for the world's biggest market on our doorstep will be treated on the same basis as if coming from Africa or Latin America.

Normally a prime minister makes programmatic speeches at a party conference, designed as much for international consumption as domestic party politics. At her party conference Mrs May was not speaking to the world or even the nation and its elected representatives, let alone the 48 per cent of the Brexit referendum voters who voted in favour of Europe, but to her beloved Tory Party rank and file.

She refused to say anything to heal the wounds of a badly divided nation. There was no acknowledgement of the 48 per cent of voters who did not fall in behind UKIP and the Tory campaign based on acknowledged lies. Instead she celebrated what she called 'The quiet revolution that took place in our country just three months ago – a revolution in which millions of our fellow citizens stood up and said they were not prepared to be ignored anymore.'

But what of the half of Britain that voted against Brexit? Were they now to be ignored? The answer was not only 'Yes', but those British citizens who were proud of and indeed accepted the concept of European citizenship, of open borders and open economy and open society, in short a post-nationalist view of the world, were crudely insulted. Speaking to her party conference Mrs May told British people who had a wider view: 'If you believe you're a citizen of the world, you're a citizen of nowhere. You don't understand what the very word "citizenship" means.'

In fact, it was Socrates who said 'I am neither Athenian, nor Greek but a citizen of the world.' Boris Johnson, who had a classical education at Oxford, might have avoided insulting the founding father of European philosophy, but to most ears Mrs May was using the language of the 1930s against 'rootless cosmopolitans' and the millions who after 1945 supported vague concepts of global citizenship as the answer to 1930s nationalisms.

She certainly appeared to contradict Winston Churchill, who told a conference in Amsterdam in 1948:

> We hope to reach again a Europe in which men will be proud to say 'I am a European.' We hope to see a Europe where men of every country will think as much of being a European as of belonging to their native land – and that without lessening any of their love and loyalty to their home and birthplace. We hope that wherever they go in this wide domain, to which we set no limits in the European continent, they will truly feel – Here I am at home, I am a citizen of this country too.

She went on to criticise those who did not vote for the UKIP/ Tory anti-EU line. 'They find your patriotism distasteful, your concerns about immigration parochial, your views about crime illiberal, your attachment to your job security inconvenient.' It was language straight from a Nigel Farage speech and she went on to proclaim: 'Our judges sitting not in Luxembourg but in courts across the land' and 'The authority of EU law in this country ended forever.'

In fact, it has been the ECtHR in Strasbourg that has more often overruled British judges, not the ECJ in Luxembourg. In a landmark ruling in March 2016, the ECJ judges backed Britain to the hilt by rejecting an attempt by the EU to move the $120 trillion trades and clearing in euros out of London and into the eurozone. The ECJ judges that Mrs May so casually attacked support the British government's argument that trading in currencies was part of the Single Market and therefore as long as Britain was in the EU, the role of London as a global financial hub should be upheld.

The ECJ acts as a commercial court and an administrative tribunal to resolve differences between countries or between the European Commission and national governments. On the whole it has supported the Margaret Thatcher vision of an economically liberal open market with no national protectionisms. It has not helped trade unions who wanted their own members protected from the often harsh winds of competition and a European-wide labour market. Many international organisations have their own tribunals or courts whose decisions are respected by member states of their relevant treaty organisation.

By telling the world that Britain would no longer respect or have anything to do with the ECJ, the Prime Minister was denouncing the very core of the Single Market. And yet in the same speech she stated: 'I want it to give British companies the maximum freedom to trade with and operate within the Single Market – and let European businesses do the same here.'

So in one sentence she trashed and rejected the institution that upholds and protects the Single Market and then a minute or two later she said it was her ambition for British firms to maximise use of the Single Market! Party conference speeches by prime ministers are notorious for being the work of many hands but it is surprising that no one picked up and ironed out the glaring contradiction. It was also worrying that neither Mrs May nor her staff worked out that the crudeness of her attacks on Europe and on internationalism would produce a negative backlash. The influential German *Süddeutsche Zeitung* reported 'Britain had changed into UKIP-land. Before, Great Britain was pragmatic and open to the world. Since the Brexit vote the government's nationalism gives foreigners the feeling that they are at best only tolerated.'

But for the Tory Party faithful who disliked and distrusted Europe and all its works, Theresa May's scorn and contempt for the EU brought them cheering to their feet. She was thus confirmed as prime minister by her conference and will face no challenge unless she fails in major policy areas.

But her confirmation as undisputed party leader was bought at the price of raising the concern, anger and determination of her fellow heads of government in Europe.

Margaret Thatcher was an economic liberal, while Old Etonian Tory prime ministers such as Harold Macmillan and David Cameron were cultural and social liberals. In the name of provincial southern English Tory nationalism, May began burying Tory liberalism and internationalism at her party conference. Her successor as home secretary, Amber Rudd, said that firms in Britain should publish lists of names of foreigners whom they employed. This suggestion sent a frisson of fear around the world, as the idea of naming aliens was utterly alien to Britain, where no one carries an identity card and most national institutions, from premier league football clubs to major banks or universities, are saturated with non-English talent. The elite sport of polo depends entirely on foreign-trained stars and it is hard to imagine any part of British sport, culture or business that can flourish if barriers to Europeans coming to work in the UK are introduced, with discriminatory entry permits to live and work in Britain. Even in Britain there was a strong reaction to the suggestion from Amber Rudd that firms should publish such lists. Writing in the *Sunday Times*, David Cameron's former political guru and Number 10 adviser, Steve Hilton, described the idea as like 'tattooing their arms'.

7

EUROPE REACTS

On the very day that the Prime Minister denounced Europe and in particular the European Court of Justice (ECJ), the guarantor of the functioning of the Single Market, EU leaders including Angela Merkel, François Hollande and Jean-Claude Juncker met in Berlin at the European Industrialists' Roundtable. The German Chancellor said that Britain could expect no concessions on the fundamental freedoms of Europe. If lorries, investment funds and consultancies can cross European frontiers without let or hindrance then so can European citizens, was the message. 'If we don't insist that full access to the Single Market is tied to complete acceptance of the four basic freedoms, then a process will spread across Europe where everyone is allowed what they want', Mrs Merkel said.

The European press seized on the bizarre proposal to publish lists of foreign employees, seen as a throwback to 1930s ideas of national preference. No one could understand Mrs May's main statement that the ECJ would have no more say in UK trade issues. The ECJ is essentially a commercial court and one that decides on disputes between national governments and the European Commission; it does not send people to prison. But the ECJ is indispensable as an arbitration tribunal for the inevitable disagreements between nations and different organisations within nations that have opened their borders to allow unfettered movement of goods, service, capital and people to take place. How will the world's investors regard a Britain that appears determined to minimise its access to 500 million middle-class consumers?

The day after Mrs May's attack on Europe that brought her party faithful cheering to their feet, I found myself at dinner with former French president François Hollande in Paris, and then with Prime Minister Manuel Valls and Jean-Claude Juncker, the EU Commission president, at a seminar the next day. Michel Barnier, the European Commission Brexit negotiator, was at both events – linked to the twentieth anniversary of the Jacques Delors Institute's *Notre Europe* initiative.

President Hollande's language on Brexit was even tougher than that of Mrs Merkel. He began by saying that Jacques Delors had to handle the rebate negotiations with Margaret Thatcher. 'Mrs Thatcher wanted to stay in Europe, but she wanted a cheque in return. Now the UK wants to leave and pay nothing. That is not possible.' The reference to the British rebate was underlined later by a remark from Luxembourg's prime minister, who said: 'When Britain was in the EU the UK government wanted endless opt-outs. Now Britain is leaving the EU it wants endless opt-ins.'

In Paris President Hollande was adamant in response to Mrs May's activist-pleasing conference speech.

> The UK has decided on Brexit, I think even a hard Brexit. We have to accept the UK's willingness to leave the EU. We have to be very firm. If not, we would put in danger the fundamental principles of the EU. Other countries would want to leave the EU to get the supposed advantages without the obligations.

Hollande underlined his point: 'There must be a threat, there must be a risk, there must be a price. If not, we will enter a negotiation that cannot end well.' Jean-Claude Juncker nodded in agreement. Michel Barnier listened intently.

The excellent Paris correspondent of the *Financial Times*, Anne-Sylvaine Chassany, was at the event and her strictly factual account of the French President's remarks was read around the world as a rejection by Mrs May of any compromise on the terms of Brexit, so Britain would be cut off from existing access to the EU's Single Market. If the British Prime Minister insisted the UK was now 'sovereign and independent' then so too were foreign exchange dealers from Manila to Milan. They began selling sterling. The pound sterling crashed in global trading. The UK HSBC bank says that the pound is now a political currency (as in 1966/76 or 1992/3) and we should expect very great volatility and a reduction value against the dollar and euro.

The next day Juncker used the word 'intransigent' to describe the EU's position ahead of the Article 50 negotiations. Speaking alongside Manuel Valls, again with Michel Barnier present, Mr Juncker told European business leaders not to be seduced into having private sectoral discussions with the UK. 'I hope major groups of European industry do not engage in secret discussions in dark rooms, curtains drawn, with British government envoys', he said. 'One cannot have one foot out and one foot in, with the foot out destroying what we have built. On this point we have to be intransigent. I can see the manoeuvring', the Commission President insisted.

For all that, Juncker and Valls stressed that a federal United States of Europe was no longer on the agenda. Both men insisted on the primacy of the nation state, with Valls saying the EU 'should supplement the nation state, not replace it'.

Pascal Lamy, the former WTO director and European Commission veteran, told me he thought the entire process was now 'political' and that he believed Brussels would not agree to sectoral discussion on future trade access to the EU until there was an overarching 'institutional agreement'.

In London, as the dust settled on the conference season and the routine of exchanges in the House of Commons became the political stories of the day, the political elites remained in denial as to the extent to which no one in the EU wanted to reward the UKIP/Tory campaign to lead the UK out of the EU.

Merkel, Hollande and Juncker were saying on the record that Britain would not be given any favours. Having opted, under poor leadership, in their view, to do terrible damage to Europe, there can be no special case for the UK by which Britain keeps its existing Single Market access but can start discriminating against European citizens. All candidates to be French president made clear they will not seek to grant the UK any favours and indeed all of them have said that Britain, after Brexit, should move its frontier for passport and other entry clearance checks from French to British soil. This could mean mammoth car and lorry queues in Dover and Folkestone, as well as economic migrants and asylum seekers facing no British police checks on the French side of the Channel.

Prime Minister May's aggressive assertion of English nationalism and sovereign independence is identical to that of nationalist-populist and illiberal political movements in France, Germany, Hungary, Poland and elsewhere in Europe. She may not see it in those terms and she remains a life-long member of the Conservative Party, which has a long pedigree of liberal economics and tolerance about what is 'foreign'.

But her language was extremely hard and uncompromising and produced an equal and opposite reaction from Europe. There was a cold fury amongst EU heads of government that the UKIP/Tory win means the end of a Europe as it had been built with their support and which for all its failings was better than any previous Europe.

Some in Britain turned their hopes to the arrival of a new president of France in 2017. François Villeroy de Galhau, the governor of the Bank of France, downplayed the possibility. 'There will be no change in the position of Paris nor in my judgement in that of Berlin after the elections there in 2017', he told me. Villeroy de Galhau grew up in the Strasbourg region, with family members living across the Rhine, and knows German and Germany well. He reflects the calm solidity of all senior French officials that Brexit is a British problem and that France, Germany and other EU member states will have to get on with life without Britain.

As the prime minister of Belgium, Charles Michel, told the German newspaper, the *Frankfurter Allgemeine Zeitung*: 'I'm for close relations between the EU and Britain, but one has to tell the truth: Britain won't be able to stay outside of the EU and, at the same time, enjoy all the advantages [of membership]. If one were to accept that out of weakness, one would be opening the door to a dismemberment of Europe.' His colleague, the Danish prime minister, Lars Løkke Rasmussen, also made clear that the success of the Brexit campaign of lies against Europe was not likely to lead to Denmark supporting concessions that Brexit campaigners insisted other European democracies would concede once the nation had voted to leave. 'We need to be extremely careful that the side that leaves [the EU] doesn't get particular competitive advantages on its way out. We all want a peaceful divorce, but when you agree to part ways – and in this situation, only one side wants to part ways – then we need to protect our own interests first.'

Ireland's prime minister, Enda Kenny, supported his Belgian and Danish colleagues by declaring on Irish radio early in the autumn of 2016 that he didn't know what the horizon for Mrs May's vision of Brexit was, adding, 'The best place that Britain could be is to have access to the Single Market as is now – but that means that they must accept one of the fundamental [EU] principles, which is migration and free movement of people [...] And let me tell you that around the European Council table that is an issue that will not be given in on.'

From Rome, Italy's trade minister, Carlo Calenda, warned that if London imposed restrictions on Italian and other European citizens arriving in Britain and seeking to work or rent property it would be badly received. 'The more they [British politicians] are going to regulate and limit the presence of EU citizens in the UK, the more we are going to limit the presence of UK goods into Europe', he declared.

The negotiator appointed by the European Parliament is the former Belgian prime minister, Guy Verhofstadt, who was vetoed by Tony Blair in 2004 in his bid to become president of the European Commission. He added his voice to other EU leaders by insisting that 'If [the] UK wants access to the single market, it must also accept the free movement of citizens.' Britain's Brexit minister, David Davis, showed his diplomatic skills by describing Verhofstadt as 'Satan' in the House of Commons. It is not quite clear when the European Parliament would have to ratify any negotiated agreement on Britain leaving the EU, but it is likely to be after the end of Article 50 negotiations, which should be the autumn of 2018 to allow the elected governments of 27 member states and the European Parliament to agree the withdrawal agreement before the new Commission and newly elected European Parliament begin operations in May 2019. The decision in 2009 of the Conservative Party to break links with all its sister centre-right parties in the federation known as the European People's Party means that Tory ministers and MPs have very little contact or networking relationship with elected politicians in other EU member states.

After Prime Minister May's aggressive anti-EU speech at her party conference in October 2016 the reaction from other key EU leaders became much more resolute, following the example of Chancellor Merkel, President Hollande and Commission President Juncker.

Michel Sapin, France's finance minister, explained it thus:

Negotiations must be as cooperative as possible, but there are principles. And on principles, none of the remaining EU member states will give in. […] One thing is certain: after Brexit, things cannot be the same as before Brexit – it is also a way to respect the vote of the British people. They wanted a change, there will be a change.

Jeroen Dijsselbloem, president of the Eurogroup, returned to the EU's favourite metaphor for how the UK will be treated outside the EU. Britain, he said, 'won't get just the cherry-picking part of the deal' in talks on exiting the EU.

To be sure, during the course of negotiations many previous statements can become 'inoperative', to use the euphemism from American politics of the Nixon era. But rather too many European heads of government have said unambiguously that if London starts to impose visas and residence or work permits on their own citizens, then that, at least, will be seen as a hostile act, which means Britain cannot expect to continue its existing automatic unfettered access to selling goods and services across Europe. By any standards, the loss of the Single Market of some 500 million (minus the UK) consumers and clients will present a major economic challenge to Britain.

Mrs May went to see the prime ministers of Denmark and the Netherlands to explain her position. She was received politely. One person who was present at the meeting in Copenhagen with Lars Løkke Rasmussen said that Mrs May just sat there and said nothing beyond polite banalities. After the Dane, Mrs May met another centre-right prime minister, the Netherlands' Mark Rutte. The British prime minister tried to butter him up by talking of a 'mature, cooperative relationship with Europe', but the Dutch leader replied coldly that 'It is evident that we will also have shared interests in the future, but the fact remains that very complex negotiations lie ahead.'

He made clear that in his view the Tory/UKIP obsession with restricting the rights of the Dutch and other Europeans to work and travel to Britain would mean the end of UK access to the Single Market, stating: 'This is not a menu to choose from.' Already May's language about 'Europe' as a place from which her country was separate rather than a part of would grate on the ears of her fellow prime ministers. They are as proudly Danish or Dutch as she is British, but they do not consider 'Europe' to be a foreign land with which they must forge a 'mature, cooperative relationship'. They are part of Europe, as is Britain. And the Danes and the Dutch are not frightened to say so.

Conventional thinking always positions the EU nations of milk and butter – the Nordic countries and the Netherlands – as automatic British allies. They all speak English, they like free trade, they are monarchies and they don't do the vision thing. But they all face strong xenophobic, racist and anti-European parties which use exactly the same populist and demagogic language as the Leave campaign. There was a surge of support for EU membership in the region following the Brexit vote. Yet still in the Netherlands 40 per cent of voters were ready to back leaving.

So for Rutte in the Netherlands and other Northern European leaders it was vital to show that Tory/UKIP anti-EU campaign's victory was not going to be rewarded by governments across the Channel agreeing to demands that the Brexit government now hoped might be granted. If Britain could start imposing restrictions on the travel and working rights of other Europeans and yet still keep unfettered access to European consumers for its foreign-owned banks in the City and for other firms, then why shouldn't the Danes, Swedes, Finns or Dutch anti-Europeans demand the same?

It is the raw politics of survival in play. If Theresa May said 'Brexit means Brexit', the leaders of Denmark and the Netherlands retorted 'Europe means Europe'. It is a club with agreed common rules, not a pick'n'mix buffet from which the Brexit Brits could take what they want. British diplomats have decades, if not centuries of experience of divide and rule, playing off one nation or set of countries against another, of offering enough to break apart a common front. But the politicians of Europe also know that unity is strength and if they allow the Leave Liars the right to claim victory then bit by bit continental Europe would become a new Balkans.

Mrs May also made a speech at Lancaster House in January 2017 which set out her view that Britain would leave the Single Market and the Customs Union – a complete amputation from the EU as a trading area. The message was repeated in a so-called White Paper. Normally a White Paper sets out in some detail government policy, but such is the volume of laws, agencies, the issue of EU citizens in Britain, financial services 'passports', the Northern Ireland border question, as well as financial commitments, that a document setting out a complete list of what will have to be negotiated before Brexit is 100 per cent consummated would be more like an old-fashioned telephone directory.

Yet at the same time the Prime Minister insisted she would keep access to the Single Market as 'frictionless' as possible and avoided the more intemperate anti-EU language of her aggressively Europhobe ministers, such as Boris Johnson and Liam Fox, let alone one of her predecessors as Tory Party leader, Iain Duncan Smith, who was always ready with a quote or soundbite at the faintest suggestion the nation was not entirely united behind the rupture with Europe. Was Mrs May keeping the door just a tiny bit ajar to coming to an economic deal with the EU once political Brexit took place? The words 'Single Market' or 'Customs Union' or 'agricultural policy' or 'immigration' or 'right to retire in Spain' were not on the ballot paper. The question was whether to leave the EU. That is perfectly feasible without destroying the British economy or massively restricting the rights that British citizens have got used to as citizens of Europe as well as their own nation. This is why Britain can both withdraw from the European treaties and no longer be part of the integrated political European Union yet still stay in Europe and still work constructively with the EU. This paradox has yet to be fully explored but as the memory fades of Brexit day 23 June 2016, it is likely to come to the fore.

Michel Barnier, who heads the EU team in the Brexit negotiations, is a heavyweight European politician. He has held top positions in French centre-right governments, including those of foreign minister and agriculture minister – one of the most sensitive ministerial posts in Europe. He did two stints as an EU Commissioner. He is a tall, trim, silver-haired Savoyard and loves the mountains he hails from and where he still lives when he can get away from Paris and Brussels. He has had far more heavyweight ministerial and European negotiating experience than any of his British opposite numbers. David Davis, about to enter his eighth decade, is three years older than Barnier. For nearly two decades between 1997 and 2006 he had little to do except promote anti-Europeanism. Barnier found time to learn quite passable English, while his opposite number in London remains stoutly monolingual, like most of his cabinet colleagues, including the Prime Minister.

Like all French-trained politicians and officials, Michel Barnier thinks in 1–2–3 triptychs. He has chosen three areas for his Brexit divorce triptych.

1. The UK has to accept responsibility for its financial liabilities and obligations.
2. There should be a solution for the future residence rights of the estimated 3.5 million EU citizens who live in the UK and those who may come to live and work in Britain before the date of formal UK withdrawal from the EU. A solution should be found for the estimated up to 2 million UK citizens living in EU member states.
3. There should be a special arrangement for Ireland to seek to preserve that status of peace that has been achieved in the twenty-first century after decades of conflict resulting in 3,600 killed by terrorists and many thousands wounded when there was a strong, physical border with customs checks between the UK in the form of the six counties of Northern Ireland and the rest of the island of Ireland.

At first sight Barnier's triptych should be easy to sketch out and colour in by the professional negotiators the EU and the UK will set to work on finding an agreement. But each one of the three areas to be filled in is fraught with difficulty. Public and political opinion in both the UK and EU member states has never confronted such an issue before – namely a decision by one of the world's largest economies and democracies to withdraw from the world's biggest open-border trading bloc, which has managed to secure peace and the sharing of laws and democracy between more than 30 nations (the 28 EU members plus those in the EEA and EFTA), as well as those seeking to join.

To read or hear the daily comments in 2017 by pro-Brexit, anti-European politicians and commentators in the press and on the BBC, the UK withdrawal is just the first step in a bigger nationalist campaign aimed at destroying the EU and returning to a Europe of rival nation states behind closed borders. Anti-European nationalist British politicians, for example, floated the idea of sending British military forces to Spain over the question of Gibraltar as the UK citizens of the tiny British enclave will have a different status once they are out of the EU and lose all rights to freely cross the border into Spain. Single Market trade between Gibraltar and Spain within the Customs Union will change when the UK gets its full Brexit.

The anodyne point that future relations between Spain and the UK on Gibraltar will be a bilateral issue between Madrid and London, including for example the right under EU aviation rules for planes to overfly Spanish territory to land on the very short Gibraltar airstrip, was turned into an orgy of anti-Spanish hate by anti-European Conservative politicians. One of them, the former party leader, Lord Howard, who has been an obsessive anti-European ever since he threatened to resign from John Major's cabinet in 1992 over the rights of British workers under Social Europe obligations, went on television to compare the Gibraltar issue with the Falklands conflict of 1982, when, as he told viewers, another woman prime minister had sent a Royal Navy task-force to defend the interests of British citizens living there.

The bombast might be dismissed as an eccentric statement from an retired nationalist Tory, but it was reinforced by the serving defence secretary, Michael Fallon, who boasted about Britain 'going all the way' to defend Gibraltar. The anti-European press enjoyed publishing details of the relative power of British and Spanish naval and other armed forces.

The rest of the world looked on in amazement at this jingoistic display, with its talk of war with Spain over Gibraltar, when all that had been noted was that outside the EU all questions of the rights of Gibraltar and the people living there to access and trade with Spain would no longer be guaranteed by EU laws and rules but return to a purely bilateral status between London and Madrid. No Royal Navy armada will set sail to attack Spain as in the sixteenth century but the explosion of nationalist, chest-beating anti-European fervour showed how difficult the negotiations might be to reach a mutually agreed final point in March 2019, when the UK is no longer a signatory to EU treaties. Mrs May made a speech in front of Number 10 and accused unnamed European political leaders of using Brexit to influence the British election. On the contrary, acting on the advice of the right-wing Australian political consultant Sir Lynton Crosby, who ran the campaign for Boris Johnson to be mayor of London, it was, sadly, the Prime Minister seeking to whip up nationalist anti-European fervour to help win her election.

Britain will have to pay a price to leave the EU and also accept that millions of European citizens will be able to live in Britain, despite the claims made by the pro-Brexit campaign that the number of Europeans in the UK was putting excessive strain on public services like housing, health and education. Indeed, Mrs May described in October 2015 as 'unsustainable' the arrival of Europeans into her country.

To sugar the pill, Barnier is dangling the carrot of a provisional agreement on tariff-free movement of goods and agricultural products between the UK and the EU, which he would like to see as part of the withdrawal package. It would not cover services, which represent about 80 per cent of the UK economy – including most importantly the huge financial services provided by the City of London, which since the 1980s have been a major money earner for Britain. In addition, the EU would expect rules-of-origin obligations to be respected, which could mean that most made-in-Britain foreign, notably Japanese, cars might fall short of having enough of their total value actually produced in the EU not just assembled on Nissan, Toyota and Honda assembly lines.

Free trade in agricultural products would help Northern Ireland, where the main export is dairy and meat products. But it would not easily work if the UK also left the Customs Union in 2019 and started to import much cheaper food, which the globalised agro-industry corporations in the Americas and the Asian-Pacific region can supply at prices which would drive most UK, Irish and indeed European small farmers out of business.

If Britain wanted to take advantage of the offer of free trade in goods as an interim agreement until a full and final trade agreement was reached sometime in the 2020s, it would have to accept in the interim continuing obligations to respect EU laws, including, possibly, freedom of movement.

Thus, while the UK would lose all right to influence EU policy and its laws, thus becoming a rule-taker not a rule-maker with a sort of half-in, half-out status rather like Norway, the British prime minister could say that henceforth all laws applying to Britain's relationship with Europe were made in the British parliament and not in Brussels and Strasbourg. It can so happen that Westminster decides to abide by EU laws and directives just as the Norwegian (and to a lesser extent the Swiss) parliaments do, but at least it would be a UK-only decision and law-making process.

To get to that point will require enormous political skill and a competent coherence on the part of British politicians. But any such compromise may reignite open warfare on the European question, which had divided the Conservative Party for 30 years, much as the question of free trade, the rights of Catholics or Ireland did in the nineteenth century. The Labour Party remains in opposition for the foreseeable future. The Liberal Democrats, despite an increase in votes in the general election, will take many years to recover the status and size of parliamentary representation they enjoyed up to 2010, when their ambitious, career-seeking leadership decided to become very junior partners in the Conservative government of David Cameron and paid a price in the disappearance of 50 Lib Dem seats in 2015. Scottish MPs are now nearly all supporters of nationalist separatism.

Barnier also insists that as part of his tariff-free trade offer, the UK must agree to be in full compliance with all EU social and environmental laws and regulations, and Barnier has met with trade union and Green organisations to stress this point.

He is worried not so much about political opposition to the process he is overseeing in Britain but also a backlash from within EU member states, such as one saw arise in opposition to the TTIP between the US and the EU and to CETA, the Canada–EU trade deal.

If he is seen as being too generous to the UK, then there will be problems from within different political groupings and lobbies in the EU. Mrs May likes to proclaim that 'no deal is better than a bad deal', as if it was a threat. It is not clear if she means the deal at the end of the Article 50 negotiation on the Barnier triptych plus tariff-free trade in goods that conform to EU rules of origin or if she means the full and final deal, which will not be negotiated for up to a further ten years. When the UK joined the six nations in the European Economic Community in 1973 its rule book, derived from the Treaty of Rome, was much smaller. Even so there was a transition period of seven years to allow the UK to adjust to being a member state. Now the UK is leaving a 28-strong EU which has grown in scope and reach, with many of its scores of thousands of rules and directives actively promoted by

London to strengthen the internal Single Market or to encourage the enlargement of the EU to take in ex-communist countries in central, east and south-east Europe.

The right of EasyJet and Ryanair to fly anywhere in Europe or the power to demand that EU member states return wanted criminals to face justice in the UK are just two small examples of common rules that will have to renegotiated once the UK has left the EU. Therefore, if it took seven years after 1973 to bring UK laws into conformity with EEC rules, it is safe to assume that it will take up to a decade before a full and final Brexit is agreed.

Barnier has created a high-level team of the best negotiators in the EU, called the T50 team. They work behind sealed-off doors on the fifth floor of the European Commission's Berlaymont building. Special security walls have been installed to prevent eavesdropping by British spy agencies. Barnier's own office is smaller than other Commissioners' offices and the entire floor is modest, with utilitarian, Ikea-style furniture.

He described his priorities:

I have met all 27 heads of governments. The UK represents 16 per cent of the EU budget. There are those which are net contributors, about half of them, and the other half which are net recipients. The net contributors cannot pay any extra and the net recipients cannot have their income reduced. This is of the highest importance.

On agreeing rights of EU citizens in the UK and UK citizens in the EU he said this was essential, with no question of imposing an early cut-off date (for example, the date of the referendum or the date of the Article 50 letter). It would apply from the moment the UK left the treaty. I pointed out that no one has any idea of the names or whereabouts of all EU citizens in the UK. It would be a massive task to identify and list them all. It was against all British traditions to start listing and categorising people for a specific purpose. Of course, people's names are there for National Insurance, TV licence or council tax reasons, but they are just names and do not identify nationality, nor dependants. Some 170,000 EU citizens in the UK have applied for permanent residence, with one in five rejected. If government agents arrive in towns and communities all over Britain trying to list and identify EU citizens (but not immigrants from Pakistan, Bangladesh, Brazil, India and other countries), it would drive people off registers and into the black labour market. There may well be political grass-roots protests against the drawing up of lists of those who can stay and those who must be excluded, which in the British liberal traditions of no identity cards smacks of what a repressive regime does.

Barnier shrugged his shoulders, as if it was just a question of extra government resources in the UK. He had been told that the problem started in 2004 when the UK did not impose the seven-year transition period on citizens of new EU member states (A8) from Eastern/Central Europe. He was surprised when I said the UK already had several hundred thousand Poles and other Eastern Europeans who came to the UK from the 1990s onwards, when the end of communism meant the end of travel visas. There was a community of 250,000 Poles in the UK dating from after 1945 and Ryanair and EasyJet were operating several flights a day between the UK and Polish and other A8 member states by 2004. The UK economy was based on low-paid, taxpayer-subsidised employment, with employers encouraged to hire the cheapest possible labour. The biggest employer of EU citizens is the NHS. But state employers are exempt from freedom of movement obligations. Britain could do much more to train British citizens for jobs and introduce other measures of internal labour market control without violating freedom of movement rules, as other EU countries or Switzerland have done. I pointed out that Ireland had 180,000 Polish workers – 4 per cent of the Irish population, compared to

1.7 per cent of the UK population that was Polish. There were no attacks on Polish workers by Irish politicians or the Irish press. Similarly, there are 1.1 million Romanian citizens in Spain but there are no attacks by rightwing Spanish politicians or the press about the presence of so many Romanians. In other words, the problem in the UK was a political one caused by the deliberate highlighting of Poles and EU immigrants by anti-EU political forces. He took a note of this and clearly had not heard these arguments.

On Ireland, he wants a 'soft' border but equally there will have to be customs controls between Ireland (EU) and Northern Ireland (non-EU). He said he had told the French government that there will be *dédouanement* points (custom clearance controls) on all French coastal towns where British ships and ferries arrive, as well as for lorries and cars via the Eurotunnel. He seemed to assume that the UK would leave the Customs Union, as Mrs May stated in her January 2017 speech and subsequent White Paper.

He took it for granted that the UK would seek a free-trade agreement with countries like the US but said this would not be easy to achieve. On people movement into Ireland and thence into the UK in Northern Ireland, he said he thought Dublin would exercise control at entry points in Ireland. If tariffs or duties on imported food and agricultural products were different in the UK and the EU, then there would be problems for cross-border traffic in Ireland. I also explained the anger that many Catholic nationalists in the six counties of Northern Ireland would feel as they once again faced a border controlled from London which separated them from their cousins and fellow Irishmen and women in the Republic of Ireland.

On Gibraltar, he said it was not part of his negotiating remit at all. The UK outside the EU or outside an EEA arrangement meant that British citizens in Gibraltar would be third-country nationals with no EU-based right to live across the border. That would be a separate bilateral UK–Spain issue, not one for his team to negotiate.

He said he would like to conclude a tariff-free trade agreement covering goods traded between the UK and the EU. This was an ambition to be realised during the negotiations. It is indeed a very ambitious agenda to cover UK payments, citizenship rights and Northern Ireland and a no-tariff trade deal in goods. The latter would have to be strict on rules-of-origin details, which will impact on all products made in the UK with components imported from outside the EU, notably cars, and so on.

He hopes his free-trade plan can include agricultural products, and he has in his team people from his cabinet when he was French agriculture minister, including his Norwegian policy adviser and speech-writer. He said financial and other services or aviation would be settled later under future agreements negotiated into the 2020s. He stressed that any free-trade deal would have to include a full British commitment to respecting EU social and environmental rights. In Barnier's view, the opposition that could prevent any deal may not come from Britain but from European protest movements that derailed the proposed US–EU TTIP and nearly stopped the EU–Canada CETA. 'I must have absolute guarantees from the UK that there will be no social or wage or environmental dumping as part of any free-trade deal. That is essential. I am meeting environmental and Green lobbies and trade unions and have stressed this point.'

At no stage since his appointment has anyone heard Barnier criticise or attack the UK, and the language of punishment for the British vote is not part of his vocabulary. His first political engagement was to campaign in 1973 for France to accept Britain into the EEC, which was opposed by traditional Gaullists and when the Socialist Party leader and future president François Mitterrand abstained. He campaigned for a 'Yes' vote in the 1992 French referendum on the Maastricht Treaty and for a 'Yes' vote in the 2005 French referendum on the Constitutional Treaty. He won the former and lost the latter. So Barnier has no problems about accepting referendum results and sees his task as the latest if not the last he has been given in a long career at the highest level of French and European politics. I have never known him to raise his voice or be unpleasant about politicians. He takes life as it comes and gets on with the business in hand.

He has little room for manoeuvre, as the 27 government chiefs have told him that Britain must accept its liabilities and pay its bill and the EU will not throw away its rule book to appease UKIP or accommodate UKIP fellow-travellers in the cabinet.

The ball is firmly in the British court. Depending on how she plays it, Mrs May will have a workable Brexit treaty, leaving the nuts and bolts of the UK's future final relationship with the EU until the 2020s. Or she will not be able to tell the truth to her party, the press and the nation and Britain will crash out of Europe with unforeseeable consequences for the economy and society and the unity of the monarch's United Kingdom.

PART TWO

WHY BREXIT HAPPENED

8

THE ESTABLISHMENT WAS WARNED BREXIT WOULD HAPPEN BUT BURIED ITS HEAD IN THE SAND

Brexit was rightly seen as a monumental change in the politics of one of the leading democracies, following one of the biggest defeats of a state establishment in postwar history. So, again, the puzzle remains, why did no one see it coming?

In the middle of the morning on the day of the referendum I came out of the BBC's Broadcasting House after an interview for French radio. Eighteen months previously, in January 2015, I had gone there to see an old friend, Jim Naughtie, one of Britain's great broadcasting journalists. I gave him a copy of the first edition of my book *Brexit: How Britain Will Leave Europe*. He took it and rifled through the pages. 'This is very interesting, Denis, we'll definitely get it on the *Today* programme.'

I was one of the first, if not the first, to use the term 'Brexit' and had never doubted that if it came to a populist plebiscite Brexit would occur. That is why I wrote my book as a kind of wake-up call and warning. I hoped that with a serious, respected academic publisher,

I.B.Tauris, bringing the book out in January 2015 it might provoke some discussion and I would be able to alert fellow citizens to just how likely it was that a Brexit referendum would end the way it did.

After the referendum the social affairs commentator Sunder Katwala, a clever and thoughtful man, wrote of 'Britain's *surprise* vote to leave the EU' (my italics). Surprise vote? That is precisely why I wrote my book. It was an effort to lift the veil from the eyes of London's liberal intelligentsia elite, as well as the ruling politicians around David Cameron, who deluded themselves that Brexit could not happen and were surprised when it did.

The call from the Radio 4 *Today* programme to discuss my book's Brexit thesis never came in 2015 nor in 2016. My warnings went unheeded by the grandees of the BBC. Despite having a network of friends, some dating back to my days as a BBC journalist in the 1970s, I could not persuade a single BBC news and current affairs programme to discuss the argument that Britain would cut itself out of Europe unless serious work was done to counter the lies and propaganda against Europe from much of the press, many leading politicians and well-connected business executives who had persuaded themselves the EU prevented Britain from flourishing. The same was true of old friends who run the main newspaper comment pages on *The Times*, *Guardian*, *Daily Telegraph*, *Independent*, *Financial Times*, *Evening Standard* or the *New Statesman* or any of the monthly political magazines. The book was reviewed in the *Times Literary Supplement* and *The Economist* and I was interviewed about it for the *Observer*.

The wilful refusal by the London political-media elites to accept that Brexit was likely reminded me of the famous *Daily Express* headline, 'There Will Be No War in Europe', splashed on the paper's front page just before 1 September 1939, the day the Wehrmacht invaded Poland. It is one thing to blame Brexit on the campaign of lies in the spring and early summer of 2016 and the years of anti-EU propaganda that preceded it, but so often in the past when the British are given a warning that something bad is going to happen they prefer to bury their heads, ostrich-like, deep in the sand.

On that humid referendum day in June after my French radio interview I found myself in a Café Nero opposite Broadcasting House. As with other media in Germany, Poland, Belgium, Denmark, the Netherlands or the United States, editors in France were willing to allow some space for my arguments that the plebiscite vote would be to quit Europe. By chance I bumped into Professor Anand Menon of King's College London. He is one of the nation's foremost academic experts on EU politics and organised an impressive team of experts to comment on the referendum in the months before the vote. I asked Anand what the result would be.

'I know the English', he replied without hesitation. 'They will bottle it. They don't have the nerve to vote to leave', he said with all the assurance of a top professor. He was in good company. On the same day, Peter Kellner, for decades one of the best number-crunchers on British politics and founder of the successful polling outfit YouGov, tweeted that the result would be 55–45 in favour of Remain.

Andrew Cooper, a close confidante of David Cameron's (who gave him a peerage) and another political insider who had gone on to make money via setting up a polling firm, Populus, was one of the trio that headed the official Stronger In campaign set up to defeat Brexit. On 22 June 2016 he told both his fellow directors in the official Stronger In campaign that Remain would easily win. A Number 10 official working on the campaign to keep the UK in Europe told me that same confident but utterly wrong message was conveyed to the Prime Minister.

It would be unfair on many friends in public life with deserved reputations for political insights to publish the names of all those who between 23 January 2013, when David Cameron announced his plebiscite, and 23 June 2016, when his gamble failed, insisted to me face to face, at seminars or conferences, over a drink or at a dinner party that there was not the slightest chance of Britain voting to leave.

But I was disappointed that in the 18 months before the Brexit vote took my country out of Europe there was something close to a complete *omerta* amongst the media and other elites as to the chances of this happening. I claim no special powers of political prediction. But from the moment in January 2013 that David Cameron announced his plan to hold a plebiscite on Europe, I was convinced the answer would be 'No' to Europe.

There have been many articles and several instant books detailing the intricacies of the weeks and months running up to the Brexit vote on 23 June 2016. British political journalists are superb chroniclers of great political moments, with an eye for detail and a joy in describing the flawed personalities of those who seek endorsement from citizens in the raw contest of political choice. I enjoyed reading them. They answered the 'who' and the 'when' but not the 'why'. They are like books on the events of May/June 1940 in France. The details of the defeat of France are fascinating, as are the accounts of the Brexit campaign and its political dramatis personae. The verbatim quotations recorded by Sir Craig Oliver, press secretary to David Cameron, vividly disclose what the principals said about each other. Andrew Gimson, a fine writer on contemporary politics, explains how the Tory anti-European campaign deliberately told lies about the Australian immigration system in order to hoodwink voters. The journalists Tim Shipman and Gary Gibbon produced excellent accounts of the campaign. But the real story is not what happened or how low and mean most of the principal political actors were but why it happened and what the consequences are.

Like George W. Bush invading Iraq, those who won the vote for Brexit had an easy victory but no plan, concept or vision of what to do once their 'victory' had been secured. The almost instant way David Cameron handed over to Theresa May was hailed as a fine example of how Britain does politics. The new prime minister sailed into Downing Street on a carmine sea of political blood. One by one all the more likely successors to David Cameron, including those who had spearheaded the Brexit victory leading to his ouster, dag-gered each other in the front, back and everywhere else in the big-gest peacetime political blood-letting in any modern democracy in decades.

But the place of Brexit in British political history is far more than the alarums and excursions of the spring and summer of 2016. In fact, the daily twists and turns and the extraordinary political fall-out in the days immediately after 23 June 2016 are less important than the con-text in which they should be set.

The swings and roundabouts of the 12 months between the Commons second reading on the EU Referendum Bill on 9 June 2015 and the decision to leave the EU on 23 June 2016 are fascinating for political commentators, but the reasons we voted to leave can be found in the politics of 10, 20, even 50 years previously.

The myth dies hard that Britain only ever wanted to be in an eco-nomic relationship with the rest of Europe. When the Labour govern-ment rejected the Schuman Plan to form a European Coal and Steel Community in 1950, Labour politicians did so explicitly because they wanted to exercise full political control over the nationalised steel and coal industry rather than share such power with others.

When General de Gaulle twice in the 1960s rejected Britain's appli-cation to sign the Treaty of Rome he did so for political reasons. The Labour leader, Hugh Gaitskell, opposed entering Europe in 1962 on the grounds that it 'would mean ending a thousand years of history', and he was talking politics, not commerce.

When in 1983 the Labour Party put in its election manifesto a Brexit pledge – to quit the European Community – again it was on political grounds. For the Labour Party of Michael Foot, Tony Benn, Peter Shore and Denis Healey such power-sharing as was implicit in all EU treaties since 1950 was unacceptable. They dreamt of building socialism in one island – in the case of Healey and Shore with the pro-viso that a Labour UK was subservient to the United States on most geo-political and strategic defence issues. The British voters gave that Labour Party just 27 per cent of the votes cast in the 1983 election.

In the 1990s, anti-EU Conservative MPs like Michael Howard, Iain Duncan Smith, Norman Lamont, Bernard Jenkin, Liam Fox and Bill Cash launched their movement for a referendum. A Commons vote to hold such a referendum on the Maastricht Treaty was defeated. I took part in nearly all Commons debates on Europe between 1994 and 2012 and the question was always about politics, not about a trading area.

So is it now possible to have done with the cant that the British only wanted to be in a trading relationship with Europe, a giant market, and the wily continentals seduced us into sharing a political bed the better to enable Europe to be the dominatrix ruling over a politically castrated John Bull? From day one there has been politics in European construction and all enforceable laws require a political decision to enable their existence.

Removing Britain from Europe was an act of supreme political will. It was achieved by clever politicians of high ambition with bottomless purses, media support without parallel in any other political campaign in British political history and a sustained, enduring ideological commitment. They triumphed over weaker, less organised, under-endowed politicians who did not know what they really believed in, were not burning with ambition for their nation to keep its status as a major European power, unable to summon up inspiring words and infected by years of appeasement of Europhobic populism.

There are good economic arguments for staying in the EU, but the question turns, has turned and will always turn on a sense of politics and the national interest which elected politicians exist to define and serve.

I set out my arguments in *Brexit: How Britain Will Leave Europe*, right at the start of 2015. But the complacency and smugness of the pro-Europeans in Britain could not be shaken nor could they be stirred into taking action to prevent Brexit once Cameron announced his referendum.

British voters or perhaps more specifically English voters, I was told, were natural conservatives who always opted for the status quo. That comfort blanket of belief ignores the wonderful strand of 'fuck youism' in the English mindset. The English cut off a king's head in 1649 and stood alone in 1940 when economic common sense suggested a deal with Hitler to preserve the empire and British wealth. The English were the first into the industrial revolution and first out of mass agricultural employment and the first into a full-blown *financiarisation* of the economy in the 1980s.

The British gave up an empire without the dreadful wars of France in Indo-China or Algeria. Then in 1982 we launched an armada across thousands of miles of ocean to reclaim a few rocks and meadows and sheep in the southern Atlantic.

It is not so much that Albion is *perfide* but at times the English are crazy and do things that the great and the good do not believe will happen.

Many white working-class voters voted for Brexit just as they had followed Enoch Powell and other purveyors of xenophobia over the years. Labour MPs fretted over these absent voters. Yet studies by Oxford University's Professor Danny Dorling, Britain's leading social geographer, showed that Brexit was won by the white middle classes – the so-called A, B and C1 social categories – while 80 per cent of British Asians, who tend to vote Labour, supported remaining in Europe. It is too simplistic to say this was a vote of the plebs against the elites, the old against the young, those with university education against those without. There were groups within groups and each social, educational, income or age category contained those for and against Europe. The real problems were that the Remain camp, despite its diplomas and highly educated directors, lacked core political intelligence and campaigning ability compared to the Leave camp.

That is true across Europe. There is a self-satisfaction amongst pro-Europeans that history ended a quarter of a century ago when Francis Fukuyama wrote his famous book and the Treaty of Maastricht was enacted, creating European citizenship and declaring the birth of the European Union in place of its quarrelsome nation states.

Brexit should be a wake-up call to all in Europe that the owl of Minerva has yet to spread her wings and that the EU is not a finished or even accepted project. New and powerful political forces within and outside Europe are lining up against European cooperation and unity. It is too easy to depict or denounce anti-EU forces as marginal and extreme. They are driven by a sense that there is too much power and wealth concentrated in the hands of the few, not the many.

In his book *Brexit: What the Hell Happens Now?* (2016), Ian Dunt has correctly described the EU as a 'well-meaning but internally con-tradictory experiment in transnational political organisation. For everything that is sensible, there is something absurd. For everything regrettable about it, there is something to be commended. It is demo-cratically flawed, but also nothing like as monstrous or opaque as its critics would have you believe.'

The EU conforms to Kant's reminder that 'out of the crooked tim-ber of humanity no straight thing was ever made'. The EU is the cre-ation of flawed humans, not pure rationality, let alone divine intention. The flaws have perhaps been more in evidence this century than in the first decades of European integration after 1950. Has Brexit delivered a mortal blow to the EU or in this game of lose-lose will Britain emerge as the biggest loser?

Figures like the German chancellor, Angela Merkel, and the out-going French president, François Hollande, came out strongly to regret and deplore Brexit, as did the chiefs of the European institutions. But most of these are in the closing days of their time as political leaders. Brexit may be seen as a modern equivalent of the United States reject-ing the Treaty of Versailles and the League of Nations. It was a foolish, bad and sad decision by America, but it was far more damaging to the hopes of a stable and prosperous Europe and the world in the 1920s and 1930s.

A different, less fateful comparison might be with the decision of France in 1954 to reject the European Defence Community. This was set up with the full backing of the US to try and create a united European defence policy and organisation to counter the Soviet threat and avoid the then delicate and difficult question of de-Nazified Germany joining NATO. French nationalists and left populists won a majority in the National Assembly to vote down the treaty, which was in parallel to the treaty setting up the European Steel and Coal Community – forerunner of today's EU.

Unlike the isolationist decision of the US Congress to turn its back on Europe in 1920 with its disastrous consequences, the decision of French populist-nationalists to reject common European defence three decades later spurred on the rest of Europe (minus France) to greater defence integration in the framework of NATO. The paradox of what might be called the Frexit vote spurning European defence integration is that it began creating a Euro-Atlantic community of nations, economically open, free societies under the rule of law, which has – until the Brexit vote – proved remarkably resilient.

Might Brexit finally get Europe's blinkered leaders to find the imagination to begin a reform programme that begins to answer the question of solving the EU's growing, deepening problems?

9

THE BREXIT GENERATION

In the 1990s there was talk of an 'E' generation of pro-Europeans taking over political control in Britain. It was indeed true that the New Labour leadership of Tony Blair, Gordon Brown and Peter Mandelson and their younger epigones was pro-European. They took over from an 'E' generation of Conservatives like Ken Clarke, Chris Patten and Edwina Currie. Liberal Democrats like Paddy Ashdown, Charles Kennedy and Menzies Campbell were also part of this next 'E' generation and meshed easily with Labour in their commitment to the EU. This sentiment found expression in the title of a book by Mark Leonard, *Why Europe Will Run the 21st Century*, published in 2005. Leonard was the son of Dick Leonard, a life-long pro-European Labour MP who worked for *The Economist* in Brussels. Mark Leonard had set up the European Council on Foreign Relations, which turned into an effective and respected think-tank in parallel with the Centre for European Reform set up in the 1990s with the similar aim of making European affairs more central to British political life.

This was the 'E' generation at work, and it was especially linked to the rise of the Labour Party to governing power, 1997–2010, and the growth in parliamentary seats of the strongly pro-EU Liberal Democratic Party. In parallel, however, there was the slowly growing

'B' or Brexit generation in the Conservative Party, in the media owned by off-shore proprietors who paid no tax in Britain and in the case of Rupert Murdoch was not even a British citizen, and in a darker under-growth of hostility to foreigners articulated by nationalist parties like the British National Party (BNP) and UKIP.

This 'B' generation of the right was descended from the politics of Enoch Powell. It was nationalist and nostalgic. Often it was crudely Germanophobe. Its elite leaders talked of sovereignty and the suprem-acy of the House of Commons. Above all it was obsessed with immi-gration. In May 2014, the leader of the anti-Semitic racist BNP, Nick Griffin, lost his MEP's seat in the European Parliament election. He was asked by the BBC if his defeat meant that voters no longer wanted to vote for a racist party. 'Oh, no', was his reply, 'they have found another one to vote for.'

Thus UKIP emerged as the leading political expression of the 'B' or Brexit generation in British political life. The key demand from an early phase of the 'B' generation was to bypass parliamentary democracy and use a plebiscite to obtain their goal of quitting the EU. The mid-nineteenth-century French leader Louis Napoleon used plebiscites to avoid having to rule under a parliamentary regime. From a very early stage, those opposed to Britain playing a part in Europe had sought to counterpose a populist plebiscite to the House of Commons deciding on an international treaty committing Britain by law to accepting common rules on aspects of its economic life, in particular.

Calls for a referendum were a staple of the European debate from the 1960s onwards. There was even a Referendum Party, formed by an eccentric, vain businessman, which stood in a few seats in the 1997 election without much impact. But the 'B' generation took off after 1997 as the new leader of the Conservative Party, William Hague, decided to make anti-Europeanism the dominant theme of his efforts to denigrate Tony Blair and revive the moribund Tory Party.

The 'B' generation vanquished the 'E' generation on 23 June 2016. In America, it might be called the 'T' generation after the Tea Party and now President Trump, who has ushered in a new era of politics hostile to many of the values that Euro-Atlantic leaders had shaped since 1945.

This is particularly true in England. The elite establishment in London and across England was predominately Eurosceptic from at least the start of the twenty-first century, if not before. The Conservative Party turned against Europe after Hague became leader. All three candidates for the Tory leadership in 2005 were hostile to the EU. The Labour Party had its Eurosceptics, especially amongst an older generation of politicians who had matured in Labour's fervid anti-European atmosphere of the 1970s.

The language of UKIP and the Conservatives on Europe overlapped, and even merged. UKIP and its mouthy leader Nigel Farage used language about the EU that had already been put into circulation by senior Conservatives. William Hague offers a good example of a politician who began the process of turning the Tory Party into a fully-fledged anti-European political grouping, describing the euro in 1998 as 'a burning building with no exits'. In December 2016, Farage took Hague's metaphor a stage further, describing the EU as 'a burning building that is catching on fire'.

This common Hague/Farage, Tory/UKIP language can be seen elsewhere. In general it was the vivid and extravagant denunciation of Europe from senior Conservative leaders that set the media tone. UKIP just spoke out loud, very loud, what many Conservatives thought and could be read every day from the late 1990s in many newspapers.

It is fashionable to depict Farage as the main instigator of anti-EU feeling in Britain. In fact, he simply copied and pasted attacks by top Tories, including all Conservative Party leaders since 1997. Farage's language was little different from that of former Conservative chancellors like Nigel Lawson and Norman Lamont. Farage was what Lenin would have called a 'useful idiot' as he amplified Conservative Party language about Europe and harried and chased Tory leaders until finally Cameron gave way and conceded the longstanding UKIP demand for a plebiscite on Europe.

It was not just Conservatives. Labour anti-Europeanism, dating from the 1960s, was never eradicated. Bernard Donoughue was a Labour peer and for a short while a shadow and then a government minister under Tony Blair. He had served as a special adviser to James Callaghan in the 1976–9 Labour government. In the diary he kept of his Blair years, Donoughue revealed the age-old suspicion of Germany that was still not eradicated on the left half a century after the end of World War II. He wrote that '[the French] are tied to the Germans, restoring the European Reich that Hitler started to build in 1940–45', and then as a junior agricultural minister in 1996, he held that the Germans 'behaved as if they owned the EU. [...] The other nations defer to them as if it's still 1941.'

I was struck during the Brexit plebiscite campaign, in all the debates I engaged in with Conservative MPs and MEPs and with pro-Brexit commentators and economists, how very early on in their arguments against Europe there would be an attack on Germany as a new hegemon that was twisting the EU and the euro to be instruments of German *Machtpolitik*. It led the leftist economics academic Jamie Galbraith to describe Greece as a 'European colony', the kind of leftwing demagogy about Europe that was as damaging to any clear understanding of the EU as the rightist demagogy of a Nigel Farage or Boris Johnson.

The media establishment, in the sense of the papers owned by proprietors who paid no tax in the UK, such as the *Daily Mail*, the *Daily Telegraph*, the *Sun*, *The Times* and their Sunday sister papers, were relentlessly hostile to the EU. Newspaper proprietors and editors rarely reveal the source of their editorial inspiration. In the 1980s, Rupert Murdoch had been involved in a titanic struggle with print trade unions over his desire to use new technology which eliminated many print union jobs (even though overall there are more employees working in printing today than ever before). British print unions were amongst the most combative, confrontational and politicised of any craft unions. The 1980s was the decade in which such trade union power was severely weakened to the point of elimination.

But then suddenly the European Commission president, Jacques Delors, appeared at the TUC in 1988 to reaffirm the importance of trade unions as social partners in the process of European integration. Delors was reflecting the German or Nordic model of social partnership, not the strike-happy, multi-union highly political British newspaper unions. In 1992, Prime Minister John Major made much of obtaining an opt-out from Social Europe rules and directives. In turn, the trade unions, the mortal enemy of press proprietors and many editors in the late 1970s and 1980s, became the loudest champions of the EU on the grounds that 'my enemy's enemy is my friend'.

Moreover, in the 1990s Margaret Thatcher remained a potent force behind the scenes, especially with her favourite newspaperman, Rupert Murdoch, and there can be little doubt that she encouraged his already deep-rooted anti-Europeanism. Since the beginning of this century, the business establishment (in the sense of the Confederation of British Industry (CBI) and the British Chambers of Commerce) produced report after report criticising the EU for regulation and red tape. If ever a word of praise was found for the EU or for the idea of open trade Europe operating under common rules, it was very faint indeed.

The super-rich in the City, like Rodney Leach, who was close to Mrs Thatcher, or Stuart Wheeler, financed anti-European campaign organisations like Open Europe, and in the latter's case, UKIP. Many had made their fortunes by speculating against different European currencies. They hated the arrival of the euro, which shut down that aspect of financial trading and did not like any suggestion from the European Commission that cross-frontier financing trading needed regulation. Even under the nominally pro-European

Tony Blair, key elements of the state apparatus never stopped complaining about Europe. The Treasury under Gordon Brown and his Labour and Tory successors spent most of their energy blocking, rubbishing or undermining any EU initiative that hinted at a bit more fairness in the way banks and businesses conducted their affairs. Blair's press operation in Downing Street always found reasons to run down any EU proposal and played up Blair wielding vetoes over directives.

Yes, there was the occasional pro-EU piece in the *Financial Times*, while the *Guardian* handed over its comment pages to fluent writers like Sir Simon Jenkins, Owen Jones, Paul Mason or Giles Fraser to mock and denigrate Europe. Almost the entire economist establishment took against the euro and the *Guardian*'s economics editor, Larry Elliott, wrote a book denouncing Europe's single currency in 2016. The UK and indeed the world's liberal-left pontificators from Yanis Varoufakis to Joseph Stiglitz have spent more time trashing parts of the EU they don't like than arguing in favour of European integration and the existence of the EU. Indeed Stiglitz became the darling of Brexit circles when he published a book shortly after the plebiscite vote saying the creation of the euro was the main cause of European woes and the single currency should be dismantled – a repeated assertion and demand of Brexit spokesmen like the three 'N's' (Nigel Farage, Nigel Lawson and Norman Lamont).

Professors Stiglitz and Varoufakis are entitled to their views, and as clever professors have the right to tell others what to think. But if the EU is finally buried, the nails in its coffin will have been hammered in as much by the global and British left commentariat as by rightwing nationalists.

Not all of these economists or *Guardian* editors and BBC presenters were anti-European in the sense of a Nigel Farage or other longstanding Tory Europhobes. Many opposed Brexit. But they had shaped even in the liberal *bien-pensant* establishment such a climate of contempt for anything associated with the EU that they created the culture from which full-on Brexit campaigners drew sustenance.

The economics writer Tim Harford has written that 'most of the British and international political and business establishment' were supporters of Remain. It is true that when confronted with what line to take on actually leaving the EU many political and business leaders – not all but a majority – supported Remain. But the damage had been done. The same establishment Harford quoted had, for the most part, been consistently Eurosceptic all this century and had provided the oxygen for the Leavers of Brexit to gain credibility. Like William Hague, for example, they thought they could be as contemptuous of the EU as they wished. Like the former Conservative Party leader, they enjoyed the applause of the anti-Europeans as it rolled in but assumed that at the final moment the people would listen to them and understand that the constant criticism of the EU was not meant to lead voters to put a cross in the Leave box.

Voters, however, drew a different conclusion. If all these clever political leaders and the chiefs of business in the CBI or the British Chambers of Commerce, as well as the majority of journalists who wrote opinion-shaping arguments, had been saying such negative things about the EU for a decade or more, then surely their advice should be followed. Voters thus drew the obvious conclusion and voted accordingly. What William Hague and the CBI sowed they reaped.

Thus my belief that Mr Cameron's plebiscite would end the way it did was not due to any special powers of prediction. They were based on 40 years of active political engagement, getting my shoes dirty and my body tired as I knocked on doors to ask people to vote. Whether in the West Midlands and London in the 1970s, in by-elections in the 1980s and then in South Yorkshire mainly since 1992, I kept coming up against this hostility to the presence of immigrants, to foreign accents heard in Tesco and Asda, to any outsider telling us what to do.

I set out reasons in my first book on Brexit. I discussed other reasons in a more passionate, shorter book, *Let's Stay Together: Why Yes to Europe*, published as a contribution to the Brexit campaign debate in April 2016. I published an article for the excellent Brussels paper *Politico* in November 2015 listing 12 reasons why a Brexit vote was likely.

One or two people shared my fears and doubts, such as Charles Grant, the director of the Centre for European Reform. Yet the main writers on British politics and the EU for the *Financial Times* or *The Economist* all patted me politely on the back and in a friendly way said, 'Don't worry, Denis, the vote will be to stay In.'

To be fair, that was also the view of many Leavers. In late March 2016 I found myself skiing with Daniel Hannan, the forthright anti-EU Tory MEP, who has been a tireless advocate, using a brilliant pen and fluency of speech in support of Britain leaving Europe. He said to me 'Your lot will win', and made the same prediction when we debated at Winchester in May 2016. Daniel, like many politicians, may sensibly always prepare for the worst in the hope that it won't happen, but although we disagree on Europe I have always found him rigorous and clear in his analysis of what he believes is good for his country.

The caution of the Leavers concerns me less than the complacency of the Remainers. But who were the Leavers?

10

THE LEAVERS

There are numerous way of reading the Brexit vote, none of them entirely satisfying. Start with the big numbers. There are 65 million people in the UK and 1,269,501 more voted to Leave than to Remain. There are 46,499,537 voters eligible to vote in the plebiscite, so the majority to leave was 2.7 per cent of the total electorate. Put another way, only 37 per cent of UK electors voted to leave Europe. If the referendum electorate was the same as those who voted in the Scottish referendum of 2014 when everyone over 16 had the right to vote and assuming that like 18–24-year-olds, the 16–18-year-old cohort had voted strongly in favour of Europe, then the majority for Leave might have been even smaller or not exist at all.

A majority of one, it is often said, is all that is needed in a democracy and the vote for Leave was clear. Mrs May chose to portray herself as the leader of the 37 per cent of the electorate who voted to leave Europe. That position was justified in electoral terms in May and June 2017. But neither in the plebiscite in 2016 still less in the elections the following year were the details given on what the new status of those who voted for Brexit vis-à-vis the rest of Europe is and what advantages or rights they may lose once all the terms to be negotiated on Britain's full and complete withdrawal from Europe are made public. Few if any of these facts were known or debated during the Brexit campaign in the early summer of 2016. At that stage a full post mortem on the questions of who voted or did not vote and why they voted will be of use. Political scientists who work on election data are presumably working over the results. The Brexit plebiscite was a watershed in British constitutional and political history. It was promised insouciantly by David Cameron in 2013. Its reverberations could last for the rest of the century.

In the 1979 referendums on Scottish and Welsh devolution it was agreed that 40 per cent of all eligible votes had to say 'Yes' for the vote to be valid. In other countries, the bar is set higher, with 50 or 60 per cent, even two-thirds of votes, needed in a referendum before such vital constitutional change can take place. The Hungarian referendum in 2016 on EU refugee and migrant policy required 50 per cent of all voters to take part and 60 per cent of Hungarians stayed at home to render the referendum null and void. It is a tribute of sorts to the generosity of the British political system that a little over one third of the total electorate can so utterly change Britain's relations with other countries and its global economic and geo-political status.

The figures below show how split and divided the nation is on staying linked to or repudiating Europe. Very roughly, the young voted for a European future and the old voted for a nostalgic English one. London, England's beating heart, Europe's biggest city-region, voted to stay linked to Europe, but in the smaller towns of England the vote was hostile to Europe. Women under 50 voted for Britain in Europe. Older women voted against Europe. The English said 'No' but two of the most distinct national components of the United Kingdom – Scotland and Northern Ireland – voted 'Yes'. Mr Cameron's referendum split the nation.

Female Votes			
Age 18–24	Age 25–49	Age 50–64	Age 65+
Remain 80%;	Remain 54%;	Remain 40%;	Remain 34%;
Leave 20%	Leave 46%	Leave 60%	Leave 66%

Male Votes			
Age 18–24	Age 25–49	Age 50–64	Age 65+
Remain 61%;	Remain 53%;	Remain 39%;	Remain 38%;
Leave 39%	Leave 47%	Leave 61%	Leave 62%

Over the next period, the majority for Brexit will slowly vanish. In the three years between the Brexit referendum and the European Parliament elections in 2019, 1.26 million British citizens over 65 will die and 2 million will reach the voting age of 18, according to Age UK. Given that 70 per cent of young voters were in favour of Remain and 64 per cent of over-65s voted to Leave, the pro-European camp will increase by 1 million and the Brexit camp go down by 756,000.

The Leave vote came top in nine out of the UK's 12 regions and nations, with only London, Scotland and Northern Ireland having a majority for Remain. There were specific reasons in Northern Ireland, with its large Catholic, nationalist population, along with many farmers who do not want to see different agricultural subsidy regimes between the UK and the Republic of Ireland, which inevitably leads to smuggling and price distortions. In Scotland, the vote was also influenced by national sentiment mobilised by the pro-EU Scottish National Party against the ruling Conservative establishment.

London had long slipped its UK moorings and become a global megalopolis. According to the 2011 census, 36.7 per cent of London citizens are foreign-born and London had the most Commonwealth or Irish citizens who were entitled to vote in the referendum. There are 250 foreign banks operating in London and more than nine out of ten members of the British Bankers Association are foreign-owned, as the City became in effect the Wall Street for the entire EU. Many American, Asian, African and Middle East firms choose London for their EU headquarters. Londoners work as lawyers, estate agents, restaurateurs, private school directors and teachers, doctors, chauffeurs, personal trainers and in other ways for the hundreds of thousands of European citizens who live in the capital. Russian oligarchs own football clubs and newspapers in London and do huge amounts of business in euros and in the EU from their London offices.

London is also home to Eurosceptic think-tanks, and anti-EU newspapers, the cohorts of anti-EU commentators writing for online as well as print media, and above all the Conservative Party establishment. But for anti-European Britain, London was a headquarters to radiate out the anti-EU message, not a well of Brexit votes. And any speaker at a City seminar or lunch in the last 15–20 years has faced many an anti-EU question or statement from London business executives. As Simon Nixon of the *Wall Street Journal*, who patrols the City, reported, there was strong support for Brexit amongst employees in 'hedge funds, asset management and insurance and domestic-focused equity market. One senior banker reckons that up to 40 per cent of participants in every meeting he attended this year [2016] were enthusiastic Brexiters.'

But taken as a whole, London made so much money from the EU and from being the most welcoming EU capital for foreigners from anywhere in the world, helped by the English language and the validity of legal contracts drawn up by London lawyers for very large fees and the use of London lawyers and judges to act in commercial disputes. It was therefore likely that many Londoners would vote for their own direct economic interests. Commentators later sought to link the Brexit vote to the level of education or income – with those without university degrees or not well paid more likely to vote Brexit. Yet in London the better-off, comfortable suburbs like Bexley and Hillingdon with Tory MPs voted Leave and poorer boroughs like Tower Hamlets and Newham voted Remain. Anti-Europeanism is at its heart a political project and if Britain is to think afresh on its future as a European country it will require political leadership and a new set of political arguments.

In the rest of England the picture was reasonably clear. In the West and East Midlands the Leave vote was 59.3 and 58.8 respectively. In Yorkshire, the Humber and the North East, which saw the biggest casualties in terms of the destruction of heavy industry jobs in mines, steelworks and shipyards from the 1980s onwards, more than 58 per cent of the little over 4 million votes cast were for Brexit. Only 19,000 Eastern European citizens worked in the North-East region of England – 1.49 per cent of the total population of 2.61 million. The North-East had benefited massively from EU structural and regional subsidies and was home to the important Nissan car plant, with its linked supply chain firms. Nissan and other foreign-owned car-makers in England export nearly 80 per cent of their cars to the EU. Despite this clear link between the economy of the North-East and Europe, the region swallowed the anti-EU UKIP/Tory propaganda and voted clearly for Brexit. By contrast, in London, home to more than 1 million EU citizens, the vote not to cut links with Europe won a majority.

The Brexit vote came at a time of economic unhappiness for many. In Britain, average real wages fell by 10 per cent between 2007 and 2015 according to the London School of Economics Centre for Economic Performance, which added that this was the longest continuous fall in workers' wages since the 1930s.

Thus the high employment figures, which included the 6.2 per cent of the British workforce coming from the EU, went hand in hand with a slump in working-class purchasing power. The UK's increase in GDP as measured by purchasing power parity – the usual international comparator – between 2000 and 2015 was smaller than that of Germany, France and Spain. Sadly, the UK's press is so insular and so keen to boost the image of a 'Great' Britain the journalists rarely look behind the news releases put out by politicians who want to persuade voters that thanks to their leadership the people of Britain are getting richer and better off. Studies by the Resolution Foundation and others have shown that EU workers did not have much impact on UK wage levels, but if there was no formal link it was an easy claim to make, as the anti-European campaigners did relentlessly after 2005, that wage levels were depressed by the arrival of new European workers.

Modern British economic management under Labour as much as Conservatives and their Liberal Democratic helpers, 2010–15, has created as many losers as winners. For northern working-class communities which saw many Eastern European workers finding jobs while they and their children were unable to secure a living family wage it was easy to believe that EU migration was a problem. Meanwhile, those with capital and investments did well, as the stock market has risen by 115 per cent in the years 2009–15.

Moreover, 495,000 council houses were sold under Labour between 1997 and 2009, but in Yorkshire and the Humber region, which recorded a high Leave vote, only 24 council houses were built. Figures dug up from the Office of National Statistics by John Healey MP reveal that the regional share of UK output has fallen in every part of the country since 2010, other than in London and the South-East, where it has risen. According to Healey, the Gini coefficient measure of regional inequality has risen in every year since then. The South Yorkshire MP points out that 'house prices are 93 per cent higher in London compared to the low-point after the global financial crash, but in other parts of the country they haven't recovered at all, leaving thousands of households in negative equity'.

A report by the Joseph Rowntree Foundation asserts that it was working-class, less-qualified, 'left behind' communities in England and Wales who were mostly likely to back leaving the EU. As we have seen, this does not explain the London or Scotland votes, and mono-causal explanations for the 37 per cent of the electorate who believed the enticements of the Leave campaign should be treated with caution. Labour, Conservative and Liberal Democrat ministers who held office in the twenty-first century all bear responsibility for their socio-economic model that left so many outside London and the South East poorer and liable to blame any external cause for their reduced status. They voted against whoever was in power. To begin with, in the early 2000s, they backed the BNP in local and European parliamentary elections and then increasingly UKIP won support from voters who felt the established governments seemed keener on promoting global capitalism than building a fairer, sharing society and economy at home. When the chance came for a massive vote against the three parties who had failed to deliver the labour market holy trinity of good jobs, fair pay and social provision – especially in the form of affordable housing – many voters may have enjoyed the novelty of having a chance to give most big-name politicians a kicking, especially as they were told money would flow into the NHS.

It has become a cliché to say the Brexit vote was a revolt of the masses against the elites. This is too simple. The pro-Brexit camp was led by elite, wealthy men and women perfectly at home at the annual gatherings of the world's rich and powerful in Davos or at Bilderberg conferences. The struggle to stay in Europe was between two establishment elites. The side with most money and most populist passion won. But it was a victory for an elite establishment.

So we know that 17 million people voted for Brexit and 16 million did not. But how permanent and how porous are those voting blocs?

Already by August 2016, the majority for Brexit had evaporated, according to a Bertelsmann Foundation survey. This showed that 56 per cent of British citizens wanted to stay in the EU compared to 49 per cent when a similar poll was carried out in March 2016. A YouGov poll in February 2017 showed a 46–42 split, with the majority of those polled saying the Brexit vote was a mistake. Other polls showed different results and it will take some time for public opinion to settle on the question.

An interesting opinion poll carried out in November 2016 asked voters if they felt more or less confident about their future as a result of the referendum. Sixty-three per cent replied that they felt less confident and 37 per cent that they felt more confident. The figure reflect the share of the total electorate who voted for Brexit – 37 per cent and the 63 per cent who either actively voted against Brexit or did not vote.

The Brexit vote pitched a modern Britain that is no longer a white-only nation against an older Britain. Many modern British are of course white and yet their parents or grandparents came from abroad. Just as the most fervent of believers are often those who have converted to a new faith, so the loudest upholders of Britishness against the EU – such as top Tories Michael Howard or Boris Johnson or Priti Patel – have recent ancestors from outside Britain. Ms Patel worked for the UK Referendum Party, headed by the businessman Sir James Goldsmith, who was an early proponent in the 1990s of a plebiscite to cut Britain off from Europe. Her devotion to anti-EU ideology got its reward with swift promotion though the ranks of the Conservative Party to cabinet office under Theresa May.

According to the polls carried out by Lord Ashcroft, two-thirds of those describing themselves as Asian voted to remain, as did three-quarters of black voters. Nearly six in ten (58 per cent) of those describing themselves as Christian voted to leave; seven in ten Muslims voted to remain.

These are fascinating figures and as interesting as the more predictable social class indicators. Brexit was a rejection of British multiculturalism. Of those who defined themselves as 'English not British', 80 per cent voted to Leave, irrespective of social class. Those who see themselves as 'British not English' voted 60 per cent for Remain. Brexit can therefore be seen as an assertion of white English monoculturalism.

Academics have drawn a parallel with the independence referendum in Quebec, where 95 per cent of English-speaking Quebeckers voted to stay united with Canada and support the increasingly multicultural

Canada that was coming into being by the time of the referendum in 1995.

In other words, referendums, including the Brexit one, tend to be about nativism and nationalism, not simply the question on the ballot paper. Those who shape the final interpretation and response to 23 June 2016 have to work out why the majority in non-white and non-English Britain voted differently from the rest of England outside London.

A ComRes poll for the *Independent* newspaper showed that 49 per cent of those who voted for Leave thought that securing Britain's economic future via a good trade deal was a priority, against 39 per cent who said reducing immigration was the main purpose of Brexit. Eric Kaufmann, Professor of Politics at Birkbeck, University of London, has carried out further research. When asked two months after the referendum, 'What is the most important issue facing Britain today' only 5 per cent of Leave voters mentioned poverty or inequality, but 41 per cent of Leave voters said immigration was the most important issue for today's Britain. In fact, Britain is ninth in the league table of EU countries with a sizeable level of movement of other EU citizens to live or work outside their borders. The region which recorded the highest Leave vote was North-East England, where only 19,000 people from the countries that joined the EU after 2004 live or work.

Professor Kaufmann conducted a poll asking if people would pay to see immigration reduced. Sixty-two per cent said 'No', they would not take any hit in their income to see migrant numbers reduced.

One reason for voting Brexit was offered in a tweet by a Mr D. Kingler, who explained his Brexit vote thus:

I don't have a video player anymore because of the filth today and adult programming upsetting my wife and daughters. I am 75 years old and can actually remember when we did not put up with this nonsense. That is why I voted alongside the many proud British people to take our country back. Sick of it!

Perhaps it is reasonable to vote to leave the EU to get rid of the bru-
talised humiliation of women represented in the extreme forms of porn
found via social media on the internet. There were many reasons why
people voted Brexit and many reasons why they might change their
mind. Professor Adrian Low of Staffordshire University, who tracked
the shifts of public opinion in the months after 23 June 2016, has
looked at the 29 per cent of the electorate who did not vote. Amongst
these non-voters there is a majority of 41 per cent to 26 per cent in
favour of staying in Europe. Of course, non-voters forfeit their right
to decide the future direction of travel of a nation. Yet one of the early
decisions of Mrs May's Brexit government was to announce that henceforth British citizens living in Europe would be able to vote in British
elections. Had this been in place before the plebiscite, then Brexit
would have been lost. Is the will of the people the will just of those who
cast a vote or should it also reflect the will of those who, for whatever
reason, did not cast a vote or those who were denied a vote?

A post-Brexit survey carried out by the respected British Election
Study organisation found that 6 per cent of those who voted Leave
regretted this choice. Several experts in opinion polls believe that 4 per
cent of the Leave vote would now vote not to quit Europe if given a
second chance. One opinion poll showed that if a new political party
was formed that fought elections just on the basis of opposing Brexit it
would win more votes than the Labour Party. Another poll by BMG
published in November 2016 showed Remain on 45 per cent and Leave
on 43 per cent. These are opinion polls, not actual voters going to cast
their vote. They show, however, that there is no solidity of support for the
kind of full, hardline Brexit that many government ministers support.

Certainly the pro-Brexit press was alive to this danger. As the media
commentator Andy Beckett wrote, the referendum result 'was an outcome for which the tabloids had campaigned doggedly for decades, but
never more intensely – or with less factual scrupulousness – than this
spring and summer [of 2016], when the front pages of the *Sun*, *Mail*

and *Express* bellowed for Brexit, talking up Britain's prospects afterwards, in deafening unison, day after day. Two days before the referendum, the *Sun* gave over its first ten pages to pro-Brexit coverage.'
Rightwing Tory money raised to campaign against Brexit was channelled via the anti-European Northern Irish Democratic Unionist Party.
Political donations do not have to be declared in Northern Ireland as
a security measure. The money was used to pay for wraparound front
and back pages of the free *Metro* newspaper to call for a Brexit vote just
before the referendum. This occult and possibly illegal financing helped
to win the vote, but Britain's Electoral Commission, which is meant to
stop improper use of political donations, was asleep on the job.

There will be a long interval between the excitements of the vote on
23 June 2016 and a major revision of public opinion. Much, indeed
everything, depends on economic developments. If the pound reverses
its sharp decline, so that on summer holidays in 2017 and 2018 British
holiday-makers feel their Brexit currency is buying as much as it did
before the Brexit vote and if the key indicators of growth, inflation and
inward investment which seemed very wobbly directly after the Brexit
vote turn out to be solid and booming, the fears over Brexit will fade
away and the vote will stand. If by the beginning of the 2020s, the EU
has rolled over and accepted that Britain and its foreign banks and firms
can have the same access to the broader EU market as before the Brexit
vote, then there will be no rethink.

But if that is not the case, then Conservative MPs will begin to fret
and worry. Some are devout in their opposition to Europe. Most are
pragmatic and have not been elected to see the economic status of their
electors and local businesses suffer.

Britain will wait a while before a final and definitive decision is
taken about the nation's relationship with Europe. Neither should the
Brexit ideologues declare game over nor those who see a European
future for Britain hoist the white flag and accept British isolationism.

11
THE CAMPAIGN

The Leave campaign was very much a male affair, with minor slots reserved for the Labour MP Gisela Stuart, who had come out as being hostile to the EU after losing her post as a junior minister in Tony Blair's first Labour administration after the 2001 election. She was close to Derek Scott, a veteran Labour anti-European whom she married in 2010. She was joined by Kate Hoey, an Ulsterwoman and veteran Labour MP who had long been anti-European and had good media fluency. Leave enjoyed the support of two former Tory chancellors, Nigel Lawson, aged 84 and Norman Lamont, 78, and the posthumous support of Labour's former chancellor Denis Healey, who in his last interview before he died in October 2015 said he would vote to leave the EU.

Most remarkable was the disloyalty of David Cameron's two predecessors as Conservative Party leader, Michael Howard and Iain Duncan Smith. They may feel that the faithlessness came from the Prime Minister, as Cameron had never shown any pro-EU leaning as leader of the Conservatives after 2005 and prime minister until the beginning of 2016, when he seemed to have finally understood that a British prime minister isolating Britain from Europe was not to the nation's advantage nor would history deal kindly with a prime minister who initiated such a rupture. The two former party leaders campaigned vigorously

against their successor. Cameron looked weak, unconvincing and without authority as he tried to persuade the nation to vote down Brexit.

But Cameron was his own worst enemy as he made no serious preparation to win the campaign. Even in May 2015, it would have been
possible for Cameron to delay or defer his plebiscite, as he had done
with the promise to hold one after 2010 on the Lisbon Treaty. But no
one in the higher reaches of the state apparatus was willing to say 'No,
Prime Minister' to David Cameron, any more than they were willing to
say 'No, Prime Minister' to Tony Blair over the invasion of Iraq.

Officials who worked in Number 10 now admit privately that the
Referendum Bill was rushed through parliament in too much of a
hurry. 'I am still kicking myself that we did not extend the vote to
16- and 17-year-olds as we did in the Scottish referendum', one senior
Number 10 insider told me. Another Number 10 official told me,
'Right-up to the last minute the Prime Minister was convinced that the
British people would never vote to leave Europe. He just believed it was
an impossibility.'

In addition, Cameron had been deliberately making it harder for
younger voters to be on the electoral register. He ordered a new system
to be put in place. Previously a parent, the owner of rented-out flats or
a university recorded who lived in a family home, rented flat or student
accommodation. Each person thus notified to the electoral registration
body in each municipality could vote. Now Cameron insisted each vote
had to be registered individually. The chances of students and other
young people living away from home making the effort to get their
names on the electoral register were not high. This meant that there
was a 9 per cent drop – around 1.9 million – between 10 June 2014
and 1 December 2015 in the number of 18- and 19-year-olds who were
eligible to vote.

This gerrymandering was aimed at helping the Conservatives in the
2016 London mayoral and municipal elections, as on the whole young
voters don't vote for rightwing candidates. Cameron insisted on forcing

through changes in October 2015 designed to help his party and had a Commons majority to do so. But in consequence a large number of young pro-EU votes were not available for his referendum.

Having placed his own obstacles in the path of victory, Cameron and the Number 10 apparatus went to sleep for nine months. The Prime Minister continued to denigrate the EU. He described Brussels as 'bossy and bureaucratic', which was not language designed to generate pro-EU votes. The whole tone of senior Conservative Party discourse in the summer and autumn of 2015 remained as it had been since the party had been changed by William Hague into one ideologically hostile to the EU, even if it stopped short of UKIP demands to quit.

There was no political preparation by Cameron to win the plebiscite he had now legislated for. None of the long arms of the Conservative Party, 10 Downing Street or high-level state officialdom reached out to try and get business to talk to employees or even to square the press. Ministers were not despatched to find arguments in favour of Europe. Indeed many of Cameron's key ministerial team – people like Iain Duncan Smith, Michael Gove, Chris Grayling and Theresa May – continued stoking anti-European fires as they blamed the EU for too many foreigners working in Britain or pointed the finger at low economic growth across the Channel.

The principal Leave campaign linked to the Conservatives was organised by a veteran rightwing but very effective campaigner, Matthew Elliot. He had turned an obscure campaign outfit called the TaxPayers' Alliance into a much-quoted source for attacks on Gordon Brown as chancellor (1997–2007) and then prime minister (2007–10). Elliot's speciality was to package statistics into media cluster bombs so that one number emerged and all the normal qualifications and setting-in-context a responsible economist, statistician or tax expert would feel honour-bound to include just fell away. There was endless money in the City or in Mayfair hedge funds for anti-European propaganda and organisation. Elliot had already set up a Brexit front organisation called

Business for Britain and his network was ready to roll out as soon as the campaign started.

Some Tories hedged their bets and stayed close to David Cameron just in case he won. Sajid Javid, the business secretary, said he would have never entered the EU, would have voted 'No' in 1975 and would vote 'No' in any referendum on a future treaty. Oliver Letwin also said that 2016 was not the time to leave Europe, but when the next treaty revision came around, then the opportunity would arise. These were the advocates of *Brexit interruptus* – withdrawal but not just yet.

After her tirade against the EU at the autumn 2015 Conservative Party conference, Theresa May was seen as a natural to lead the Brexit campaign. But she is a cautious, hesitant politician and stayed nominally loyal to her prime minister, though she made no effort in the campaign to help the Remain camp. On the contrary, in late April 2016 she made a speech saying Britain should withdraw from the European Court of Human Rights and the European Human Rights Convention, which would mean leaving the Council of Europe. This was not on the referendum ballot paper, but after the EU itself, the ECtHR was the most hated institution amongst anti-Europeans and the Europhobe press. So Mrs May was sending a clear message of reassurance to Tory Eurosceptics that she remained with them. Even if they did not win EU withdrawal she would urge withdrawing from the European Convention on Human Rights and in consequences the Council of Europe.

Once the Brexit vote was decided and she became prime minister, May quietly dropped the ECHR pledge as an immediate priority. Leaving the EU was the bigger prize. But her public statement calling for withdrawal from the ECHR had cynically served its purpose in reminding Tory activists who would elect the new leader that she was one of them in disliking Europe.

Like his predecessors as party leader William Hague, Iain Duncan Smith and Michael Howard, David Cameron whipped up campaigns against immigration to use as a political stick to beat first Tony Blair and then after 2007 Gordon Brown. Cameron foolishly made promises to reduce the level of immigration as an absolute number if he became prime minister. The more he talked up immigration, the more voters took the issue seriously. In the 25 years since Mrs Thatcher became prime minister, the population and demographics of Britain had changed. The population grew by 10 million to today's 65 million. Birth rates went down and life expectancy increased. Having been until 1980 a nation with a net emigration figure, Britain became a country dependent on incomers to do all essential work. The fast-food chain Pret A Manger says that of 50 applicants who seek employment – and salaries can eventually reach £43,000 a year – only one is British. The rest are hard-working Europeans serving us coffee and well-made sandwiches. The economy was reshaped to be employment-rich but income-poor. As women entered the workforce households still needed to have children looked after, homes cleaned, ageing relatives cared for and goods ordered online delivered to homes by an army of white-van drivers and Deliveroo-type courier services, while new fleets of taxis from Addison Lee or Uber ferried customers around. These low-pay jobs were largely done by immigrant workers from within the EU or further abroad. It was the way the British economy functioned.

Inevitably the two camps became dubbed Remain and Leave. The Leave camp split into two groups – one based on the Conservative Party and one based on UKIP. The off-shore-owned press pumped out Brexit propaganda independent of either the Tory or UKIP campaigns, nominally separate but seen as one, since both used the same language of dislike of foreigners and made the same claims about the money that would flow to British households once outside the EU.

UKIP set up its own Leave campaign, very publicly bankrolled by an insurance salesman who had made billions, and Nigel Farage toured the country making the same speech that he had been making for 15 years. Farage, a speaker of conviction and passion, has the demagogue's gift of distilling a complicated set of interlocking relationships into simple slogans. All UK laws are made by the EU. Not true. Britain pays £350 million a week to the EU. Not true. There is no growth in Europe. Not true. The EU or the 'Europeans' had caused the unemployment in countries like Greece and Spain. Not true.

But the demagogue is not interested in truth. He wants to arouse emotions and present a dragon that can be slain – if the people will only fall in behind the Leader. In fact, there was little to choose between the Tory Leave campaign and the UKIP Leave campaign. Both were the culmination of more than 20 years of attacking the EU across the board.

It was surreal to hear a senior Tory, Andrea Leadsom, say on the BBC Radio 4 *Today* programme shortly before the Queen's Speech in May 2016 that 60 per cent of all UK laws were decided in Europe, as if Her Majesty the Queen was in Brussels taking dictation from Commission officials on what she could or could not put in her speech announcing future legislation. No one on the BBC's flagship current affairs programme challenged this palpable untruth.

Another pro-Brexit minister, Penny Mordaunt, was challenged when she kept insisting that 75 million Turks were about to join the EU with the right to travel and live and work in the UK and that Britain could not stop this happening. When the BBC interviewer, who knew a little about the EU, pointed out that the UK had a veto (along with 27 other member states), she snapped, 'No, we don't' and continued to maintain what was a complete untruth or, in plain English, a lie.

The Leave battle-bus was emblazoned with a slogan declaring that if the UK left Europe there would be £350 million a week to spend on the NHS. Again a lie, as the UK gets back from the EU its mammoth agricultural subsidy budget, £700 million annually for university research, regional subsidies of hundreds of millions of pounds for

South Yorkshire, Wales or Cornwall, as well as Erasmus scholarships and funding for environmental and cultural projects. Boris Johnson blustered when tackled on this point, but the damage was done, as scores of millions of TV news viewers saw Johnson and other Leave Tories standing in front of the bus with the untrue slogan beamed into their homes.

A Leave leaflet pushed through letter-boxes said that 'Britain's new frontier was with Syria and Iraq' and another one showed a map which stated that Turkey was 'set to join the EU'. In a slightly different tint next to Turkey were its neighbours, Syria and Iraq, as if those countries were about to join the EU with the right to freedom of movement.

At the beginning of the campaign Boris Johnson said that the EU was following in the path of Hitler in seeking to create a super-state. Even by Johnsonian standards the lie was grotesque and over the top. Johnson of course blustered, as he always does, and said his remark had been misinterpreted, but he knew exactly what he was doing in planting in voters' minds the insinuation that being in the EU was something Hitler might have wished for. In his biography of Winston Churchill, Johnson has written of 'the Nazi European Union' and of 'this Gestapo-controlled Nazi EU'. He was making a point about Hitler's plans to dominate Europe but the smear against the EU and the obsession with quoting and linking Hitler to the European Union – which was set up precisely to ensure that the disasters of the 1930s could never happen again – is part of Boris Johnson's pathological need to denigrate Europe by any and all means possible.

Johnson and other Leavers were indeed inspired by a demagogue who said 'If you tell a big enough lie and tell it frequently enough, it will be believed.' The politician in question ran Germany between 1933 and 1945 and consolidated his hold on power with a sequence of populist plebiscites.

The obsession of the Leavers with Hitler was a theme of their rhetoric. As the economist Professor John Van Reenen of the London

School of Economics (now with the Massachusetts Institute of Technology) wrote:

> For me, the nadir came a few days before the vote when one of Leave's leaders, Michael Gove, compared me and my colleagues to paid Nazi scientists persecuting Einstein. This was apparently in response to a statement we signed (including 12 Nobel laureates) warning of the economic damage from Brexit. At least one of these derided experts had grandparents murdered in the concentration camps, so one can imagine how Gove's statement – supported by Boris Johnson – made them feel.

Many election promises and campaign declarations are denounced for being elastic with the truth. Campaigning to stay in Europe, the then chancellor, George Osborne, cited a Treasury study that households would be £4,300 worse off in the event of Brexit. Alas for Osborne, he had made too many erroneous forecasts in his six years as chancellor for such a specific figure to be believed. After Brexit the *Mail on Sunday* reported that the slump in the value of the pound caused by the referendum result meant that all British holidaymakers going to the continent in July and August 2016 could expect to pay an extra £200, while expat British pensioners would see their UK pension lose £400 a month thanks to the low pound. Back in Britain the pensions advisory firm Hymans Robertson warned that following referendum vote, 'The cost of purchasing an annuity [which provides a guaranteed income for life] is up by as much as 30% since Brexit.' A survey by the firm of 600,000 employees, factoring in new economic assumptions post-Brexit, shows that only 25 per cent now have a good chance of meeting the level of retirement income regarded as appropriate by the Department for Work and Pensions (DWP), and that 50 per cent have an extremely low chance of reaching that level. The company concluded that the Brexit vote is having 'terrifying' effects on the pension schemes of millions of British workers, with 75 per cent of people now expected to have a retirement income below the government's recommended level.

An important aspect of the Brexit campaign was the extent to which it was based on complete and utter lies spoken by men and women intelligent enough to know they were not telling the truth. There is an absolute difference between citing projections of what may or may not happen, offering different policies for running the country or quoting reports drawn up by economic experts and telling 100 per cent demonstrable lies. There could have been no objection if Boris Johnson, David Davis, Nigel Farage or Andrea Leadsom had argued that Britain would be better off outside the EU or that EU rules and directives were bad for Britain. But they didn't. They cranked up fear against foreigners who had come openly and legally to work in UK businesses, to pay taxes, to rent homes, and whose only problem for the Leave campaign was that they were European.

They told lie, after lie, after lie. By comparison Donald Trump seemed permanently attached to a lie detector as he screamed his own abuse at Mexicans or Muslims or at Hillary Clinton, as everyone at once challenged and took apart Trump's false assertions. In Britain, perhaps it is the beguiling tones of an Eton and Oxford classicist, Boris Johnson, or the reassuring Scottish voice of the former GP, Liam Fox, who can get away with fabulations that if uttered in a general election by either of the two main contenders for Downing Street would be pounced on by journalists. But on Europe any lie can be told without fear of correction.

The MEP Richard Corbett usefully listed the main lies from the Leave side.

1. We send £350m a week to Brussels.
2. We can't stop Turkey joining.
3. We can't stop a European army.

4. We are still liable to pay eurozone bailouts.
5. The UK rebate can be changed against our will.
6. Our VAT exemptions will be ended.
7. Cameron's deal was not legally binding.
8. EU law is adopted by unelected bureaucrats.
9. We can't control our borders in the EU.
10. Criminals arriving in Germany can get EU passports and come over here.
11. Health tourism costs us billions.
12. EU needs UK trade more than vice versa.
13. Past referendum results have been ignored.
14. Auditors still refuse to sign off the accounts.
15. CAP adds £400 to British food bills.
16. British steel suffers because of the EU.
17. Irish border will be unaffected by Brexit.
18. UK can't deport EU criminals.
19. UK is always outvoted in EU decisions.
20. Sixty to 70 per cent of laws come from the EU.
21. Renationalisation of industries is impossible.
22. We get no veto on future treaty change or integration.
23. The budget ceiling can increase without our consent.
24. We thought we were only joining a free trade zone.

Corbett has provided chapter and verse on each of these 24 Leave lies. Once key Leave figures like Boris Johnson, Andrea Leadsom and Liam Fox were in the cabinet they hoped that their untruths from the Brexit campaign would be quietly forgotten. But they should not be, if ever politics in Britain is to regain any confidence from a British public now thoroughly disillusioned with the way politicians seem utterly indifferent to any notion of honesty or truth as their open lies for the most part go uncorrected and unpunished.

As mentioned, Nigel Farage's UKIP Leave campaign and the Tory Leave campaign were indistinguishable. Both focused on immigration to the exclusion of most other themes. Those who hoped there might be a rational debate on the nature of modern sovereignty and a real balance-sheet discussion of the pros and cons of the Single Market or the City of London enjoying trillions of euro-related trades or being the centre for clearing the common currency were disappointed.

In a report analysing the campaign, the Electoral Reform Society (ERS), based on extensive polling, said no one believed the Prime Minister or any of the pro-European politicians campaigning against Brexit. 'Towards the end of the campaign nearly half of voters thought politicians were "mostly telling lies", Katie Ghose, the chief executive of the ERS, said. She added:

> This report shows without a shadow of a doubt just how dire the EU referendum debate really was. There were glaring democratic deficiencies in the run-up to the vote, with the public feeling totally ill-informed. Both sides were viewed as highly negative by voters, while the top-down, personality-based nature of the debate failed to address major policies and issues, leaving the public in the dark.

Nigel Farage was pictured in front of a poster with the slogan 'Breaking Point' showing a long, snaking queue, shabbily dressed, Levantine-looking, mainly young, people with the clear implication that they were typical of the citizens who were now working in Britain. In fact, the picture was from a border crossing in the Balkans of desperate refugees fleeing Middle East wars. With Britain outside the Schengen zone there was no obligation on Britain to accept any of them. But the bigger the lie and the more frequently it is repeated, the more it will be believed.

The fact that the Brexit vote was won on the basis of the biggest lies ever told in a British political campaign is unfair on many on the mainstream Leave side who were uneasy about references to Hitler and the sheer populist xenophobia against fellow Europeans. Others had longstanding and genuine concerns about sovereignty and parliamentary supremacy. But their arguments were like a gentle flute drowned by the drum beat and trumpets of great bands marching with a simple tune of anti-immigrant fear and dislike. Against the daily demagogic stirring of hate and lies and references to Nazis and Hitler, there was little that the Remain side could do.

12

LABOUR FAILS TO MAKE AN IMPACT BEFORE, DURING AND AFTER

The Remain campaign in Downing Street had little or no answer to the Leave camp's relentless focus on immigration and the arrival of foreigners in Britain. They could appeal to reason, with arguments about the contribution newcomers made to the economy and government tax receipts, but the employers who profited most from immigration had never been willing to defend the EU or directly take on the xenophobic propaganda from many Conservative MPs or the off-shore-owned press.

Many British farmers depend significantly on cheap foreign labour and subsidies from the EU. Many in the Leave campaign promised that outside the EU, Britain would import food from poor nations where farm workers had no rights. As a result, said Leave, the price of food would fall significantly. In fact by 2017 food prices were rising as the Brexit devaluation increased the cost of imported foodstuffs.

Indeed, a full application of a Brexit policy based on opening British farmers to competition from agro-industry giants in the southern hemisphere would mean the end of much British-produced agricultural produce and destroy the UK farming community. Nonetheless, both sides of the motorways of Britain in rural areas were covered with

Leave posters placed there by landowners and farmers who joined in anti-EU campaign festivals. Britain's farmers seemed happy to see the controlled, managed environment provided by the EU thrown away to allow the mass import of cheap food. They also seemed to assume that the taxpayers of Britain living in towns and cities would be willing to pay higher taxes to subsidise British farmers, especially as the automatic outlet to the Single Market dried up. Germany buys half the lamb exported from the UK, while the United States banned all imports of British meat for 20 years after the mad cow disease disaster of the 1990s.

Farmers were locked into the group of British citizens that had been told for decades that EEC or EU membership was negative for them, and when such group theory takes hold nothing can dislodge it.

All the time there was a subconscious hankering after a past when Britain, or more precisely England, was more master of its destiny. It was the England imagined by John Major, of warm beer, spinsters cycling to evensong, balmy evenings, when most films were panegyrics to World War II or camp *Carry On* farces, and 'Rule, Britannia' or 'Land of Hope and Glory' were real music, not the 'Ode to Joy' from Beethoven's Ninth Symphony. In fact, that day-before-yesterday England was one of cars that didn't start in the morning so bad was British manufacturing, long-forgotten planes like the Comet 4B, thousands of gay men sent to prison by reactionary judges and appalling treatment of women. It was white England posting notices in their houses saying 'Rooms to Let. No coloureds, No Irish'. It was an England untainted by foreigners of any sort. It was the England of Nigel Farage and the *Daily Mail* and since it was a dream and never existed it was impossible to refute because negatives can never be proven.

As the late A. A. Gill told *Sunday Times* readers:

We all know what 'getting our country back' means. It's snorting a line of the most pernicious and debilitating Little English drug, nostalgia. The warm, crumbly, honey-coloured, collective 'yesterday' with its fond belief that everything was better back then, that Britain (England, really) is a worse place now than it was at some foggy point in the past where we achieved peak Blighty. The dream of Brexit isn't that we might be able to make a brighter, new, energetic tomorrow, it's a desire to shuffle back to a regret-curdled inward-looking yesterday. In the Brexit fantasy, the best we can hope for is to kick out all the work-all-hours foreigners and become caretakers to our own past in this self-congratulatory island of moaning and pomposity.

Sadly Gill's scornful, satirical tone was lost in the hectares of anti-European, pro-Brexit propaganda that the off-shore-owned press had been pouring out for two decades. The Brexit campaign sold a dream of an England once again proud and mighty, where the beastly European foreigner knew his or her place, and that was in Brussels, Germany or France – being bossed about by England. It was and is a dream, but as Yeats told us, we must tread softly because we tread upon our dreams and those in favour of Europe have no alternative dream to tell.

Thus the efforts of the Remain campaign to talk about the ills that would befall the economy if the UK left Europe failed to land home. The campaign – dubbed 'Project Fear' – was master-minded from Downing Street and based loosely on similar tactics that had worked in the 2014 Scottish referendum.

Indeed many of the voices of that campaign, those like Gordon Brown and Alistair Darling, were sent back into action but they sounded like yesterday's men. Gordon Brown wrote a 350-page book, *Britain: Leading, Not Leaving. The Patriotic Case for Remaining in Europe*. It was published a few weeks before the referendum by a Selkirk publisher and, as always with any writing by Brown, was solid, fact-based and well argued. It had very little impact and came out too late to appear in many bookshops.

In the 2010 general election campaign, Brown had been caught off-guard calling a Labour voter in Bolton who complained of too many European immigrants a 'bigoted woman'. It was not language a prime minister hoping for re-election should have used, not just about the woman in question but the many anti-immigration voters like her. Brown had also made an appeal at the Labour Party conference for employment based on 'British jobs for British workers', which sounded like a UKIP or BNP slogan.

As chancellor of the exchequer Brown had thwarted many of Blair's pro-EU initiatives and during the 13 years of the Labour government had never been seen as pro-European. Of course he was anti-Brexit, and when he set his very considerable intellect to making the case for Europe, as he did in his Brexit campaign book, his arguments were strong. But so many of the anti-Brexit campaigners from the New Labour era were now men and women of the free bus pass generation and were no longer listened to. Other old-timers, Michael Heseltine and Neil Kinnock, for instance, made valiant efforts to speak up for the UK staying in the Europe but they came tagged as denizens of the House of Lords, the least democratic chamber of any parliament in the world, where a cheque buys the right to be a legislator.

Above all, Prime Minister Cameron turned the entire referendum into a personal vote of confidence. This turned off many Labour voters who were not prepared to back a man who had protected the wealthy through tax cuts while imposing austerity on the poor. Cameron made passionate pro-European speeches, but these sounded unconvincing from a man who had found nothing positive to say about the EU or Brussels in his whole life in politics since the 1990s. Moreover, he had been saying ever since the referendum was announced in 2015 that the UK could survive and indeed 'do fine' outside Europe. In November 2015 Cameron declared: 'Whether we could be successful outside the European Union is not the question. The question is whether we would be more successful in than out.' He undermined all the efforts of the

Remain camp, which sought to depict negative consequences in the event of the UK withdrawing from Europe, when at the end of May 2016 Cameron said 'Britain is an amazing country. We can find our way whatever the British people choose.'

This was precisely the language of the UKIP/Tory anti-EU camp. Far from representing a 'Project Fear', David Cameron exuded confidence for much of the period before the final weeks of the campaign that Britain did not need the EU as much as the EU needed Britain.

Charles Grant of the Centre of European Reform wrote during the campaign, 'I met large numbers of voters, including younger ones, who wanted to hear something good about the EU and how Britain could play a leading role in it.' There was no such language from Cameron, Osborne or the foreign secretary, Philip Hammond.

President Obama, Japan's Prime Minister Abe and the heads of the IMF and OECD and bosses of Goldman Sachs and Hitachi, along with other denizens of Davos, spoke or wrote warning about the dangers of Brexit.

But how was this playing in Bradford, Bootle, Bournemouth or Bolsover? The Stronger In/Remain campaign simply came too late in the day. It sounded and looked like the elite establishment of globalisation's chattering class.

It might have been helped if the opposition parties had commanding leaders. After Paddy Ashdown, Charles Kennedy and Nick Clegg, the Lib Dems were led by an affable but little-known MP. Labour was far worse. It had elected as leader Jeremy Corbyn, a leftist from the 1970s who had learnt nothing and forgotten nothing since that era. He was not pro-Brexit but equally had never shown any enthusiasm for the EU. He wanted a socialist Europe in which trade unions were strong, while open market trading arrangements and enforced competition rules were suspect. In the Corbyn worldview, today's EU, dominated as it is by centre-right and nationalist populist parties, should move sharply to the left.

Perhaps if he was a commanding speaker, able to dominate TV studios, find words that inspire and convey hope, Corbyn might have enthused core Labour voters, including the millions who felt they had lost out as globalisation and its EU variant dissolved borders and allowed cheap products made for slave-labour wages in Asia to fill High Streets, without any compensating social investment by government.

Corbyn refused to speak alongside Cameron; why indeed should Labour give the Tory prime minister who had called this plebiscite out of cynical internal party opportunism any slack? But in consequence Labour was absent from parade during the vital weeks leading up to the vote.

Veteran Labour MPs like Alan Johnson and Hilary Benn made Remain speeches, and the bulk of Labour MPs and MEPs did their best with local canvassing and street stalls. But senior Labour figures contradicted each other. Corbyn, for example, had a left international-ist perspective on migration and opposed any controls on people com-ing to the UK. Other Labour MPs, such as the deputy leader, Tom Watson, and Yvette Cooper, called for the EU to change its rules on free movement, which was the demand of the Leave camp and would have required major treaty change. There was no coordination or com-mon message from the Labour side. Labour's failure to develop an internally coherent message on the EU in the twenty-first century now cost the party and the Remain camp dear.

But it is far from evident that Labour's disarray made much diffe-rence to the referendum result. Labour voters had been reading the *Sun*, the *Daily Mail*, the *Daily Express* and the *Daily Star* for years and had absorbed all propaganda against the EU over the decades. Even those who took the *Guardian* read endless reports and comment articles which blamed the EU – not national government leaderships – for the continent's many economic and social problems after the 2008 crash imported from America. The *New Statesman*, a left weekly, had given up reporting on Europe (other than articles written in impenetrable academic English) and clearly found the complexities of European politics either too difficult or too dull. The *New Statesman* could find seven pages to profile in gushing prose the anti-immigrant Dutch politician Geert Wilders as the coming man in Europe shortly before Wilders was soundly beaten in the Dutch election of March 2017, but the paper regularly over many years turned down articles that were positive about Europe and EU membership.

To blame the inability of Jeremy Corbyn to make a pro-EU case for the Leave victory is ahistorical. It was the result of the long Labour years of 1997–2010 when Labour, the liberal-left intelligentsia and the media lost both voice and a coherent message on Europe. Neither Tony Blair nor Gordon Brown invested any of their leadership and communication skills in explaining the benefits of the EU to the nation. I once asked Blair on a plane trip to Brussels why he didn't speak up more for EU membership in speeches in Britain. He looked at me sadly and said: 'What can I do with the fucking tabloids we have?' The failure of all prime ministers who followed Mrs Thatcher to overcome their terror of the off-shore-owned press and simply tell some truths about the advantages of EU membership – instead of focusing on the frustrations and annoyances – helped bring about Brexit.

In his insider's account of the campaign for *Politico*, Daniel Korski, a foreign policy specialist adviser in 10 Downing Street, who worked on David Cameron's efforts to avoid Brexit after the May 2015 general election, asserts that:

> In many constituencies, especially in the North, Labour MPs never really needed to canvass the electorate. These constituencies had returned Labour MPs to the House of Commons since time immemorial. And so they remained largely uncanvassed. Many Labour MPs also did not seem to me to have the intellectual tools to have serious arguments about Europe with their constituents. They just hadn't had to do it before. Whereas every

Tory MP and would-be politician had been forced to hone his or her views on Europe, Labour – though historically and nominally pro-European – was full of MPs who struggled to make the case for the EU.

This is simply untrue. Firstly, modern Labour MPs in the north of England do as much if not more canvassing than politicians elsewhere in Britain. It was precisely through such detailed canvassing that Labour MPs felt the impact of the non-stop Tory/UKIP post-truth propaganda against Europe after 1997, when William Hague switched the Conservative Party line to hostility to the EU. Labour MPs also felt the brunt of dislike from the local white working class – which had always been silently hostile to the arrival of scores of thousands of immigrants from Pakistan, Bangladesh and India as well as other economic migrants or refugees from the Balkan and Middle East conflicts. Labour voters read the *Sun* and *Daily Mail*, where nearly every day there was a leading Tory or any number of populist rightwing Yorkshire and other northern MPs denouncing the EU and railing against European citizens working in the region.

Korski would be better advised to aim his criticisms at all the northern Tory MPs who played the English nationalist card against Europe, especially William Hague, who sat for the North Yorkshire seat of Richmond and who had used his very considerable speaking powers to ridicule and denigrate the EU between 1997 and 2010. However, Korski is right that Labour MPs, especially once Gordon Brown and his acolytes took over as national leaders in Downing Street, lost the ability to make an effective case for EU membership. This mood change was exacerbated by David Cameron, whose five years as leader of the opposition saw a rising indulgence in anti-EU lines and emotional appeals on immigration that were little different from UKIP's.

Labour under Ed Miliband found itself hounded by Tory accusations that it was responsible for the presence of so many incomers and sought in the May 2015 general election to claim it would be tougher on immigration than Cameron. So by the time of the referendum Labour had zero enthusiasm to go out and do battle to save David Cameron. Labour MPs and local party activists still did far more street stalls, door-to-door campaigning and leaflet deliveries than the Conservatives. If Jeremy Corbyn was unable to defend EU membership with style and wit, there were other effective pro-European Labour speakers – Alan Johnson or Hilary Benn, for example – but Number 10 did not know how to use them and the BBC preferred to go with more dramatic Tories like Boris Johnson and other cabinet members who were disloyal to Cameron.

Support for UKIP and the BNP in local council and European Parliament elections strengthened after 2001 as the kind of anti-immigrant feelings amongst Labour that had been suppressed but not eliminated since the era of Enoch Powell had a voting outlet. Already by 2004, before the legal arrival of EU workers from Eastern European countries, UKIP had surged past the Lib Dems to win 2.6 million votes in the European Parliament elections and Nigel Farage's career was launched.

In white working-class areas the question of 'immigrants' was constantly raised on the doorstep for Labour MPs from the 1970s onwards. After 1997 Labour changed the law to allow many more cousin marriages from Pakistan and Bangladesh so that the Muslim population grew rapidly, and as a Labour MP I met constant racist comments when canvassing for local and parliamentary elections in the 1990s. This anti-immigrant prejudice on the doorstep increased in tone and substance after 2000, when the immigrants were white Europeans and therefore could be attacked without accusations of racism.

There was resentment against the 'Kosovars' – some of the 850,000 refugees from Kosovo who fled Slobodan Milošević's genocidal violence in 1999. The Balkan wars of the 1990s, initiated largely from Belgrade, generated the first tidal waves of refugees and immigrants in post-communist Europe and began the process of making people movement a burning issue. Every Labour MP's surgery was clogged with asylum seekers from the former Yugoslavia, Afghanistan, Iraq, Zimbabwe, Somalia, Eritrea and other countries where political repression or economic despair forced people to move north to Europe.

The failure of Blair and Brown to implement fully (or to delay) EU directives like the Agency Workers Directive, the Working Time Directive or the Posted Workers Directive, all of which were designed to help the indigenous worker and protect him or her from exploitation by the mass arrival of foreign workers willing to work long hours for very low pay, made matters far worse.

Labour in government seemed keener to help those in the business world who loved the flow of cheap, docile, foreign workers from Eastern Europe rather than to try and implement EU directives designed precisely to help British-born workers.

In the normal story-telling of an election campaign, there are key moments, important events, a brilliant speech, a ghastly error, a turning point, which allow a narrative to emerge to explain the result. In the case of the Brexit plebiscite, nothing like this occurred. The Leave establishment had the better tunes and by far the better demagogues.

In other countries insurance and health schemes are based on contributions, so an EU incomer had to pay to get something. In the workplace there were much stronger social rules and works councils to stop undue exploitation. Under all its prime ministers since 1990, Britain had focused on creating as many low-pay jobs as possible and importing trained workers to do jobs that the UK's lack of compulsory training meant few British workers were equipped to fill. Some 137,000 EU citizens worked in the health care services in Britain because the Royal Colleges which impose the closed shops of the medical and nursing professions had never allowed sufficient British men and women to qualify to fill the demand.

The referendum vote was the chance to express the protest that had been simmering for decades against the existence of a two-nation Britain. One statistic sums up the fault-line. Fifty-two per cent of the British are recipients one way or another of state hand-outs – pensions, child benefits, disability allowances, education, working tax credits, social service care and so on. Forty-eight per cent are net contributors to the UK national budget – they pay more in taxes than they receive in benefits.

That was precisely the divide in the referendum – 52–48. Of course many well-off people voted Leave – 43 per cent of social categories A/ B were Leavers and many state-dependent people voted Remain. But when a nation has so many unable to earn enough money to stand on their own feet without having to be helped by a state hand-out of one sort or another, then a sense of unfairness sets in.

George Osborne's stewardship of the economy, with its relentless focus on austerity cuts while protecting the already-rich, helped fuel the anger against him and David Cameron that many believe was part of the reason for the anti-London establishment Brexit vote.

Following the financial crash, the take-home pay of the average British employee fell by 10 per cent between 2007 and 2015 – the longest continuous fall in income since the Great Depression of the 1930s. It was the areas worst hit by the great de-industrialisation of the 1980s and 1990s that saw the biggest increase in poverty and where the Brexit vote was the strongest.

> Ill fares the land, to hastening ills a prey
> Where wealth accumulates, and men decay

wrote Oliver Goldsmith in 'The Deserted Village' 250 years ago. Britain's greatest historian of postwar Europe, Tony Judt, used part of those lines for the title of his great deathbed essay – *Ill Fares the Land* – attacking the meretricious Britain that came into being this century as the gap between have and have-not Britain grew ever wider.

According to a McKinsey Global Institute report published in July 2016 the era of slow growth – what the US economist and former US treasury secretary Larry Summers calls secular stagnation – means that 70 per cent of the UK population is an income bracket with flat or declining incomes in the decade since 2006. They feel their lives and those of their children are getting no better and would like to pin the blame on someone, something.

Immigrants have been a scapegoat since time immemorial for a nation's worries and lack of direction. The question of the EU and the question of immigrants fused into one target and it was singled out to the exclusion of nearly all other themes by the Leave populists.

The same McKinsey report argues that only 20 per cent of Swedes have flat or declining income, even though Sweden has a higher percentage of foreign-born residents – 18.3 per cent compared to the UK's 13.4 per cent. In other words, it is not immigrants *per se* that make a nation poorer but the organisation of labour markets, access to public services and affordable or social housing and fair pay. In Sweden 68 per cent of the workforce is in a trade union, compared to 25 per cent in Britain.

Yet when the Swedes did hold a referendum on joining the euro in 2003 the answer was 'No'. If the method of consultation is a plebiscite and the question on the ballot paper has Europe on it then in today's slow-growth economy winning a majority appears mission impossible. So to see the issue as just a question of the masses versus the elites is too simple. As noted earlier, the anti-Europe elite establishment was more present and more focused than the pro-EU politicians.

There was a paradox in liberal elite commentators for establishment papers like the *Financial Times* and *The Economist* bemoaning the fact that the political class was so out of touch with 'ordinary' people. Yet both those papers, despite their pro-EU stance, were part of the London elite establishment that supported fiscal, labour-market and social policies that created mass resentment amongst the very people they hoped would vote in favour of David Cameron and George Osborne's appeal to stay in Europe.

Dislike of a prime minister is part of British democratic politics. The referendum allowed that dislike to be channelled into a vote against David Cameron. His friend and chancellor George Osborne produced a budget in March 2016 that proposed cuts in social payments to severely disabled people. It was widely seen as unfair and had to be withdrawn, as it was clear even Tory MPs would vote it down. It dented Osborne's authority at a crucial point on the eve of the Brexit campaign and left his reputation in tatters just at a time when he invited voters to believe his claims that they would all be massively worse off if they voted for Brexit.

When life is seen as unfair, the natural reaction is to find someone or something to blame. The rich are too rich and they're all the ones saying vote Remain! Let's give them a kicking! For years we've been saying our children need jobs but the politicians ignored us! Let's give them a kicking! We're proud of our nation, its history, its language, its culture. But we're told we must accept new beliefs, cultural practices, shocking treatment of girls and women and tolerate those who preach support for a radical religious ideology, which at its far extremes plants bombs on the London Underground. Let's send the elites who've been patronising us a message they'll finally get!

The Scots and the Welsh have been given parliaments and can vote their own arrangement, but London keeps all power in London and ignores the needs of the North and the Midlands, so let's let England arise and speak! Our sons and daughters can't find houses to live in while rich European and other bankers flock to London and make living costs unaffordable, so let's vote against them!

This was not a general election when voters look at the palette of choices on offer from different parties and leader. This was a one-off chance to vent anger, to give two glorious English fingers to the boss class, and the elites who seem to do so well out of Europe and out of cheap imported labour but have forgotten how the other half lives, especially far from metropolitan cities and university towns.

Labour, however, compounded its failure to campaign effectively against Brexit in the 13 months after the general election of May 2015. Once the vote was in, Labour seemed without strategy, tactics or spokespersons on what to do next. Some Labour MPs, dubbed 'Red UKIP' by journalists, produced their own schemes to control immigration, with regional or industry quotas or enforced residence and work permit visas imposed on citizens across the Channel.

Labour turned to lawyers, including a newly elected QC who had become fabulously rich before deciding he wanted to be an MP, to guide the party on Brexit. None had much experience of politics outside wealthy north London circles or any experience of how the EU worked. Mrs May's foolish initial decision to bypass parliament was knocked down by the courts, and Labour sought to secure a debate on the future negotiations over the UK and EU. But when the final vote came, Labour MPs were ordered to vote with the Conservative and UKIP MPs in the anti-EU and pro-Brexit lobby. Fifty-two Labour MPs saved the European and internationalist honour of Labour by refusing to obey the whips, but in meeting after meeting Labour activists were dismayed at how their party was now falling in behind Mrs May in celebrating the Brexit vote as unchallengeable. There was some argument that this was necessary to reassure Labour's working-class voters in the north of England. Labour MPs Frank Field and Dan Jarvis warned that UKIP would win Labour seats in the north of England on the back of Brexit. But when UKIP's leader, Paul Nuttall, stood in February 2017 in a by-election in Stoke-on-Trent, where the seat became vacant after the sitting MP resigned to take up a lucrative, high-profile job as a museum director in London, he was easily defeated by the Labour candidate. This, despite Stoke being the city with the highest number of Brexit voters in June 2016. The judgement of Labour MPs that UKIP would surge unless Labour adopted anti-immigrant policies was called into question by both local and parliamentary elections in 2017, when UKIP candidates fared badly. Mrs May's Conservatives have now adopted so much of UKIP's language that there is no point in UKIP existing. It is not so much that the Tories have taken over UKIP as the reverse.

On the same day as Paul Nuttall's rejection by Stoke voters, with memories still fresh of Labour MPs voting with Conservative and UKIP MPs on Brexit, there was also a by-election in the Cumbrian seat of Copeland, which had always been a secure Labour seat. Despite Labour's Brexit vote shortly before the day of the election, Labour voters deserted the party and elected a Conservative MP.

In effect, trying to secure a narrow legalistic interpretation of the Brexit vote instead of alerting public opinion in each constituency to the potential economic consequences and job losses that arise from a hard-rupture Brexit, and instead of defending the rights of British citizens to work, live, travel and retire in Europe and reciprocal rights for Europeans in Britain, Labour seemed to alternate between pandering to Brexit supporters and having no real message for the public. A way out would be to allow Labour MPs a free vote on the issue of Britain and Europe. The party was shown to be divided anyway, and at least with a free vote more Labour MPs could have shown support for the half of the nation opposed to cutting links with Europe.

The 48 per cent of the vote that was against Brexit and the 63 per cent of the total electorate that did not vote for Brexit, let alone all the young people who were disenfranchised by David Cameron ahead of the referendum, had no champion in the main opposition party. The Liberal Democrats valiantly spoke out for Europe, but the decision of Nick Clegg to endorse the austerity politics of David Cameron's 2010 government had led to the loss of 49 Lib Dem MPs in 2015 and marginalised the party as an effective player in the current Brexit debate.

In short, there was no visible parliamentary opposition to Brexit. In a damning indictment of Labour's inability play a role in the Brexit debate, Martin Kettle, senior *Guardian* political commentator, wrote that by the spring of 2017, 'Labour policy on Brexit has quietly moved in a much harder direction than many people realised. Under Keir Starmer [shadow Brexit minister], Labour's view has solidified into something that, in many essentials, is indistinguishable from the Prime Minister's hard Brexit.'

The debate on Britain's future would take place within the Conservative Party as Labour lost all confidence and coherence on the issue of Europe.

13

THE BBC'S DISDAIN FOR EUROPE WON IT FOR BREXIT

Disdain for Europe was commonplace in the salons of the 'Baby Boomer' generation who rose to the heights of the professions, media, universities and agenda-setting circles by the end of the twentieth century.

They had holiday homes in France or Spain or Italy and all had their local story about some EU regulation their neighbours moaned about. Often it was a health and safety rule insisting that swimming pools should have fences around them or a gate to prevent access by small children. Or perhaps a rule saying that fresh meat and cooked meat products could not be sold off the same wooden counter where bacterial cross-infection was possible.

Every time they met a town hall official or local farmer or perhaps a police officer or an elderly supporter of General de Gaulle they were told about the iniquity of the dreadful EU.

They clinked their glasses of Bergerac or Gavi in the holiday sun of Tuscany or the Dordogne and told each other what a dreadful, interfering, undemocratic, over-bureaucratic monster Brussels was and regaled the dinner parties back in Holland Park or Fulham with horror stories about 'Brussels'.

Over the subsequent two decades the elite London and wider English intelligentsia's scorn for Europe became the norm. All those who could never find a good word for the EU were horrified by the Brexit vote. But they had helped unconsciously to bring about the result by their constant chip, chip, chip and endless fault-finding with any and all aspects of the EU. It little mattered that their children were looked after by European nannies, the houses were cleaned by low-cost Eastern European women or repaired by Europeans charging far less than English or Scottish plumbers or local electrical firms, their right to teach, live or work across Europe was upheld by the common EU rules enforced by the Brussels bureaucracy, but still as they wined and dined one another any mention of the EU produced a sneer or a snort of derision.

The superior left-liberal member of the British intelligentsia, perhaps a *Guardian* columnist or an *Economist* editor, a university professor or retired deputy headteacher, had not been able to find a word in favour of the euro in place of all the competing devaluing or revaluing drachmas and pesetas, marks and francs that existed before. They seemed to think that a single market could coexist with a dozen currencies changing value every day according to the whims of speculators on the foreign exchange markets. They blamed the devastating economic and job-loss impact of the US banking crisis imported into Europe in 2008 not on American extreme *financiarisation* ideology but on the existence of the eurozone. They looked with contempt at the political shenanigans in Greece or the failure of politicians in Spain or Belgium to win support to form a stable government. They had nothing but scorn for the feeble twenty-first-century growth in the eurozone, even if many regions or economies in the eurozone outperformed the British economy and did so without the marked growth of inequality or the impoverished public services and old-fashioned infrastructure that held Britain and Britons back.

They spoke with contempt of 'the Europeans' – an undefined group of nameless men and women who took decisions behind closed doors which ruined the life of the southern Mediterranean peoples with whom our English salon Eurosceptics felt such affinity. They were never in favour of Brexit, but neither could they find any words of warmth or enthusiasm for the integrated Europe such as had come into being over their lifetimes. They had forgotten what it was like to wait to inch through border controls on holiday and have to pay high exchange fees to buy pesetas, lira and drachmas.

They were never in the Brexit camp and did not vote Leave, but they, along with the obvious political and media Europhobes, created the atmosphere which made the Brexit vote a foregone conclusion. Nearly all my political-media friends from the mid-1990s were in this camp. They spoke foreign languages, had worked in Europe but once back in London their lips curled as they discussed the creation of the euro or the different EU treaties. Euro- and Brussels-bashing became the norm for these salon Eurosceptics. They recoiled in horror at the vulgar xenophobia of UKIP but they tittered in agreement with their Tory and Labour friends who were always swift to blame and slow to praise anything to do with the EU. They did not join John Redwood or Daniel Hannan in writing books denouncing the creation and exist-ence of Europe as it had evolved since 1950, but they could produce learned, superior tomes that proved to their entire satisfaction that the euro was a disaster.

They never for a second believed that Brexit would happen and thought David Cameron's decision to call a referendum in 2013 was just a bit of cheap political gamesmanship, like Tony Blair's prom-ise to hold referendums on entry into the euro or on the 2004 EU Constitutional Treaty. Some were convinced – against all political evi-dence – that Ed Miliband would win the 2015 general election and thus the possibility of a plebiscite would be avoided.

The salon Eurosceptics all voted Remain but by then it was too late. Their constant undermining and disdain for the EU and its institutions had worked its way insidiously into the wider British body politic.

Nowhere was the disdain for Europe more evident than in the ranks of BBC current affairs presenters. Indeed, a major cause of the referendum result was the very poor quality BBC coverage of the lies and demonstrable untruths of the Brexit campaign. The BBC set a very low standard, broadcasting on a daily basis demonstrable lies, and other broadcasters like Sky and ITN took the cue from the BBC. BBC journalism is rooted within the journalistic culture of the day. When I worked for the BBC World Service in the 1970s, no story could be broadcast unless it had three sources, so scrupulous was BBC deontology about 100 per cent accuracy in any report. Writing news bulletins for BBC domestic radio services in that era was not quite so demanding, but there was a sense then that BBC journalism could be patient, less obsessed with 'breaking news' and above all passionate about truth and not mixing facts with opinion.

Over the years, that tradition was eroded. BBC news presenters became celebrities, earning a fortune from moderating or speaking at business and other events. It was essential to be aggressive and challenging – the journalist as a prosecution QC, not a seeker after objective, balanced truth. Nowhere was this more evident than in the coverage of Europe, where BBC current affairs programmes sounded like Radio *Daily Mail*. Their presenters could be heard, as it were, curling their lip every time they mentioned Europe. Monolingual BBC celebrity interviewers and presenters who were part of the London political-media elite opined on the state of France or Germany or Italy while hardly being able to say *Bonjour* or *Danke* with the correct accent.

Although he never could win a seat in the House of Commons, and his party never made a breakthrough at local government level, only doing well when the single issue being voted upon was Europe, Nigel Farage was treated by the BBC as a pillar of national life.

Before the referendum campaign got fully under way, 27 of the last 28 MEPs to be invited to appear on the BBC's *Question Time* were UKIP MEPs. Farage was given a national platform and allowed to make his crude anti-European propaganda points almost without challenge in the 15 years before the referendum. The justification usually given was that UKIP won a good number of votes in European Parliament elections. The party did indeed pick up votes. In the 2014 European Parliament elections, the BNP lost its two MEP seats to UKIP. UKIP became the vehicle *par excellence* for every expression of xenophobic and racist anger over immigrants, wherever they hailed from. But the number of UKIP voters never reached the 6.5 million members of the TUC or, until 2014 and 2015, the nearly 4 million who pay membership dues to the National Trust or the 2 million who attend some kind of religious service – forms of commitment and participation more demanding than casting a protest vote every few years for UKIP.

UKIP's membership was 10,000 in 2010 and rose to a claimed 35,000 in 2016. By contrast, more than half a million people paid membership or supporter subscriptions to the Labour Party at the time of the 2016 leadership contest, but no Labour leader was offered anything like the fawning, uncritical platforms that Nigel Farage was. Just 9,600 people voted in the election to choose Paul Nuttall as the successor to Nigel Farage as leader of UKIP. By contrast, at the same time 2.9 million voted in the primary election of the French centre-right to choose François Fillon to be their candidate in the French presidential election. Nigel Farage, who has never won a national parliamentary seat, obtained and obtains far more airtime on the BBC than Fillon, a former French prime minister who has been re-elected and re-elected to the French parliament, does on French national TV and radio. The England edition of *Question Time* went out 15 times in 2016 before the referendum (there are different panels in Scotland and Wales). The BBC made sure Nigel Farage or another UKIP representative was on 10 of those 15 shows. This despite the complete failure of UKIP to win a parliamentary seat in its own right in the 2015 general election. UKIP, like the BNP and all other parties who feel their share of Commons seats does not reflect their share of votes, can blame the UK's electoral system. But it is the one that exists and once-marginal parties making a broad offer to their voters can succeed in winning Commons seats, as the Scottish Nationalists have shown or indeed the Liberal Democrats, when under Paddy Ashdown and Charles Kennedy they won more than 60 seats. UKIP failed the first test of British politics – to be elected to parliament. Nonetheless, the BBC and other media treated UKIP with the utmost reverence. The BBC's uncritical fawning and promotion of Farage is one of the most shameful examples of the decline of its journalistic standards in the twenty-first century and its direct involvement in shaping political outcomes rather than waiting for voters to decide who would be their representatives in parliament and then reflecting that choice in invited guests.

The BBC never afforded the same prominence to the leader of the TUC or top religious leaders, let alone whoever speaks for the National Trust, despite the mass paying membership of such national institutions. But as the BBC became more and more infused with the values of tabloid journalism and its news operations focused on the cult of celebrity, Farage was turned into a major political figure as important as most cabinet members or senior parliamentarians in the opposition parties. He was allowed to repeat his untruths about 70 per cent of UK laws being made in Brussels, or that billions were sent to Brussels, without pointing out that billions came back as subsidies for farmers, poor regions or university research. Had any national politician made such demonstrably untrue statements, *Today* presenters or daytime TV news and politics shows anchors would immediately have challenged the untruth. But such was the low level of knowledge about how the EU actually worked that Farage could put out his dishonest propaganda without any challenge.

The problem got worse during the referendum campaign. Most BBC news and current affairs programmes take their cue and their choice of interviewees from the morning papers. Loughborough University reported that four out of five of all referendum stories, adjusted for circulation, were negative. As Martin Fletcher, a former foreign editor of *The Times*, wrote: 'Most newspapers chose wilfully to deceive, mislead and inflame […] by peddling lies and phoney patriotism.' It was perhaps hard for the BBC to stand apart from the prevailing pro-Brexit propaganda line of most of the press, but the BBC is a public service with a clear deontological duty to inform the public. It should not be an echo chamber for fashionable London newspaper contempt for the EU. Charles Grant, a former *Economist* correspondent in Brussels, went on to set up and run the highly respected Centre for European Reform think-tank in London. He is categorical on BBC journalism during the campaign.

> The BBC's performance during the referendum campaign was lamentable. […] It failed to fulfil its legal obligation to inform and to educate. When senior journalists interviewed Leave campaigners, who said things that were untrue, the comments often went unchallenged. Why was this? Having spoken to many BBC journalists – some of whom acknowledge there was a serious problem – I conclude there were at least two reasons.
>
> First, a lot of well-known BBC presenters and interviewers know very little about the EU. So when, for example, a Leaver said (as they often did) that the 'Five Presidents' Report' (a report about the EU's future drawn up by the heads of the major EU institutions – Commission, Council, Parliament, etc.) showed that a super-state was under construction, with a European army, and that Britain would have to join, the interviewer let it pass. Few BBC journalists knew that this infamous report only

concerned the Eurozone, did not mention an EU army, did not apply to Britain and had been effectively vetoed by Germany.

Grant is right. As mentioned, when I heard Andrea Leadsom repeat on Radio 4's *Today* morning news programme the standard UKIP lie that 60 per cent of all British laws were decided in Brussels – a claim regularly knocked down by the House of Commons Research Library – I wrote to the Director General of the BBC, Lord (Tony) Hall, an old acquaintance, to ask why Leadsom's demonstrable untruth was allowed to be broadcast unchallenged by the *Today* presenters, who preen themselves on being tough interviewers exposing false assertions. I received a reply from a *Today* producer saying that Mrs Leadsom was being interviewed on some other aspect of the Brexit propaganda distortions; her untrue assertion that 60 per cent of UK laws were made in Europe was just a passing remark, therefore there was no need to correct it.

This is precisely the point Charles Grant makes – namely that the BBC allowed clear and specific lies to be broadcast during the three-month campaign and thus did the public the worst disservice in the corporation's near-century of history. He went on to make a further point.

On June 21st the BBC broadcast a televised debate from Wembley Arena. Between each section of the debate, a voiceover sought to explain the factual background to the next subject for discussion. One of these voices stated that 'EU leaders are discussing the cre- ation of a European Army', which is completely untrue. When I set up the CER, 18 years ago, BBC journalists were much better briefed on EU matters than they are today. There are, of course, honourable exceptions who are well informed, and many of them regret that the BBC made only half-hearted efforts to educate staff before the campaign began.

When I started my professional life as a BBC graduate news trainee after Oxford, one of my first jobs working in the Midland regional TV newsroom was to count up during a general election the number of times the words 'Labour' or 'Conservative' were used in news bulletins. If there were more mentions of 'Conservative' or of 'Labour' I would hurriedly write a short news item to ensure that precise balance was maintained. That way the BBC could put its hand on its heart and say it was maintaining a perfect and fair equilibrium between the main parties of government.

This mechanical equilibrium, however, was not appropriate for BBC reporting in the referendum. Ivor Gaber, a professor of journalism at the University of Sussex, has criticised what he calls the BBC's 'phoney balance'. As he points out, the BBC does not give equal space to climate change deniers whenever John Humphries or Nick Robinson interviews a scientist issuing a warning about global warming. But the BBC was prepared to broadcast complete lies about Europe without any challenge.

Professor Gaber gave these examples.

- Just one day before the vote, 1,280 business leaders signed a letter to *The Times* backing EU membership. This was 'balanced' on BBC bulletins by one man, Sir James Dyson, who had long ago come out for Brexit and had moved his business out of the UK to Malaysia.
- When ten Nobel economics laureates warned of danger to the UK economy this was 'balanced' by an interview with a longstanding anti-European campaigner, Professor Patrick Minford, who has university status but at hardly the same level as Nobel Prize-winning economists of world renown.

This BBC ping-pong (also copied by Sky, ITN or Channel 4 news, as well as commercial radio stations), in which exactly equal room was given to statements that were deliberate propaganda falsifications, greatly helped the Leave side, whose repeated lies that Turkey would join the EU and the UK could not veto this, that £350 million a week would be available to spend on the NHS outside the EU, that most non-UK-born residents were from Europe or that a European Army was about to be formed helped sway voters.

The writer Catherine Bennett, who knows much about early morning BBC current affairs reporting, wrote of the BBC's referendum coverage that:

> The BBC, as well as enabling an often asinine level of argument, allowed its obsession with balance to dictate that any carefully argued observation on Brexit, deserving of analysis, be promptly followed by its formal opponent's unsubstantiated bluster. In his 2011 report on BBC science coverage, the geneticist Professor Steve Jones criticised the 'over-rigid' insistence on due impartiality that could give 'undue attention to marginal opinion'. But once again, in referendum coverage, the corporation actively required its journalists to supply this phoney balance, even when that meant, as Jones put it on science, allowing rhetoric 'to give the appearance of debate'.

As Ms Bennett argued, the BBC was intellectually unwilling to challenge what is known as false equivalence – the concept that if one side says the Sahara consists of ice then truth and balance are served as long as you get someone later on in a programme to argue it consists of sand. It's what the Nobel laureate Professor Paul Krugman describes as 'both-sidesism', where if one side says all Muslims are terrorists and the other side says all Muslims are not terrorists then one side balances the other and the TV audience has been properly informed.

Rick Bailey, the BBC's chief political adviser, asked why audiences were not informed by news presenters who like to portray themselves as fearless exposers of political dishonesty that, for example, the endlessly televised Leave claim that outside the EU there would be an additional £350 million a week to spend on the NHS was a distortion, replied the lie could be challenged on the Radio 4 specialist programme about statistics, *More or Less*, which has a tiny fraction of the audience of the main BBC news bulletins upon which voters relied for honest, truthful reporting.

Roger Mosey, the BBC's former editorial director, now master of Selwyn College, Cambridge, reported on a conversation with a senior BBC presenter who observed: 'Balance has too often been taken to mean broadcasting televised press releases. [...] Instead of standing back and assessing arguments, we have been broadcasting he says/she says campaign pieces, which rarely shed any light on anything.'

It is impossible to point to one single cause for the victory of the Brexit camp. The BBC's general approach to reporting Europe and its hero-worship of Nigel Farage and metropolitan sneering at pro-European arguments long pre-dated 2016, or even the 2013 announcement of Cameron's plebiscite. It is unfair on specialist BBC Europe correspondents based in Brussels or those who reported from other EU capitals who maintained high standards of truth-telling impartiality. But the main TV and radio news programmes were produced in London by editors, producers and celebrity presenters who had rarely if ever worked in modern Europe or knew its languages and political cultures. They reflected what they read in their preferred London-produced daily and weekly newspapers and political magazines, where a sneering dismissal of the EU had long been the norm.

The BBC had weathered many crises in its news reporting, including anger at criticisms of Churchill in World War II, or broadcasting the opposition to the Suez invasion, Mrs Thatcher's fury at coverage of Sinn Féin-IRA statements in the Northern Irish troubles and other complaints from politicians. But on the Brexit campaign, the BBC was not on the whole attacked by the political campaigners. Rather, there was a sense that the BBC had left behind its own ethical obligation to speak truth unto its listeners and the nation. There was no decision or dark conspiracy, and many in the BBC journalists network were probably Remain voters. But there was no commanding editorial hand at the BBC that allowed a better-informed decision to be taken.

Some may feel this is just sour grapes and that even if the more obvious lies had been challenged, so entrenched were views on immigrants and so strong had been the printed press propaganda against Europe over the previous 20 years that a more robust, truth-seeking BBC coverage would not have affected the outcome of the vote. But just as David Cameron's plebiscite did serious damage to the tradition of parliament being the place where the nation makes its decisions, so did the referendum do serious damage to the twentieth-century tradition of the BBC as a news broadcaster that was different from and more reliable than other sources of news within Britain. It was not that the BBC dumbed down for the referendum but rather it was not able to create a new way of debating and reporting what was the biggest political choice in British peacetime history.

The BBC did not produce the Brexit result. But the BBC's low standard of broadcast journalism and failure to expose or challenge Leave lies was a huge bonus for the anti-European camp.

PART THREE

BREXIT IN THE CHANNEL: BRITAIN CUT OFF

14

BUSINESS HATES BREXIT BUT STAYS SILENT

'I would rather see finance less proud and industry more content', proclaimed Winston Churchill as chancellor of the exchequer in 1925, shortly before embarking on policies that all but destroyed British manufacturing and helped create conditions that led to the great depression in Britain by the end of the 1920s.

That search for some equilibrium between the City and the North, between industrial engineering and financial engineering, has been greatly desired by many governments ever since. Yet the plain fact is that London, which overwhelms the rest of the UK, is in turn itself overwhelmed by its success as one of the world's financial hubs, perhaps even more important than Wall Street in terms of international financing.

After joining the EEC in 1973, shortly after the end of Bretton Woods system and the emergence of such new global economic powers as Japan or the Gulf States, with money-making cities like Hong Kong and Singapore giving the first signs of what Chinese capitalism could become, London took much of the new international financial market in raising capital and in currency trading.

Mrs Thatcher's 'Big Bang' deregulation of the 1980s and the image of London as the epicentre of finance capitalism attracted every unsentimental money-maker in the world. One can moralise about them, but as money flowed in and through London every bank in the world needed an office or an operation, big or small, in the Square Mile.

But the so-called Big Bang – in essence a move from slow-moving paper and handshake transactions to round-the-clock, seven-days-a-week on-screen trading – did not make London the Wall Street of Europe. This was entirely due to the European Single Act and the aggressive dismantling of barriers to financial business done across Europe. The European Commission enforced common rules on accounting and on fund management so that the cosy cartels of local stock exchanges and financial trades were burst apart. As European firms demolished national borders using the Single Market competition rules that reduced national regulation that were hidden barriers to commerce, they needed somewhere to raise money and London was the obvious hub. Above all, the concept of EU citizenship with the right of free movement to travel, reside or do business anywhere in the EU worked enormously to London's advantage.

London firms could hire anyone they wanted from anywhere in Europe. London became France's sixth biggest city, there were so many French bankers and finance sector professionals working and living in London as successive French governments made little effort to reform the French economy to ensure that Paris or other French cities would get a greater share of the financial industry. British universities delivered graduates with high-quality degrees in mathematics and other subjects who would produce the algorithms and computer programmes that drove the constant search for higher return on investment.

According to economist Douglas McWilliams in his 2015 book *The Flat White Economy*:

In the five years to 2013 London fintech (financial technology) growth was twice that of Silicon Valley. The UK and Ireland (which is, in practice, chiefly a London measure) account for more than 50 per cent of European Technology venture capital measured by number of deals – and 69 per cent measured by funds invested.

The new oligarch class from energy- and raw-material-rich states like those of the former USSR and from Asia loved to come to London to invest their money, buy or rent elite property, send their children to elite private schools and splash their money in Bond or Sloane Street or expensive restaurants, all of which generated work and incomes for hundreds of thousands who in turn kept the London economy churning.

Commercial law has for centuries been an expertise of London lawyers and judges, as the British merchant class came to accept that the arbitration of a court was preferable to more direct conflicts. London lawyers did well drawing up the contracts for all this new financial business activity. Having English as London's language helped. Chinese, Japanese and Korean businesses could use English as a common language, as could all Europeans.

Unlike some centre-left governments exemplified by François Hollande's initial 75 per cent tax on high incomes or his 2012 election statement that 'the enemy is finance', the Labour governments of Tony Blair and Gordon Brown bent over backwards to keep London as Europe's capital of finance. By 2016, a staggering US$120-trillion volume of business in just one financial area alone – the buying and selling of euros and other financial products linked to the euro, as well as clearing these sales (the process by which banks act as the guarantor for purchases and sales of a currency, taking a profit from each transaction) – was being done in London.

Hedge funds proliferated and English-speaking London became the place where every new bit of financial engineering invented in America most swiftly transferred. To be sure, the excesses ended in the crash of

2007/9 and the deregulatory zeal of Washington and London is rightly criticised for the disastrous state of the Euro-Atlantic economy since 2009. But the money rolled in and the City in 2015 was paying more than £66 billion in taxes – £20 billion more than the UK's defence budget and only £20 billion less than Britain's education budget.

According to Nicolas Véron, a senior fellow at the Bruegel think-tank in Brussels and a recognised expert on international finance, London outside the EU is unlikely to attract the kind of money and people that made London in the period between Britain voting to stay in Europe in 1975 and voting to leave Europe in 2016. There will not be a dramatic change, but as he argues, 'In the EU, national and euro-area authorities have been effectively prevented from discriminating against UK-based firms thanks to the Single Market framework and its enforcement by the European Commission and the European Court of Justice. Such protection will erode when the UK leaves.' Véron argues that 'Recognising the high probability of the City hollowing out as a consequence of Brexit is not about "talking down" the UK economy but rather acknowledging an impending tragedy – terrible news not just for London and England, but for Europe as a whole.'

Great trading cities like Venice that have grown rich by becoming the centre of international commerce go into decline when they are cut off from new centres of trade. When it is no longer possible to do euro trades in London and when there are problems getting a visa to fly into London to work and live, when German and Swiss business executives can no longer treat London City airport as if they were getting a tram in Munich or Zürich, then smart new cities which do not oppose free movement and welcome the supervision of the European Commission, European Central Bank or the European Court of Justice instead of treating them as enemy organisations in the manner of a Boris Johnson or a *Daily Mail* or *Daily Telegraph* journalist are likely to start to get some of the business that London has made so profitably its own since the 1980s.

Already several European capitals have sent recruitment missions to London to try and entice finance houses to relocate. Paris has offered major tax incentives and allowed UK firms to contemplate a move to La Defense, the Canary Wharf-type business centre at the end of the Metro line on the west of Paris.

James Gorman, the CEO of Morgan Stanley, has said 'onshoring' to Europe is inevitable. 'We will have to move employees and their families to our offices in Europe to keep doing business.' Anthony Browne, head of the British Bankers Association, went further when he warned that:

> Most international banks now have project teams working out which operations they need to move to ensure they can continue serving customers, the date by which this must happen, and how best to do it. Their hands are quivering over the relocate button. Many smaller banks plan to start relocations before Christmas [2016]; bigger banks are expected to start in the first quarter [of 2017].

Browne is a cautious man, not given to making dramatic statements. That British banks authorised him to come out with a warning that London faced a significant drop in its income as the City lost business was significant. He pointed out that banking is the country's biggest export industry by far and 'the current trajectory threatens not just tariff-free trade, but the legal right of banks to provide services'.

Japanese banks in London issued a warning that they would have to move out of London in 2016 if no guarantees were given that the government would maintain Britain's Single Market access and the right of UK-based banks and investment funds to have a 'passport' to work anywhere in the EU. British bank bosses preferred to talk to ministers behind closed doors. As with British exporting firms, they did not want to be seen as openly opposed to the new prime minister, who has a reputation for bearing grudges and remembering everyone who opposes or criticises her. But their silence meant that public opinion was not mobilised, and constant reassurances from the pro-Brexit press that Brexit Britain was heading for a radiant economic future were left unchallenged.

London fund managers managed £1 trillion of savings and assets on behalf of investors based in the EU across the Channel and the UK's Investment Association – the trade body for asset managers in Britain – produced a report after the Brexit vote which said their member firms would lose jobs as money would move out of London, which would no longer have access to unfettered trading in Europe. Pro-Brexit economists like Gerard Lyons, who was economic adviser to Boris Johnson when mayor of London, pooh-poohed any such suggestions and insisted that London had a bright future managing 'Islamic finance' and dealing in China's currency. London would remain 'the major financial centre of Europe', he insisted.

This optimistic view was not shared by Mark Boleat, policy chairman of the City of London Corporation. Boleat agrees with Anthony Browne that it is inevitable that jobs will be lost. 'Some activities will no longer be able to be conducted from London. Some employment will simply stop as the volume of business can no longer be supported by the higher costs', Boleat said. The City UK, a lobbying group set up to challenge the Brexit campaign, reckons that 70,000 City jobs will go once London is cut off from the EU. Another report by the management consultancy PWC put the figure higher at 100,000 lost jobs.

Between 2008 and 2014 more than one third – 35 per cent – of Britain's total foreign direct investment arrived in the form of investment in financial service. Overall the industry earns a trade surplus of £22.8 billion, with more than £10 billion coming from trading in the Single Market. City lobbyists who went to see David Davis, the Brexit minister, said he did not deny the figures but told them it was a price worth paying to regain British 'independence and sovereignty'.

By contrast, the chancellor of the exchequer, Philip Hammond, told the Conservative Party conference that voters did not support Brexit 'to become poorer'. But that appears to be inevitable. Sterling has seen one of its biggest ever devaluations. According to Dr Angus Armstrong of the National Institute of Economic and Social Research (NIESR), 'the pound has fallen by 17% against the dollar; more than the Wilson devaluation and the aftermath of Black Wednesday ERM debacle in 1992'. Harold Wilson famously said after he devalued the currency in 1967 that 'The pound in your pocket is worth the same.' That isn't true 50 years later. Britain's net worth is now one sixth less than it was on 22 June 2016. And assuming the government is prepared to see trade and market access reduce in order to achieve what it considers to be the mandate from the 37 per cent of the electorate who voted against Europe, then Britain will become a poorer economy with much smaller revenues for the government to serve the nation unless it chooses to increase borrowing massively and pass on giant new debts to future generations. As Armstrong notes: 'The pounds in our pocket are worth less and we won't have more of them.'

The fall in value of the Brexit pound means that everything we import – from food, wine, energy, Audis, MacBooks, iPhones to Ikea products and sports clothes – will get more expensive, as will holidays abroad and air fares.

Conversely, any product made in Britain for export should become cheaper – unless they contain components, as many do, which are sourced from abroad and now will cost more as a result of the Brexit pound. And while goods destined for Europe or America are a bit cheaper, the cost of exporting – travel, hotels, professional services – goes up as the Brexit pound has far less purchasing power outside the UK. Tourists coming to Britain will find the price of clothes and entertainment and hotels has gone down – but if hotels, bars, cafés, taxi firms, restaurants and the tourist and catering industry no longer can employ hard-working young Europeans they will have to put up prices.

The car industry, which depends entirely on the decisions of for-
eigners in Japan, America, India and France to sustain investment in
Britain, faces a very difficult time. Mary Barra, the chief executive of
General Motors, which makes Vauxhall cars in England, blamed 'the
UK referendum and the resulting devaluation of the pound' for the
US$400-million loss GM Europe said it would post in the second
half of 2016. This Brexit devaluation led General Motors to look at
selling their European operations – Vauxhall in England and Opel in
Germany – to the French firm Peugeot. Rationalisation could follow,
leading to the closure or reduction of Vauxhall operations in Britain.
The promised bonanza of growth, trade and jobs that the Leave Liars
said would follow if only the electorate voted to quit Europe seemed far
away. German car-makers said they had lost 9 per cent of their sales in
Britain as a result of the Brexit devaluation and said on the record that
the UK car industry would disappear if its Japanese- and Indian-owned
producers could no longer export freely without tariffs and customs
checks to all of the Single Market.

In the aftermath of Brexit and the blunt 15-page memo the Japanese
government sent Mrs May declaring that they counted on her to stay
in the Single Market, Carlos Ghosen, the outspoken head of Nissan,
announced that the firm might not build its new Qashqai model in
Sunderland if the UK left the Single Market. Around 42,000 jobs
in the north of England are linked to the Nissan plant there, in addition to directly employed workers in the plant itself. This led to a
panic meeting between Mrs May and Ghosen and an emergency flight
to Tokyo by Greg Clark, the business secretary. He is reported to have
handed over written documents stating Nissan would be protected or
compensated for any change in rules or tariffs in the event of a full,
destructive Brexit. There were calls for the statement to be made public,
as every other firm exporting to the EU scratched its head and asked if
they too would get taxpayers' money to compensate them if selling into
Europe became more difficult. Ghosen later underlined in the French

weekly *Le Point* that Nissan's investment in Sunderland was an investment 'in its European operations, not specifically in the UK'. He added
that if 'walls are erected between the UK and the EU, investment will
go down'.

Jeremy Warner, the acute and well-informed *Daily Telegraph* writer
on business affairs, noted that the Japanese will regard the British government's letter 'as tantamount to a sovereign obligation, or even international treaty'. 'Already', Warner went on, 'the attitude of corporate
Japan to Brexit is that it amounts to a form of treachery, in that when
Japanese companies agreed to invest in the UK it was on the understanding that it would give unrestricted access to Europe's single market.' Half of all Japanese investment in the EU is in the UK, with 1,000
Japanese multinationals using Britain as a gateway to Europe.

For the proponents of Brexit, betraying the trust that Japan and
other foreign investors in Britain had that the UK would conserve their
access to Europe is of little consequence, as Britain becomes a different
better nation once it stops cooperating under EU rules to trade freely
with 27 other rich nations. But as Mr Warner concludes with pitiless
logic, if the government 'is to compensate Nissan for tariffs, then it
would have to do so for the rest of the motor industry, if the motor
industry is to be compensated, then logically almost anyone facing
tariffs in exporting to Europe would have to get the same treatment'.

The mayor of London, Sadiq Khan, accused the government of
economic 'self-sabotage' and pleaded with Theresa May to drop the
destructive Brexit approach which many in her party, in the UK and
the Europhobe press were urging on her. 'If the proper agreements
aren't negotiated, there will be serious knock-on impacts with jobs and
billions of revenue lost – something that would hit the entire country,
not just London', Khan told a City of London Corporation banquet.
'My motivation is not about protecting old City institutions just for
the sake of it or presenting a London-centric approach. It's about protecting our country's economy – protecting jobs, promoting growth

and safe-guarding prosperity for the next generation', he said. While the car industry represents less than 1 per cent of the UK economy, banking, finance and professional services contributed £190 billion to the UK economy – almost 12 per cent. But these points were being made by Boris Johnson's successor as mayor of London. They were not being made by the new Foreign Secretary, who, many political commentators noted, was still trying to position himself as the man who could take over if Mrs May stumbled.

15

FIXING AN EXIT: TRADE

Forty-nine per cent of all the exports in goods and services from the UK go to countries which live under EU laws and trade agreements. If Britain continues to reject those common rules and laws following a formal political Brexit, in the sense of no longer being a signatory to EU treaties, then the economic dislocation will be the greatest ever experienced in history. In the period after Brexit, it was as if everyone became a trade expert. Unlike Canada, where the government has 300 trained professionals who work on Canada's different trade deals with other countries, or the United States, where major, well-staffed trade think-tanks comment and advise on the work of a very senior official, the US Trade Representative (USTR), the British government has very little experience or expertise in trade negotiation.

There are 550 highly skilled, experienced trade negotiators working for the EU Commission compared to an estimated 40 Whitehall officials working on trade in London. Since 1973, responsibility for UK trade other than on minor specific issues has lain with the European Commission, which has signed 50 major trade pacts with other world partners. If and when Brexit is consummated all these trade pacts will have to be renegotiated with Britain. As Peter Mandelson, who served as an EU Trade Commissioner, said, free-trade agreements 'do not come free, do not cover all trade and take ages to agree'.

Jason Langrish, a senior Canadian trade diplomat, says that the negotiations for the Canadian–EU trade deal known as CETA were conducted in a friendly atmosphere, but he points out:

> I certainly did not think that the scoping, negotiation and the ratification of the treaty would take more than 10 years. The next generation of bilateral agreements go beyond trade, touching upon behind-the-border issues such as standards, regulation and opening government contracts to competitive bidding. This complexity means that the deals take years to negotiate and conclude. In our amped up media environment, there are special interests making noise at each step in the process, ensuring that trade and investment deals are a marathon, not a sprint.

Every EU member state will be looking to protect its own exports in any future EU–UK trade agreement. According to Professor James Galbraith, who was an adviser to Yanis Varoufakis during the latter's flamboyant but forlorn efforts as Greek finance minister to try to get the EU to pay extra money for the programme of government initiated by the left-populist party, Syriza, the Dutch government insisted that a condition for granting any EU financial help for Greece was that the use-by period on a bottle of milk should be seven days, not, as was the norm in Greece, three days. This was designed to help Dutch dairy exports and it is a minuscule example of how trade issues insert themselves into negotiations between the EU and other countries.

The EU agreed, for example, to allow imports of British beef after the 'mad cow' outbreak led to a global refusal to allow it to be exported. While the United States, all Commonwealth countries and even the then British colony of Hong Kong slapped a ban on British beef exports which lasted more than a decade and long after all British cattle were proved to be free of the malady, the UK was able to require that the EU market be open to British beef sales. Outside the EU British meat exporters will have no such protection. Fifty per cent of all British lamb is sold to one country – Germany. The Germans are notoriously sensitive to food safety issues and all it will need is a minor outbreak of foot and mouth and once the UK is outside the EU its sheep and lamb export markets may close down.

For the time being the UK is still in the EU so the situation does not arise. But as Cecilia Malmström, the EU Commissioner for Trade, an energetic Swedish liberal politician who has spent most of her political life in the European Parliament and is now into her second term as an EU Commissioner, told the BBC, 'First you exit and then you negotiate the terms of the relationship.' For the advocates of Brexit, all other EU member states would simply roll over for the UK as they want to continue to have access to the UK market. Certainly, the British will want to drive in BMWs, drink French wine, shop at Ikea, Zara and H&M and will expect their Lidls, Aldis and Icelands to be full of cheaper imported foods.

But first the UK has to leave the EU and that means beginning negotiations under Article 50 of the EU treaty. This allows an EU member state to quit the EU. Article 50 allows for two years to conclude these negotiations, though with agreement of both the UK and the EU this deadline can be extended. The mayor of London, Sadiq Khan, and other politicians, including the respected Andrew Tyrie MP, then chair of the Commons Select Committee on Finance, urged a policy of strategic patience on Mrs May and pointed out that the EU faced two major elections in 2017 – in France and in Germany – that could see new leadership emerge in the EU's two leading member states and thus it would be prudent for the UK to wait until it could see the political lie of the land before embarking on the formal two years of Article 50 talks.

However, in the first period after her arrival in Downing Street thanks to the Brexit vote Mrs May clearly felt she had to appease

fellow-travellers of UKIP in her cabinet and the bulk of Tory Party militants with whom she appeared to be in permanent communion. She
thus made clear her preference for what became dubbed 'hard Brexit',
cutting Britain out of the Single Market and Customs Union. But most
agreed that coming to a new set of rules for trade in goods and services
with the EU27 would happen after the formal withdrawal from EU
treaties sometime around Easter 2019.

The Article 50 negotiations will turn out to be a damp squib unless
the economic situation in Britain deteriorates so fast that public opinion turns on the Brexit hardliners and Tory MPs respond by refusing
to be rushed out of Europe and call for the Article 50 talks to be suspended or even revoked. At all events, the Article 50 negotiations are
not about what should be the new terms of trade between the EU and
the UK. These would be the subject of a different and protracted negotiation between Brussels and London. First exit and then draw up the
terms of a new relationship, as Cecilia Malmström has pointed out.

Writing in *Le Figaro*, Mrs May asserted, 'We will seek the greatest
possible access to the European single market through a new, comprehensive, bold, ambitious free trade agreement.' These are fine words but
are the same as those used to launch the Transatlantic Free Trade deal
between the US and Europe which foundered on political opposition
on both sides of the Atlantic. Putting the meaningless, clichéd adjec-
tives 'new, comprehensive, bold, ambitious' will strike a chill into any
trade negotiator's heart. Australia and New Zealand have been trying
to get a trade agreement on imports and exports of apples since 1921,
but it has proved impossible.

Mrs May is outlining trade talks that can last a full decade if not
longer and which will allow 27 EU member states to let their peculiar-
ities and internal political lobbies play a part in refusing ratification if
they do not obtain their wish-list.

That is why more fervent Leavers, like the Conservative politician
John Redwood, have said all that is needed to be done is for the UK to

repeal the 1972 Accession Act which took Britain into Europe. That is certainly a possibility, though it is doubtful there is a majority in the Commons or Lords for such a unilateral repudiation of the UK's relationship with the rest of Europe without any substitute agreement being in place. It would mean that not only could the other members of the EU and EEA impose their own conditions on trade with Britain but so could the rest of the world, as Britain would no longer have the benefits and protections of being party to the EU trade rules with other countries.

Any country could impose tariffs or the more problematic non-tariff barriers to trade. The UK exports about 49 per cent of all its exports of goods and services to the EU, while the UK market for the rest of the EU is about 3 per cent of its total GDP, according to economist Jonathan Portes of the NIESR. If the UK unilaterally left the EU, as John Redwood and others who think it is just a matter of repealing the 1972 Act argue, Britain would be left naked, without any trade treaty or agreement anywhere in the world. The Uruguay Round of trade negotiations began in 1986 and concluded in 1994. The Doha Round of WTO negotiations began in 2001 but broke down and were suspended in 2008 as the United States and Japan refused to make concessions acceptable to other partners. Of course it is possible to negotiate a trade deal if Britain accepts every one of the other parties' demands. The United States would be happy to sign a deal with Britain on condition the NHS could be taken over by US medical and pharmaceutical interests, the BBC no longer enjoyed its state tax in the form of the licence fee and British-based airlines had to buy Boeing planes, not Airbuses. So when Brexit ministers promise quick trade deals around the world the rational person just looks at how long every modern trade deal has actually taken.

The World Trade Organization established rules for trade in products but since more than two-thirds of UK exports are in services (banking, finance, insurance, education, culture, creative industries,

amongst others) these important sources of UK wealth cannot be protected by the WTO. Today, the UK is a WTO member by virtue of its
EU membership. It would remain a WTO member but not have access
to the markets of other WTO members without first agreeing to their
terms and demands for trading with Britain.

It might be assumed that such support would be automatic, but any
state that has some deep-lying difference with Britain – Argentina on
the Falklands or Spain on Gibraltar or many countries that object to tax
havens situated in British-controlled crown colonies and territories –
could demand bilateral negotiations and concessions from London in
exchange for support for WTO membership. Drawing up all the legal
schedules, even within a WTO framework, can take years. The EU, for
example, has quotas on every product it imports – chickens from Brazil
or wheat from Australia. Post-Brexit, the EU would have to adjust these
quotas and Britain would have to negotiate its own new share.

Altering the terms of trade in agricultural products sounds easy
when declaring that Britain will open its borders to any and all food
imports. But we should not forget the powerful farming and land-
owning lobby in Britain, which is especially close to the Conservative
Party and well represented in the House of Lords. The farming lobby
raises considerable political heat if it finds its sales to the UK market
undermined by much cheaper products and its exports abroad coming under protectionist challenge with the WTO unable to help in
any way. Major global agro-industry multinationals in Australia, North
America and Brazil can supply Britain with nearly all the food we con-
sume at a much lower cost than British farmers can. It remains to be
seen if the Conservatives will be happy to see UK farming eliminated
in order to swell the profits of globalised food giants.

While writing this book I went to my local post office to send a
book to my daughter working as an English teacher in Andorra and my
niece who lives in Geneva. The counter clerk gave me a customs form
to fill in because, as he explained, both countries were 'not EU'.

Up to the moment of Brexit, Britain is part of the Customs Union. This means I can send any packet or were I a businessman despatch any lorry from London to Lublin in Poland or Lamia in Greece on the same basis as if I were posting a packet or despatching a lorry to Liverpool. Outside the Customs Union I would lose these rights. Every British business would have to fill in numerous customs forms every time a good or service was sent for sale to Europe.

British manufacturers of, say, high-tech 3D printing equipment can take their products to any trade fair from Finland to Bulgaria in the boot of their car as if still in the UK. If they go to Switzerland, they have to show they have the appropriate papers to bring in their products.

A customs union works by its members abolishing all control of goods and services crossing their frontiers, but in exchange there are common duties or tariffs agreed by the members of the customs union on goods coming into the countries within the customs union. It means that the customs union as a whole – in this case the EU – negotiates on behalf of all its members trade agreements with other countries.

Free trade is not quite free. Each trading nation, or trading bloc of nations in the case of the EU, keeps a certain control over its national economic interests. The United States has what are called Buy American Acts which stipulate that certain products can only be bought if produced inside America. Automobile production, for instance, has been protected by external tariffs, which is why Ford and General Motors (known as Vauxhall in Britain or Opel in Germany) opened factories in Britain and Germany as the tariffs imposed on exports from America were a response to US protectionism in the Buy American legislation.

In the 1970s exports of reliable Japanese cars surged into America and Europe, even if they were more costly with the extra tariffs imposed on them. Customers were prepared to pay the higher price in order to have a car that started each morning. But in due course Nissan, Toyota and Honda opened automobile production plants in the US to be able to be part of the giant US single market rather than navigate exporting and trade rules. Once Britain joined the European Economic Community and its Customs Union, and Margaret Thatcher set up the Single Market, Japanese car firms opened manufacturing plants in England so as to sell their cars across the European market.

To be sure, if the product is much desired or has high status, it will be sold independently of tariff or custom duties. But just as we have no customs barriers or tariffs on goods produced in Yorkshire or insurance or banking services carried out in London and sold in different parts of the UK, so there are none within the Customs Union of the EU.

All this will alter when a full Brexit takes place. Leaving the Customs Union would mean every good coming into the UK and then sold on to Europe would need to be checked or stamped with appropriate paperwork confirming that the product and any component elements in it were in conformity with EU norms and standards. The implications for Ireland are extremely serious. Assuming that Ireland stays in the Customs Union but the UK, including Northern Ireland, has left it, that means all trade between Northern Ireland and Ireland would have to be checked for controls on content and to prove that the correct duty had been paid.

One of the claims by hardline Brexiters is that a closed frontier between Northern Ireland and the Republic of Ireland once the UK left the Customs Union and Single Market would present no problems. Owen Patterson MP, the pro-Brexit former Northern Ireland secretary, told the BBC that the parallel is with trade across the US–Canada frontiers. He said electronic customs clearance could be used to avoid any delays at a UK–Ireland frontier in Northern Ireland.

Leaving to one side the political implications for fundamentalist Irish nationalist republicans of British frontier posts, the comparison with the US is far-fetched. There are thousands of trucks crossing both ways between Canada and the US but they mainly carry motor cars and car components between the major US auto manufacturers – the 'Big 3' – which for decades have operated as single unit on both sides of the Great Lakes.

There are relatively few crossing points between the US and Canada, unlike the hundreds of small roads that criss-cross the 499 km Northern Ireland border. US–Canada trade is very large shipments of finished goods between the same firms, who have sophisticated logistical computer systems in-house. Most 'exports' from Northern Ireland to the South are agricultural and goods products. There is very little agricultural trade between the US and Canada. Many firms in Ireland are in effect all-Irish and have used the Single Market, the absence of border and customs controls and the right of any European citizen – British, Irish or continental – to live and work everywhere in Europe to create a harmonious common economic community.

Dublin hopes to maintain the longstanding Common Travel Area (CTA) between Ireland and the UK. But if any EU worker can drive, walk, bike or row across the UK–EU border the hard Brexiters want, it will not be possible to sustain the CTA since rigorous entry and exit controls will be needed along the Northern Ireland border.

So the idea that there is a computer solution to cross-border trade is fanciful. There is simply no comparison between the type and extent of trade within the island of Ireland and that between the US and Canada.

An even more worrying trade scenario opens if Scotland, following a hard English Brexit, does finally opt for independence and custom posts have to be set up from Berwick to Gretna Green.

There are customs checks, for example, for goods coming in from China but none for goods arriving from Europe. For airports and ports it would mean creating a giant new bureaucracy to deal with this red tape. Even if computerised, the customs data still needs inputting and verifying. The UK employs about 5,000 customs officials today but this number would have to increase fivefold in order to meet all obligations under WTO rules. The US employs 47,000 customs officers, though the share of imported goods into the US is half the size as a percentage of economic activity as in Britain. So leaving the Customs Union, as many hardline Brexit politicians in UKIP and the Government demand, would require a massive and expensive recruitment of a new bureaucracy to manage the flow of components and finished goods into and out of the UK.

On the other hand, staying inside the Customs Union means accepting that the EU does your trade negotiations. Turkey, for example, is in the Customs Union (except for agricultural products), so Turkey does not negotiate separate trade agreements but accepts what the EU trade agreements stipulate. For hardline anti-EU Tories the whole point of Brexit is that Britain can have a glorious future negotiating its own trade deals. Staying in the Customs Union means limiting Brexit to political withdrawal from EU treaties, which may make sense to most practical businesses selling goods and services across Europe. On the 23 June 2016 ballot paper none of these variations on what 'leaving' the EU were spelt out and certainly never explained by Leave Liars.

Outside the Customs Union, checks would be required on trains, lorries and cars coming through the Eurotunnel. When I worked in Geneva in the 1980s, cars were regularly searched as they crossed back from France to check if any Swiss resident had bought beefsteaks in France, where meat was cheaper. This was eliminated as Switzerland accepted EU rules and free movement as part of maintaining its economic trade advantages with its EU neighbours. Mrs May and her Brexit ministers do not want to roll the clock back to the 1950s and 1960s when trade was heavily controlled by bureaucracy. But Brexit is the politics of unintended consequences and unless she and the Conservative government truly want to extend Brexit to all profitable economic relations with the world's biggest market she will have to adapt to reality. The idea of every British holidaymaker or Eurostar user or all the lorries who use the Eurotunnel or cross-channel ferries queuing up for inspection is not attractive, but if the UK leaves the Customs Union it may be hard to avoid.

Outside a customs union, a country that wants to do trade has to prove the origin of goods and show that appropriate duties and VAT are paid, which will require firms to hire form-fillers galore. We will see the Dover ferry and Eurotunnel terminals transformed into giant lorry and car parks, possibly stretching back up the motorway as vehicles wait for their customs clearance. But there is no obligation on France to spend millions of taxpayers' euros on expanding facilities at Calais just because of a political decision to leave the Customs Union by anti-European politicians in London.

The UK exports £150 billion of goods each year to the EU. Dr Andrew Grainger of Nottingham University's Business School, an expert on trade and freight transport, reckons that the extra cost of customs checks and red tape, hiring new customs officers and building new facilities could be 'an additional cost to UK–EU in the order of several billion pounds a year'.

An example quoted in the *Financial Times* is given by Tim Sarson, tax partner at KPMG. He cites the examples of the chemical industry, a key UK exporter. This is because of 'the complexity of the supply chain that starts with oil being pumped out of the North Sea and ending in, say, a bottle of perfume or a stick of lipstick. Customs officials would have to assess the origins of products at every stage.'

The government's computer system for its customs services dates from the 1980s, and while the private sector can certainly come up with new systems of electronic customs checks, the undoubted fact is that outside the Customs Union movement of goods in and out of Britain is going to be costly and complicated, with major new burdens on firms to record and account for all goods they trade.

So the trade logic would appear to dictate staying in the Customs Union. But the ideological logic dictates otherwise. Trade did not feature much in the Brexit referendum. Because Britain has been united with other European nations on trade policy since 1973 there are few experts and no politician who has ever specialised in trade issues. Analyses of why people voted have produced no evidence that people voted to see massive customs barriers between the UK and the rest of Europe, but unless there is a rethink on how Britain wants to take Brexit these will soon have to be in place.

Trade has become a new arena of political contestation for both the left and the right. Leftwingers in recent years have seized on trade as a mobilising issue. Mobilising against the US–EU or the Canada–EU trade agreements has used many of the same exaggeration/simplification techniques of the Brexit campaigns. TTIP, the Transatlantic Trade and Investment Partnership agreement between the EU and the USA, has been blocked as politicians on both sides of the Atlantic have preferred to side with street protests than stand up for free trade. There is always a justification for a protectionist measure and it needs the kind of mass mobilisation that did away with the protectionist Corn Laws in England in the mid-nineteenth century to overcome the natural fear of change and disruption that allowing citizens to choose amongst the cheapest goods and services that can be put on offer will provoke.

So the Brexit ideologues, headed by the newly created minister of international trade, Liam Fox, want a complete rupture with the Customs Union. Staying in it means accepting the trade deals that the EU could negotiate with the rest of the world, though even Dr Fox had to backtrack a little as the evidence mounted in Whitehall that leaving the Customs Union would damage British interests.

This is unacceptable to the hardline Leave Tories. They want nothing to do with Europe, and they cannot admit that it might actually benefit British business to at least stay in the Customs Union. It does indeed mean conceding control – in the sense of trade policy – to the UK's soon-to-be former partners across the Channel. And since the purpose of the Brexit vote was 'to take back control' it follows that sensible cooperation within a customs union must be rejected.

Of course firms in Britain can keep selling manufactured products to Europe – and anywhere else that will buy UK goods and services. The UK sells more to Greece in the EU than to New Zealand, an English-speaking Commonwealth nation. Pakistan and Venezuela and every other member of the WTO can sell into the EU if they produce goods or services which interest the European consumer. But the WTO does not cover services, which constitute 80 per cent of the UK economy.

Outside the Customs Union anything made in the UK can face a tariff. This is perfectly legal under WTO rules. In 2015, the UK's main exports of goods (not services) to the EU were:

1. machines, engines, pumps: US$63.9 billion (13.9% of total exports)
2. gems, precious metals: US$53 billion (11.5%)
3. vehicles: US$50.7 billion (11%)
4. pharmaceuticals: US$36 billion (7.8%)
5. oil: US$33.2 billion (7.2%)
6. electronic equipment: US$29 billion (6.3%)
7. aircraft, spacecraft: US$18.9 billion (4.1%)
8. medical, technical equipment: US$18.4 billion (4%)
9. organic chemicals: US$14 billion (3%)
10. plastics: US$11.8 billion (2.6%).

The EU imposes a 10 per cent tariff on cars imported from the United States. Outside the Customs Union, Brussels could place a similar tariff on all the Japanese cars made in Britain as well as the Jaguar and Land Rover vehicles made by the Indian firm, Tata. After the referendum, pro-Leave enthusiasts were saying that the UK could make an offer of tariff-free trade with the rest of the EU. This would certainly help Britain. Forty-nine per cent of UK exports of goods and services go to the EU. But only 16 per cent of EU exports of goods come to the UK. (It is important to remember that it is trade in services that is the real money-maker and where the UK runs a healthy surplus with the EU. But services are most vulnerable to non-tariff barriers and the WTO membership does little to force nations that do not want to buy services to do so.) So making an offer not to impose tariffs on imports from the EU may sound generous but it is mainly to the UK's advantage. In exchange the anti-Europeans want to limit and discriminate against EU citizens who want to work, start up firms and contribute to the UK economy and its tax base.

In addition, outside the Customs Union, all the chemical, plastic, metal, pharmaceutical and other products will have to go through rigorous customs checks and form filling before going on sale in the EU. British firms can today use the CE kite-mark, which tells consumers the product is safe and meets high, commonly agreed standards. But if Mrs May persists in saying Britain cannot accept any ruling from EU regulatory bodies and panels, all of which accept the ultimate authority of the European Court of Justice, British goods will no longer be able to use the CE kite-mark. Aerospace is an important export for the UK, as all the wings for the hugely successful Airbus are made in Britain. The consortium of EU nations that makes the Airbus have spread out the manufacturing of its body, wings, avionics, internal furnishing and engines so that each participating EU nation gets a share of the profit that comes from this collaborative EU enterprise. But outside the EU there will be pressure from other nations to have the current wing production factories reshored in the EU and no longer in Britain.

There will be a row and legal fights, but outside Europe Britain will be in a markedly weaker position. The arbitration court for any trade dispute within the EU is the European Court of Justice but Mrs May says she wants nothing to do with it. So where does a British exporter turn if unfairly treated by a European competitor – the comment pages of the *Daily Telegraph*? Certain industries can now only raise capital and make a world-beating product by operating across frontiers. That will become more awkward, not impossible but much more difficult, as the

UK no longer wants to abide by the common rules, laws and standards agreed at EU level.

Ahead of the 2017 presidential election, France just rolled over and gave up on a trade deal with the US. In their search for votes, Hillary Clinton and Donald Trump also trashed the trade deals that the Obama administration had tried to craft with transpacific as well as transatlantic partners. Outside the EU and outside the Customs Union, Britain will have little, if any, influence on regional and global trade policy. Mrs May in her speech to the Conservative Party conference in October 2016 made much of proclaiming that workers' rights are 'not just protected, but enhanced under this government'. Yet increasingly, organised worker groups and trade unions are at the heart of protectionist politics and protests against free trade. Is the Conservative Party, having been, for most of the last century and a half, a free trade party, going to revert to preferential trade deals, quotas and bilateral arrangements open to challenge in the WTO?

And if Britain seeks to use its post-EU status to create Britain as a new centre for low-cost exports and a giant off-shore entrepôt for exporting to the EU, will the EU and trade unions and businesses across the Channel accept what many will see as unfair advantage accruing to Britain using its non-EU status to avoid the common rules that are applied across Europe? As a business leader in France who handles European affairs for Medef – the French equivalent of the CBI – told me, 'It is up to the UK if you want "hard" or "soft" Brexit but no one in Europe will accept "dirty" Brexit by cheating on all international rules on taxation and treatment of workers to obtain unfair advantages by tax or social dumping.'

The big area of economic gain for Britain since the Thatcher era has been services – especially financial services, management consultancy, creative and cultural industries and above all universities. These economic sectors are not covered by the WTO. They depend massively on people movement from the EU. There appears to be no government assessment of what leaving the EU would mean for these profit centres. Similarly, no evidence was presented by the Leave campaign about the new burden on exporters post-Brexit, who will have to go through complex, costly and time-consuming rules-of-origin tests in order to be able to ensure that third-country products, any sort of goods or component parts, are not transiting through the UK to avoid paying the EU's Common External Tariff.

There are many ways of using regulatory mechanisms to put disguised barriers in the way of foreign products. Inside the EU or its Customs Union, Britain was not subject to such hidden protectionisms or could successfully appeal against them, though so far it has not been able to persuade free-trade America to drop its Buy American laws. Outside the EU, Britain loses all chances to influence EU trade rules in a direction that would help the modern British economy.

The many foreign firms from North America, Japan, South Korea and increasingly China that have come to the UK during the last 35 years of what is called globalisation have done so to avoid paying EU customs duties and tariffs and probably, more importantly, not to have to submit products or services produced in the UK to regulatory controls since, by definition, doing business in the UK was doing business in the other 27 member states of the EU.

All this is put at risk. It is the first time in Britain's economic and trading history that we have been prepared to contemplate a serious reduction in our economic strength as a result of a populist plebiscite promoted by openly xenophobic politicians and won on the basis of hate and lies.

Another problem is the WTO, which supervises global trade in goods – but not services, the UK's main export. Outside the EU, the UK reverts to its existing status as a WTO member. Today, the UK ambassador to all the United Nations organisations based in Geneva, such as the World Health Organization, the International Labour Organization and others, also represents the UK at the WTO. The ambassador has little to do on WTO affairs except attend regular coordination meetings with other EU ambassadors and the EU official who represents all EU nations at the WTO. Trading relationships between EU nations and the rest of the world – tariffs, quotas, agricultural quotas – are handled by the EU.

Outside the EU Britain would have to negotiate an agreement with 163 WTO nations, each of which has its own trade priorities and needs. New members about to join the WTO include Bosnia and Sudan, who will have their say on what the terms of Britain's external trading rules will be.

A key area will be agriculture. UK farmers know what their subsidies are at the moment, as they are agreed under the EU's Common Agricultural Policy (CAP). Developing countries complain that CAP subsidies stop a flow of cheaper agricultural products coming into Europe. It is not just developing countries. Britain would have to negotiate its farming policy agreements within a WTO context and few Commonwealth countries, to take that network of nations, will open their market to British goods unless Britain drops all barriers to what they want to export, including their students wanting to study at British universities and then work for a few years in Britain to burnish their CVs.

Within the EU, important segments of the British economy, including agriculture, are enveloped within the 28-nation trading bloc that has very great clout at the WTO. Outside, Britain will be very exposed.

There will have to be difficult negotiations with the EU and the WTO on the British share of the current EU quota system agreed with the WTO for reduced-tariff food products like chickens and beef. Any trade negotiation goes to the heart of what we eat: arguing over what share of an existing quota Britain gets to keep will not be easy, nor fast.

Any unilateral British subsidy or tariff for UK farmers or industries like steel which face competition from lower-priced products made in China, for example, can be challenged at the WTO. Trade panels at the

WTO, with roughly the same power as the European Court of Justice, can declare such post-Brexit subsidies or tariffs illegal. The WTO itself rarely, if ever, votes on such issues, which are decided by consensus. But consensus requires agreement, and many WTO members will not seek to offer Britain preferential treatment.

There is agreement between the EU and the WTO on tariffs the EU can apply. So automobiles imported into the EU, including the UK, have to pay a 10 per cent tariff and textile goods or wool products have to pay 12 per cent extra duty. Outside the EU, made-in-Britain automobiles, suits or sweaters will face these tariffs for anything exported across the Channel or into Ireland. Brexit ministers claim that these tariffs will not be applied. But why should France and Germany or Italy and Spain and other EU member states offer a privileged relationship with the UK not offered to French- or Spanish-speaking countries elsewhere in the world, let alone to the United States, China or Russia?

Many have forgotten that the main advantages of EU and Single Market membership are the application of rules and regulations and standards that are applicable across the member countries. This reduces transaction costs and creates a level playing field for business. The European Commission works at preventing monopolistic or oligopolistic abuse; containing state aid and other support from national governments that favours domestic producers; and opening up access to public procurement opportunities across the region. The benefits to both market participants and customers have been significant.

Two examples are the agreement on open skies, with a major increase in the number of airlines in Europe, including Britain – especially low-cost airlines benefiting people on more modest incomes in Europe. Similarly, the recent reduction in EU-wide mobile roaming charges allows millions of British people on holiday or travelling in Europe to pay lower mobile phone costs thanks to tough regulation of the Single Market. We have seen a real increase in consumer surplus in these two areas alone, as low-cost aviation and phones have become a reality, with significant extra economic activity in both home and host nations as a result. Outside the EU, Britain loses access to the proposed single market in digital services and energy as well as a capital markets union, which will see many more individual national cases of discrimination in favour of domestic players gradually disappear.

Car factories in Spain – Europe's biggest car-producing nation after Germany, France, Italy, Slovakia and Romania – will be delighted to see Nissan, Toyota and Honda cars made in England become more expensive, especially as the Brexit devaluation of the pound sterling will be seen as giving British exporters an unfair advantage. Once outside the EU and an independent member of the WTO, the UK would have to follow 'most-favoured nation' rules on trade. This means that Britain has to offer the same terms of trade to all countries and not just pick and choose which countries can export into the UK without duties or tariffs. A way around this is to negotiate a separate trade deal once the UK has left the EU with major countries like the US, Japan, China, India, Brazil or South Korea and of course with the EU.

But such trade deals are now politically highly charged and can take years to negotiate. They all require ratification by national and regional parliaments. As we have seen, political opposition has blocked both the major trade deals between the US and Pacific nations and the US and the EU. There is no evidence that outside the EU, Britain will have the clout, the charm or the negotiating genius to shape advantageous trade deals without years of negotiations. The European Court of Justice has ruled that the proposed EU–Singapore trade agreement has to be ratified by all EU national parliaments and where national law so stipulates, regional parliaments.

A UK–EU trade agreement subject to the same ratification process could take not just years to negotiate, as every national government made sure its objectives were upheld in the final agreement, but also years to ratify, as any group of national parliamentarians raised objections and sought a populist majority against Britain in their own domestic political setting. An EU trade agreement with Peru and Colombia was signed in June 2012. By 2017 it still had not been ratified in three EU countries and could not enter into operation. The stated objective of Mrs May to achieve a quick EU–UK trade deal does not seem realistic

One intriguing suggestion made by Michael Emerson, of the Centre for European Policy Studies, is that the UK copies some of the proposals in the EU–Ukraine Association Agreement and its Deep and Comprehensive Free Trade Agreements (DCFTA). These allow a common set of rules governing:

• technical standards and regulations for goods
• trade 'remedies' (e.g. anti-dumping)
• competition policy
• intellectual property rights
• public procurement
• trade-related energy rules (e.g. on pricing)
• basic rules for services
• taxation (namely VAT).

But they do not include financial services, which are vital for the UK unless it wants to lose the global money-making role of the City, which has become a global financial hub since the 1980s thanks to UK membership of the Single Market. Moreover, if the UK agrees to abide by common EU-determined rules but like Norway do so outside the framework of EU treaty law, then Britain loses both voice and vote and will still have to abide by EU decisions and directives, something UKIP, many Conservatives and the anti-EU press say is unacceptable for a 'sovereign and independent Britain', to use one of Mrs May's favourite slogans.

In the initial period after Brexit, when new ministers were encouraging free trade in slogans, there was a fatuous suggestion that Britain would offer a complete free trade deal to the EU and therefore all problems are solved. But Britain – at least those who exult in the Brexit plebiscite outcome – appears to want to return to a world of stronger national borders, whereas open or liberal or free trade requires the fewest barriers possible to exchange of goods, capital, services, people, ideas and information.

Britain can demand but is unlikely to get just free trade in the areas where it thinks barriers should be removed but not in areas that matter to other countries. Thus all trade deals are negotiations and, forgive the pun, based on trade-offs. If Britain rejects the Single Market and quits the Customs Union, as Boris Johnson told Czech journalists in Prague would happen, then trade in and out of the UK will be very different. It will be free but severely limited and the centuries-old tradition of Britain basing its wealth and power on maximising trade at all costs will have come to an end.

16

EUROPEANS *CHEZ NOUS* AND BRIT EXPATS IN EUROPE

One major problem arising from Brexit is the status of more than 2 million British citizens who live, work or have retired in EU member states. The figures vary according to what source is used but a report prepared by the Institute for Public Policy Research for the government in 2010 and drawing on national census data, passport estimates and the UK Department of Work and Pensions reckoned there were 2,112,700 British citizens living in other EU countries. The level of official registration varies from nation to nation. Many ex-pat Brits maintain a presence in the UK but spend most of the year in their homes in warmer regions of southern Europe. What will their rights be after Brexit?

Under the Treaty of Maastricht each national of an EU member state is also a citizen of the European Union. It means we as Brits have the right to be treated in the same way as nationals of any EU country we choose to go and live or work in.

The concept of non-discrimination in employing workers goes back to the very beginning of helping to bind Europe together. It was written into the first European Coal and Steel Treaty in 1951. After the

1930s, when nationalist politicians tried to ban hiring of workers on ethnic, religious or national grounds, it was felt important that workers in dangerous, dirty industries like coal and steel – which had always been dependent on hiring workers from outside the region or country where they were located – should be hired on the basis of their willingness to do the job and not barred from work because they did not speak the right language or carry a specific passport.

It was in this period that the UK was directing demobilised Polish soldiers who stayed in Britain to work down mines and the *Windrush* was bringing in the first wave of black immigrant workers from the West Indies to work as nurses or bus conductors. In both cases there were not enough native-born Brits willing to do arduous underground work digging out or work long shifts in poorly paid public-sector jobs. Fast forward 60 years, and firms in sectors like fruit and vegetable picking, fast-food catering or care homes could never find enough British citizens willing to do the job. It might be argued that if pay was increased British workers would come forward. But the margins in many of these sectors of economic activity are such that unless we want to pay £5 for a few leeks or see the cost of looking after those in their later years become unsustainably expensive, these labour-intensive sectors of the economy have difficulty paying much more than the legal minimum wage, often topped up with a taxpayer subsidy in the form of income tax credits.

British citizens in turn have benefited from the EU's rule of non-discrimination against citizens of member states. There are many British citizens married to EU citizens who can live with spouses, have children, make homes in Britain without let or hindrance. Since Brexit many EU citizens in the UK have sought to get permanent residence – itself a precursor to seeking naturalisation as a British citizen. The process is cumbersome, with an 85-page form to fill in and up to £1,000 to pay in fees and legal advice. And at the end of the process a Home Office bureaucrat can find some reason to refuse the application. Many are just giving up and will live here illegally until such time as they are caught and possibly deported. Throughout history there has been no greater pleasure for low-skill immigration officials than to refuse some the right to enter or stay in a country. Mrs May's six years as home secretary were obsessed with foreigners coming into Britain. Now she has unleashed a new jobsworth bureaucracy making lives as miserable as possible for French, Italian, Swedish or other Europeans who have chosen to form a partnership and create a home in Britain on the assumption that their national passport was all they needed.

All that ends as a new meaner, more discriminatory Britain comes into being. Nowhere on the ballot paper about leaving the EU was there any reference to punishing and hurting people who came to marry or form partnerships in the belief that Britain was a tolerant European nation. But Mrs May has chosen to interpret the vote as a mandate for some harsh, even cruel measures that are causing misery to many. To be sure British people lived on the continent for many decades before the EU existed. However, the right to automatic residence or the ability to set up a business or take paid employment without a complicated permit application is something very recent in European history. Nations have in the past jealously guarded access to their labour markets.

The one interesting exception was the decision after Ireland became an independent republic in the 1920s to allow every Irish citizen the right to travel to Britain, to live or take work in the UK. Citizens of what was a foreign republic which stayed neutral in World War II and where dislike of England was part of the political discourse were allowed full, free movement into the UK. 'Foreigners' or 'immigrants' from Ireland (they were never called that, as the anti-EU populists reserved the term 'immigrant' for those who came not from across the Irish Sea but from across the English Channel) were allowed to buy a home or raise a family and live as normally under the suzerainty of the king or queen of England as they would under the fiercely republican regime across the Irish sea.

Research by London University reports that there are upwards of 200,000 Brazilians in the UK, mainly London. Often they arrived on tourist visas, found a job, a partner, enjoyed life and stayed. The Office of National Statistics estimates there are 197,000 US citizens living and working in the UK. So if Mrs May or any government wanted to reduce immigration or the presence of non-British citizens they could start with – or could have started with – the non-stop arrivals from the Asian sub-continent or the Americas. Instead, UKIP and Tory Eurosceptics egged on by the Europhobe press have targeted white, usually young, healthy Europeans. British expats in Spain cost the Spanish health services £250 million a year. The equivalent figure for Spaniards in the UK is £150,000. Brits in Spain are not in the first flush of youth, whereas Spanish baristas, bankers and language teachers tend to be still fit and young.

A false set of arguments has been advanced by well-intentioned people as to whether existing Europeans living in the UK can maintain the right to remain residents and work. There are 137,000 EU citizens working in the NHS and other health care sectors (along with 73,000 other foreigners). Bars and cafés, fruit picking and harvesting other vegetable crops, as well much public and private transport, would stop functioning if non-British-born labour was barred. This dependence on immigrant labour was not caused by the EU. More than a million Irish citizens came to rebuild the British economy and work as doctors, nurses, carers or in building trades after 1945 because the Irish economy and society were so badly organised the country could not offer jobs to its own people. This was a major help to the UK economy in the postwar era of growth.

Indeed the whole history of Europe has been shaped by mass movements of populations like the Portuguese into France as building workers, the Spanish and Yugoslavs into Germany as automobile workers and Italians going to work making Volvos in Malmo, Sweden. There are more than 1 million Romanians in Spain, 780,000 in Italy and 400,000 in Germany. As mentioned, the Europhobe politician Nigel Farage said he would feel 'uncomfortable' if a Romanian family moved into a house next door. There were no Spanish political parties or newspapers that exuded such crass xenophobia against the 1.1 million Romanians in Spain. That was a British speciality served up by UKIP and Tory politicians and fanned by the anti-European press.

Switzerland has the highest share of EU citizens in its population of any European state, despite the Helvetic Confederation not being an EU member state. Lack of available labour also obliged Germany, France, Britain and the Netherlands to open frontiers to hundreds of thousands of Muslim immigrants from Pakistan and Bangladesh into Britain, from Turkey into Germany, from Morocco, Tunisia and Algeria into France and Belgium and even from far-off Indonesia and Surinam into the Netherlands. It would be delightful to believe that the native true-born English worker is going to do the exhausting, sometimes dirty and dangerous work that all recently arrived immigrant workers are willing to undertake.

This is not just something happening at the low-pay end of the labour market. Five of the six chief executives of the principal British banks are foreign-born, as indeed is the governor of the Bank of England. It is hard to see how one puts in place a fair and balanced policy of work permits and visas that covers everyone from Ireland to Estonia. Those hoping to make Brexit a success story talk of imposing work permits on unskilled workers. But what is an unskilled worker? Is it a university graduate from Italy or Spain who works as a barista in London's coffee shop economy? Is it a medical orderly or a removals firm employee with strong arms to carry heavy furniture? Picking fruit may be unskilled but before the arrival of Eastern Europeans 15 per cent of all fruit in Kent rotted on trees as the men and women of Kent were not willing to do the backbreaking work in the fields of picking fruit.

Spending eight hours a day in a care home helping elderly immobile British people on and off the lavatory and making sure they are washed and neat when their families come to visit may not require a PhD but it is vitally important work and the evidence is that many British citizens do not want to do it.

In the 1980s Britain exported its surplus workers when unemployment rose to over 3 million under Margaret Thatcher. The popular TV series *Auf Wiedersehen Pet* showed the comic side of British immigrant workers in Germany undercutting their fully unionised German comrades and working the system to maximise income and allowances. In 1978 I was President of the National Union of Journalists at a time when the union was leading a campaign against racism in the press and urging newspapers and the BBC to start employing more reporters from ethnic minority backgrounds. Today that is not an issue but in the 1970s to suggest that the all-white journalist workforce might be strengthened by openings its ranks to British journalists from a BAME background produced howls of rage and venom from reactionary newspaper columnists like Bernard Levin.

As part of the campaign I wrote to the editor of the *Daily Telegraph* after a particularly foul front-page story about an unemployed 'Asian' man, his disabled wife and his family of 12 claiming benefits amounting to £5,000 a year (£100 a week) – a princely sum in the 1970s. I protested that the *Telegraph*'s dislike of anyone being helped by the state was one thing but why identify the man as 'Asian', as there were plenty of white Brits doing exactly the same? The managing editor wrote back to say that if the paper had not used the word 'Asian' in the headline its readers 'would have assumed he was Irish'. I assume the *Telegraph* editor was not pulling my leg and meant his justification to be taken seriously. But it shows the deep, enduring prejudice against the incomers of any sort in Britain. In the 1930s, German Jews; in the 1950s, the Irish; in the 1960s, the Afro-Caribbeans; in the 1970s, the East African Asians; in the 1980s, the Pakistanis; in the 1990s, the Kosovars. Since 2000, it has been the Poles, Slovaks, Lithuanians and Bulgarians or the Middle Eastern war refugees.

For some it would be nice to imagine a Britain without immigrants. But 300 years ago Daniel Defoe wrote his poem in 'A True-born Englishman' to mock the very idea that in 1701 his country somehow had a pure blood line. A few years earlier the English had had to import an immigrant from Europe, a Dutchman, to be king. The present royal family descends from a German immigrant who arrived from Hannover in the eighteenth century and whose descendants constantly married European immigrants to strengthen the blood line of the English monarchy, including the Queen's marriage to a man of great distinction but in essence a Greek-born immigrant without a drop of English blood in him. Defoe took on UKIP and today's nationalist anti-immigrant journalists thus:

> Thus from a mixture of all kinds began,
> That het'rogeneous thing, an Englishman:
> In eager rapes, and furious lust begot
> Betwixt a painted Britain and a Scot.
> Whose gend'ring off-spring quickly learn'd to bow,
> And yoke their heifers to the Roman plough:
> From whence a mongrel half-bred race there came,
> With neither name, nor nation, speech nor fame.
> In whose hot veins new mixtures quickly ran,
> Infus'd betwixt a Saxon and a Dane
> While their rank daughters, to their parents just,
> Receiv'd all nations with promiscuous lust.
> This nauseous brood directly did contain
> The well-extracted blood of Englishmen.

To use the term 'a mongrel half-bred race' to describe the flag-waving, 'Rule Britannia'-singing devotees of UKIP and assorted *Daily Mail* readers would bring down the wrath of the Twittersphere, so let it be clear the quotation is from one of the masters of English literature and should not be taken as a comment on today's nativist populist politics. It is cited merely to underline how eternal is the obsession of some with the fear of foreign blood in our midst.

To be sure, there is a widespread belief supported by writers like David Goodhart, former *Financial Times* labour editor and director of the Demos think-tank and far from being a rightwing nationalist, that the EU's free movement philosophy must be to the disadvantage of what are called native workers – the 'somewhere' people, as he describes them. The Leave campaign brilliantly fused the latent longstanding prejudices against 'immigrants' that have been a stock of British politics since the days of Enoch Powell, with the arrival of European workers in regions and towns where few had been seen before.

Economists have identified what they call in their jargon 'compositional amenities', that is, everyone speaks the same language, shares an English Christian heritage, behaves more or less the same and life runs along predictable groves. American and British social scientists carried out a survey of 21 countries with results published in 2009 which showed that worry about the loss of 'compositional amenities' was significantly more important in explaining public reaction to immigration than economic concerns, such as the impact of foreign incomers on wages and taxes. Even if the evidence shows that immigrants help to boost economic output and that workers from Europe are massive net contributors to government tax receipts, worry, even fear, about the changing identity of a community prevails over economic arguments.

The study found that this anxiety about loss of 'compositional amenities' is higher in those with lower educational attainment. President Trump won votes by proposing to cut the United States off from its neighbour Mexico and making it much more difficult for non-Americans to come and live and work in the country.

The language of Boris Johnson and Nigel Farage, and indeed Theresa May when home secretary, about keeping European immigrants out played to exactly those fears. Counter-arguments about the economic benefits of migrant labour could not counter this sense of anxiety that

England was changing because too many foreigners had been allowed in since the time when Enoch Powell made immigration the toxic political issue it has remained since the 1960s.

That up to 400,000 French citizens work in well-paid jobs in London is something British politicians like to boast about. No one has ever bothered counting or being concerned about the scores of thousands of young Greeks, Italians and Spanish who moved to the UK after the crash of 2007/9 to create the new coffee culture in city centres.

There are fears of foreign workers in all European labour markets. France's communist leader, Georges Marchais, used to demand in the 1980s that jobs in France should be reserved for French citizens. Ski instructors on every Alp moan when British instructors turn up and offer lessons at lower rates and in fluent English to tourists. But the particular problems of the UK labour market have been made worse by British rules or absence of them.

For example, free movement does not apply to work in the public sector, for employees paid by the state. The NHS employs 57,000 EU citizens. It would be perfectly legal to reserve work in the NHS for British nationals. But that would require investment in training sufficient doctors, nurses and other hospital staff. Indeed, public-sector employment can be reserved for nationals, but much has been contracted out, with employees losing their public-sector status as they work for private-sector employers who cannot reserve jobs for national citizens.

Another mechanism is to insist on full qualifications for many jobs. This again assumes that there is a structure of obligatory apprenticeships with a commitment to offer a job at the end of the training period.

When firms have to abide by industry-wide pay agreements negotiated with trade unions as in German-speaking Europe as well as most Nordic countries or the Netherlands, it is harder to offer low- or minimum-wage jobs which do not sustain a family but which are attractive to men or women coming from countries where wages are far lower and decent jobs hard to come by.

Writing for *InFacts*, the accountant Philip Shirley has pointed out that there is no need for the government to grant the personal tax allowance to newcomers from abroad. This means that a worker has to earn £10,000 before paying tax. Tax rates are reserved for national laws and are not an EU prerogative, and it would be possible to make the tax allowance conditional on five years' residence in the UK. According to Mr Shirley:

> Somebody earning £10,000 would pay tax of £2,000 and have take-home pay (ignoring national insurance contributions) of £8,000. Such a change would be fairly easy to administer through the tax system. It would not prevent foreign workers from coming to the UK, but would have an economic impact on what they earn from the UK.

Others argue that such tax-code discrimination would be illegal and fall foul of the European Court of Justice. But it is perfectly possible to have a more proactive local or regional employment system whereby all firms have to notify vacancies to employment agencies which can then track and place employees and set up training schemes to lessen the over-easy reliance on non-locally sourced labour of any sort. It would not breach any EU law to ban employment agencies who advertise and recruit for workers in Eastern Europe in local languages when those jobs are not advertised in Britain.

Delaying access to work-related social benefits until such time as a level of social security or insurance contributions have been made is also compatible with EU rules and laws. In fact it would be no bad thing if all workers in Britain had a work identity card that carried details of National Insurance contributions, tax paid, years of residence in the UK if not a British citizen and other relevant work-related information. Anyone who carries a credit card or mobile phone is already sharing more than this level of information with private finance and phone companies. It should not take much investment to develop an identity card showing that someone had the legal right to work in the UK and had made appropriate social benefit contributions. Indeed such a card could be issued to all British citizens who entered the labour market and it would become as normal as having a driving licence.

These are all means of *internal* migration controls rather than archaic *external* controls such as quotas, work permits or travel visas. They respond to the call for managed migration but do so in a modern fashion and on the basis of supporting local workers rather than discriminating against anyone not born in the UK.

One of the old complaints about Europe was that in comparison to the United States there was insufficient labour mobility. That allegation has been stood on its head with the mass movement of millions of Europeans across borders, especially since EU enlargement to southern and then Eastern Europe after the end of fascism and colonels' rule in Spain, Portugal and Greece and 15 years later the end of communism. It is now the US which has a more static labour market and become dependent on millions of undocumented or illegal Latin American immigrant workers. In contrast, in the EU system, on the whole, everyone is listed (except in the UK) and has to pay taxes or social security insurance contributions.

Already the EU was mulling over a so-called 'emergency brake' on access to welfare benefits for the first years of an EU citizen working in another country. Again, there is little evidence that EU workers came or come to Britain to access benefits. It is rather the job offers that matter. But making official such an 'emergency brake' would ease fears, not only in Britain, about too rapid a mass arrival of foreign workers, especially in unskilled jobs.

Another mechanism would be to enforce rigorously EU social rules like the Posted Workers Directive and the Agency Workers Directive. Low-pay employers have driven a coach and horses through these directives to employ at the lowest rates possible workers from Eastern

Europe delivered by employment agencies at the expense of local British workers. Employers, including the biggest UK employer – the government – may complain they cannot be competitive if they have to meet these obligations. Yet in much of Europe, in or out of the eurozone, firms do well and employ local workers as well as European migrants.

Mrs May says she wants to see more fairness in the workplace. Measures to help British workers goes with that agenda, as well as lowering the über-attractiveness of the low-pay British labour market to EU citizens. Many firms as well as the CBI and British Chambers of Commerce (BCC) may moan, but they have to ask themselves if being excluded from the Single Market is a price worth paying if, as an alternative, the EU principle of free movement can be made compatible with more jobs and decent pay for British workers and Britain ceasing to be the employer of last resort for the unemployed of Eastern Europe.

In the end, the reason so many European workers come to Britain has been government policy directed at maximising subsidised low-pay employment rather than maximising productivity or maximising fair wages so that a worker can support him or herself and a family, without requiring taxpayer subsidy via the workplace.

It is an economic policy choice shaped by Labour after 1997 and then by Conservatives and Liberal Democrats after 2010. But there will never be enough 'truc-born Englishmen' – to use Defoe's phrase – to fill all the taxpayer-subsidised, deunionised low-pay jobs that are so central to British economic management in the twenty-first century.

Hence the real policy dilemma. Immigrant workers will only stop coming to the UK if the economy turns sour, investment dries up, there is a recession and employers stop hiring. Immigrant workers from Europe have made the modern British economy what it is. Blaming them is demagogy and nasty politics. There is an alternative, up to a point. But it means paying workers fair wages. Are British employers and government ministers ready for that?

Meanwhile, if Britain brings in new rules limiting Europeans from visiting or working or living in Britain it is likely that there will be reciprocal action against British citizens living in Europe. Already in the Dordogne region of France, where an estimated 100,000 Brits have homes, there is talk of selling up as no one knows if they will be able to keep living as freely as they have in recent years if Britain rejects the European philosophy and rules about travel, work and residence. In London there were calls for existing EU citizens in the UK today, before a full-on Brexit is decided, to keep their rights. There are 850,000 Poles now in Britain, most with Polish citizenship. But while they may be granted some special status, what of their cousins, sweethearts, grandparents who would like to visit?

The pro-Brexit Tory MP Jacob Rees-Mogg has said there is no problem with every European seeking to come to Britain applying for an online visa. Mr Rees-Mogg has clearly not spent much time navigating computer visa systems for other countries. The cost in setting such a system up and administering it would be a drain on public resources, as would the many extra staff needed at airports to check the visas. Writing in the *Financial Times*, Daniel Hannan suggested that some tolerance should be extended to needed EU workers who support the British economy or do key public service jobs. But, he added, this should not extend to being allowed to live with spouses and children. It is illegal under most international conventions, including the European Convention on Human Rights, to deny the right to a family life to a parent who has children. Mr Hannan's suggestion is untypically mean of him. It shows how confused the argument on free movement can become.

If all EU citizens can travel to the UK as tourists without first getting entry visas, they can easily slip into the informal or 'black' labour market. That is how hundreds of thousands of Europeans from former communist countries were able to come to Britain and Ireland after 1990. One of them, Laima Muktupāvela, even wrote a book about her

experiences as a mushroom picker. The Polish building workers, deco-
rators or plumbers and any number of nannies from Eastern Europe
looking after the children of middle-class British families where both
parents worked were the stuff of endless newspaper articles and reports
in the 1990s and in the years leading up to the formal entry of new EU
member states in 2004. The idea that Eastern Europeans only arrived
after 2004 is nonsense.

But the only way to stop the continuing arrival of Europeans who
can then slip into the unofficial labour market would be to impose
an obligation to obtain travel visas just to visit the UK. Even the US-
style ESTA (Electronic System for Travel Authorisation), a variation
of which the European Commission is proposing for entry into the
Schengen zone, will not help as any travel visa system, electronic or
otherwise, will not prevent the arrival of EU immigrant workers if
the UK economy needs them. A hard-Brexit economic slowdown will
mean less new hiring; whether that is the price to be paid for cutting
links with Europe may be difficult for people to accept. Imposing new
red tape and regulations on every employer to first obtain a work permit or visa and check the status of anyone who seeks a job working
in a bar, in a care home or doing some delivery work will again be
costly and cumbersome. EU citizens, for example, will be able to fly
to Dublin and then catch a train, bus, drive or hitch-hike to cross the
border into the UK over scores of small roads and once inside the UK
travel to Scotland or England.

All EU member states are required to have secure borders with non-
EU member states and if this proviso is enforced there will have to be
manned checkpoints on every road between Ireland and the UK, but
what of the paths or the loughs where the frontier runs through water
– will the UK border police have to have motor-boat patrols on all
the small lakes that straddle the two borders? When the UK system
of farm subsidies finally replaces the EU Common Agricultural Policy
there may be differential support payments for British and Irish cattle

and other livestock. No greater invitation to smuggling can be dreamt up and again short of the kind of border that existed between East and West Germany before 1990 the frontier between non-EU UK and EU member state Ireland that runs through the hills, fields and loughs of Northern Ireland will turn into a clear source of tension, as will the frontier between Gibraltar, a British territory whose citizens have UK passports, and Spain in the EU.

17

DIVORCE AND A NEW PARTNERSHIP

The Brexit ballot papers had scarcely been counted before policy think-tanks were busy preparing their own schemes for a future relationship between the UK and the EU. Indeed the European Commission produced its own proposal offering five future scenarios for the EU ahead of the celebration of the sixtieth anniversary of the Treaty of Rome, which in 1957 was the international treaty that set up the European Economic Community from which the European Union is descended.

A quick post-referendum set of ideas came from policy-thinkers associated with the highly respected Bruegel think-tank based in Brussels. Four men, who included influential opinion-formers in Paris and Berlin as well as Sir Paul Tucker, a former deputy governor of the Bank of England, called for a new 'Continental Partnership' which would allow the UK to have access to the Single Market. London could also impose quotas on EU workers, and in exchange the UK would continue to make a financial contribution to the EU budget and accept rulings of the European Court of Justice and take part in discussions – but without a vote – in EU decision-making procedures on markets, as well as on security and defence. But this runs counter to the fairly clear view of many national leaders in Europe as well as the presidents of the Commission and the Council that the four freedoms of movement at the heart of the EU – freedom of moment for capital, goods, services and people – could not be altered to give London the right to pick and choose which the UK accepted.

In effect the Bruegel-linked idea, even with its catchy title of a 'Continental Partnership', amounted to a reworked concept of concentric circles in Europe with an inner EU and an outer ring of nations consisting of the UK, Turkey, Ukraine, Norway and Switzerland which would pay a financial contribution to the EU, enjoy deep economic integration and some cooperation on defence, foreign policy and security, but not accept all the supranational rules of the current EU. In particular it would allow Britain to limit immigration of Europeans into the UK. They seemed unaware that Norway and Switzerland permitted free movement and that was a *sine qua non* for both countries' access to the Single Market.

The Bruegel authors forgot little Lichtenstein, which formed part of the European Economic Area. About two-thirds of the Alpine principality's 37,000-strong population are foreigners. The tiny nation was allowed a small derogation to slow down the arrival of foreigners seeking to buy property in remote mountain villages, but it does not amount to anything like the introduction of a fully managed migration bureaucracy which has been a longstanding demand for anti-immigrant Tory/UKIP politicians, some Labour MPs and tabloid editors.

The authors associated with the Bruegel think-tank argue that this would provide an answer to the next 20–30 years of European construction. Yet it seemed very similar to ideas of an inner and outer Europe, of two-speed Europe, or *KernEuropa* (core Europe) that have been in play since the 1970s and the beginning of the moves to greater EU integration to make the common market of the 1957 Treaty of Rome work more fully and with enhanced post-frontier trade supervised supranationally. Such ideas repeat the confusion behind the cliché of a 'multispeed' Europe – as if the initial 6, then 9, then 12, 15 and now 28 EU member states ever moved at the same speed in terms of economic development and social cohesion! One might as well refer to 'multispeed' Britain, as different regions of Britain move forward at different speeds of economic performance and living standards. But the EU will stand by its common laws and rule book. Otherwise it ceases to exist. The former French president Valéry Giscard d'Estaing published in 2014 *Europa: Europe's Last Chance*. He proposed a core EU of 12 nations consisting of the original six signatories of the Treaty of Rome in 1957 plus Poland, Ireland, Finland, Spain, Austria and Malta, but not the other central and eastern or south-eastern European countries, Greece, Denmark and Sweden and of course Britain.

Another political heavyweight from the 1970s is Britain's former foreign secretary and founder of the Social Democratic Party, David (Lord) Owen. His 2012 book *Europe Restructured* proposed an inner European Union consisting of the Treaty of Rome six plus Austria, Slovakia, Slovenia, Malta and Cyprus with Britain and other EU member states in a European Community, which would extend to include Turkey.

The Bruegel proposal is thus the latest in the long list of will-o-the-wisp moments as clever, well-intentioned men redesign Europe. Michael Maclay, a British expert on the EU, wrote his paper 'Multi-Speed Europe' more than 20 years ago. Admittedly, there is more pressure now thanks to the Brexit decision but there are no signs from the rest of the members of the EU that they are willing to be shoe-horned into inner and outer, or fast and slow, or euro and non-euro groupings just to find a place for a Britain which opts to turn its back on Europe. Nor is it clear that British politicians who have promoted Brexit see themselves joining with Ukraine or Turkey in a queue of nations that sits in the waiting-rooms of Brussels hoping to catch the attention of someone who has real power and economic weight.

In *Europa ist tot, es lebe Europa!* (Europe is dead, long live Europe!), the German writer Thomas Schmid argues that Britain should seek what he calls a 'privileged partnership' with the EU after full Brexit. Schmid singles out Britain along with Turkey and Ukraine as countries that the EU needs to find a relationship with. The term 'privileged partnership' was one invented in Germany to describe what German conservative politicians wanted the EU's relationship with Turkey to be. They baulked at the idea of full EU membership for Turkey and there has been a great deal of unpleasant Islamophobe hostility to Turkey, especially in rightwing circles in Paris and Vienna. There is every reason to criticise the lurch to authoritarian and religious rule under the Turkish strongman, President Erdoğan, who has done little to encourage support in the rest of Europe for EU membership for Turkey. Nonetheless for Britain to be placed in the same category as Erdoğan's Turkey by an influential German opinion-shaper is not quite the status that the Brexit enthusiasts envisaged for their country.

Pierre Moscovici anticipated Schmid's title with his own book of 2006, *L'Europe est morte, vive l'Europe*. It was written after Moscovici and other pro-Europeans on the French left lost the campaign to ratify the EU Constitution in the referendum held in France in 2005. It was, strictly speaking, a new EU treaty even if given the grandiose title of 'Constitution'. As in Britain, parties split and prominent French socialist political leaders, such as former prime minister Laurent Fabius, found reasons to call for a 'No' vote in the plebiscite. The French and Dutch 'No' saved Tony Blair's bacon. There was no need to hold the referendum he had promised on the EU Constitutional Treaty – a promise he made to help Labour MPs retain their seats in the general election of 2005.

Had it been held, the UK would have voted similarly to France and the Netherlands. That might have been a warning to David Cameron that to play with plebiscites on Europe was to play with fire and risk the inevitable blowback.

But ever faithful to his European vocation, Pierre Moscovici in 2006 decided that Europe was not dead despite the defeat of the constitution.

With hindsight he was right. Europe defied its grave-diggers in 2005 and also rose to the occasion in 2007/9 when European leaders, with strong leadership from Gordon Brown, one of the few who understood international finance, put in place major new institutional and political arrangements to prevent the made-in-America financial crash having the sort of impact on Europe that the crash of 1929 had, which ushered in a long worldwide depression culminating in World War II. Today all EU member states are growing – some more strongly than the UK.

For many the answer was to cut out of the EU all its weaker members like Portugal, Ireland, Greece and Spain – the famous PIGS. But the EU is neither a project nor a super-state. It is more like a family than a federation, and a family or union of nations that knows some help, tolerance and time must be allowed so that weaker or more wayward members can find their feet after a period of stupidity. More than a decade after Pierre Moscovici wrote *L'Europe est morte*, the EU is still alive and it will survive Brexit, as Schmid's 2016 title indicates. Europe is not dead as a result of Brexit, though British participation may be on hold for a while, just as the US placed on hold its involvement in international bodies like the International Labour Organization and League of Nations in the 1920s.

The intelligentsia, whether as individual writers or collected in European university departments or think-tanks, do invaluable work. But the future relationship between the UK (or perhaps parts of the UK) and the rest of Europe is for the time being a known unknown. There will be a relationship, but until the consequences of the Brexit plebiscite are fully worked out, writing about it is thumb-sucking journalism, not real politics.

At the core of all these concepts is the end of the full Single Market with its four freedoms of movement – of capital, of goods or services and of people. Thus as the different think-tanks set out their visions, the men and women of Europe who need to get themselves elected or rather re-elected were being asked to say to their voters that the UK could be the first major country since the European integration process had started which could unilaterally shut the door to other Europeans without having Europe in turn spurning other relationships, mainly economic ones, with Britain.

None of these arguments, which may make perfect sense when drafted in the libraries of Chatham House, King's College London or think-tanks on the continent, take into account the fact that 27 EU governments each face major problems with populist, often rancid anti-EU politics at home. Some prime ministers have only limited control over their parliaments. In effect Britain has to negotiate with three Europes. There is the European Commission, the European Council and the nations of Europe and the European Parliament.

A leader of Germany's Social Democratic Party and vice-chancellor, Sigmar Gabriel, has said that Britain must be seen not to have an easy or painless exit from the EU, because that would set an example that others might follow and in consequence Europe 'would go down the drain'. Gabriel said the UK should have a 'nasty exit' and be seen to 'suffer pain'. In private many other EU leaders say the same thing, though the etiquette of inter-government politeness in the EU tends to keep these remarks behind closed doors.

It is the easiest thing in the world to write in London a splendid paper or comment piece for the *Financial Times* or a political weekly or monthly sketching out a two- or three-speed multi-tier EU. But the idea that makes perfect sense to the London academic or commentator makes no sense at all in Warsaw or Copenhagen or Rome. Europe is a profoundly political construction shaped by men and women who have to return home from each EU meeting to face voters who are told by opposition parties that what makes sense at EU level is bad news for the future of the citizens who live, work and above all vote at a national level.

The director of the Royal Institute of International Affairs, Robin Niblett, has argued in Chatham House's *World Today* that an important objective for Theresa May 'should be not to complete the Article 50 process until the framework for the future UK–EU relationship has been agreed'. This seems at first sight uncontroversial. However, when he argues that the British government should aim to ensure that the European Council and the European Parliament formally approve the new framework, and its appropriate treaty base, after the conclusion of the Article 50 process, but before the withdrawal agreement formally comes into force, the head of Chatham House is getting close to enunciating a UK wish-list that has little basis in achievable reality.

As Martin Schulz, the president of the European Parliament, who was chosen as the Social Democratic Party candidate to run against Angela Merkel in the contest to be chancellor of Germany, wrote in an article on the day of his visit to see the Prime Minister and Mayor of London there is a clear 'majority in the European Parliament for insisting that the fundamental freedoms are inseparable, i.e. no freedom of movement for goods, capital and services, without free movement of persons. I refuse to imagine a Europe where lorries and hedge funds are free to cross borders but citizens cannot. I cannot accept any hierarchy between these four freedoms.'

Until judges intervened, Brexit Minister David Davis had made clear that parliament and the electorate would not be informed about the UK's negotiations – a return to the secret conclaves of Eurocrats behind closed doors that Eurosceptics always denounced. The High Court, however, made clear there was little sense Brexit supporters saying that the purpose of the referendum was that citizens and parliament should 'take back control' from secretive Brussels institutions and then keeping the British parliament in the dark about what the government would be saying and arguing as it began its preparation for negotiations.

Dr Niblett concludes his *World Today* article by suggesting that the UK should first sort out its trade and economic relationships with the

EU before even invoking Article 50. This will not and cannot happen. First comes the divorce, followed by years of wrangling over access and what the new relationship should be.

EU social legislation, including participation by UK workers and trade unions in European Works Councils and numerous directives connected to workers' rights which are now part of UK law, would face unpicking given there is a clear Conservative majority in the House of Commons and most of this legislation dates from when Tony Blair signed the Social Charter obligations of the Treaty of Maastricht. For Britain to support a policy of what is called 'social dumping' by weakening workplace rules disliked by employers will be seen as creating an unfair playing field across the Channel. Governments of the left or with social democrats in coalition, as well as MEPs and socialist or social democrat members of the Commission, are unlikely to accept any proposal from London which means the EU accepting that the UK can practise social dumping.

One of the little-known advantages of being in the EU for international firms with more than 1,000 employees in two or more EU member states and their workers is the obligation to set up a European Works Council (EWC). These bodies do not negotiate wages. That remains firmly fixed within national labour law and national custom and practice on wage setting. Germany, for example, negotiates pay covering all the workers in the same industry. To begin with the federation of regional employers in the metal or chemical or retail industries agrees a wage deal and it is generally accepted as the benchmark for the rest of Germany. German negotiators will take into account the state of the economy, any worries over inflation and the ability of firms to remain profitable in face of global competition. Thus it was possible at the beginning of the twenty-first century for German unions to agree to hold down wage increases in the manufacturing sector in order to recapitalise firms and reorganise and upskill production to keep firms competitive in the face of imports from Asia.

By contrast, in Britain, wage bargaining is still carried out company by company, often in an adversarial context. In France, politicised and ideological general trade unions quite different from the industrial unions (one industry, one union, as in Germany or the Nordic nations) or the UK myriad of overlapping unions negotiate broad agreements. But if just one of the general unions run from Paris signs an agreement it enters into force even if other, more militant general unions oppose it. A great many French labour-market practices such as working time, redundancy or the minimum wage are decided by state legislation, so unions lobby, campaign and mobilise their militants to try and put pressure on politicians rather than keep the state and politicians competing for votes at arm's length.

The EWCs therefore do not change the contours of what matters most in terms of Europe's many labour markets – namely pay and consultation over redundancies or changes in working practice. But they are an important mechanism for workers employed by the same firm to keep in touch and for the senior managers to hear about problems and try and resolve them before they turn conflictual. American multinational firms operating in Europe have set up 171 EWCs. This is fewer than German firms, which have 230 EWCs, but more than Britain with 112 and France with 128. Altogether there are 1,000 EWCs covering 19 million employees with about 20,000 trade-union-nominated or elected representatives taking part in their meetings. They are a living, functioning embodiment of Social Europe and the concept at the heart of the EU that workers should have rights and that in exchange for accepting market liberalisation across borders, including movement of workers between different labour markets, workers in Europe-wide firms must be consulted and informed.

EWCs are enshrined in EU and thus national laws of all 28 member states, including the UK prior to Brexit. EEA firms also have to set up EWCs. The British government has given a vague promise that all EU legislation currently on the UK statute book will be translated into British national law. But in the 1990s British Euroscepticism took off over the issue of Social Europe, and one of the demands of British Conservatives and business organisations is that Social Europe practices and directives should have no legal force in the UK.

In any event, the two EU directives of 1994 and 2009 which provide the legal basis for the EWC operations will no longer have force in Britain outside the EU. This will not mean, however, that British companies with operations in two or more other EU member states and employing more than 1,000 workers can escape the obligation to set up an EWC and pay for its operation.

To guarantee that the post-Brexit UK does not become a free-riding labour market which refuses to accept the common rules of Social Europe, firms with EWCs are now looking to relocate their central management offices dealing with human resources and employee relations to a jurisdiction that lies within the EU.

EWCs often need to use specialist employment lawyers with cases taken under national labour law to courts and tribunals. American and British firms will want to manage their EWC operations from a jurisdiction that speaks and writes English and has access to an English-speaking labour court system. Thus experts in the field see an increased role for Ireland, as no firm will want to run its EWC operation from a country that has repudiated EU cooperation and norms. It might also mean that while many EWCs cover firms operating in Britain and workers from the company sites can seek nomination and election to an EWC, there will no longer be a legally enshrined right for British trade unions to participate in EWCs.

EWCs are a symbolic and significant development in the history of social partnership and the relationship between capital and labour. By leaving the EU, British workers and their unions will lose an automatic and legally enforceable right to get managers to discuss European-wide operations with employees.

For many anti-European ideologues, reducing workers' rights is a major reason to quit the EU. As more and more workers feel left out of the modern economy and turn to populist demagogues who promise simple answers, often based on harsh treatment of immigrant workers, removing the safety valve of a management–worker forum like an EWC will be counter-productive. There is a further loss in the UK losing specialist lawyers and expertise in the tricky world of managing the modern relationship between capital and labour.

18

BREXIT SPELLS DANGER FOR IRELAND AND CONCERN IN SCOTLAND

If Brexit was the victory of English nationalism, might it bring back to full life Irish nationalism? The long and very violent expression of Irish nationalism in the twentieth century, including the war of national independence after 1918 as well as the subsequent vicious civil war in Ireland and the three decades of violent resistance and terror acts from the late 1960s until Tony Blair secured the Good Friday peace agreement in April 1998, still resonate in Ireland. During what are euphemistically called 'The Troubles', 3,500 people were killed. Tony Blair's chief of staff, Jonathan Powell, did much of the face-to-face negotiating that allowed the Good Friday agreement to happen. He calls the book he wrote about the process *Great Hatred, Little Room*, a fair four-word summing-up of the politics of the Northern Irish part of the United Kingdom (of Great Britain and Northern Ireland).

The power-sharing agreement which parcelled out political power between parties that had resorted to sectarian violence and revenge killings either in the name of ultra-nationalism and Catholic Irish identitarianism or in the name of a Protestant supremacy and unquestioned allegiance to a London-based monarch who ruled over England, Wales and with less certainty over Scotland suited the politicians, who swapped their weapons for iPads and iPhones but did nothing to bring the two communities together. The election for the 108-strong Northern Ireland Assembly in March 2017 showed the two communities as divided as ever. The pro-Brexit Democratic Unionist Party (DUP) gained just one more seat than the pro-EU Sinn Féin, which saw an overall increase in its vote. The preferred solution of Sinn Féin and other nationalists to the problem of Northern Ireland being forced out of Europe by a Conservative/UKIP vote in England is the creation of a united Ireland, which of course would remain a member state of the EU.

The Protestant–Loyalist–Unionist and the Catholic–Nationalist–Republican communities in Belfast and other parts of the north-west corner of Europe's most westerly island live in what in Ireland is called the Six Counties (of Ulster) and in England Northern Ireland. They live in separate communities, as distinct as those under apartheid in South Africa. They almost all go to different schools, worship in different churches and while on the whole the peace agreement mediated by the US government of Bill Clinton still holds, no one can say that this region of Europe has found out how to live without tension and in harmony together.

The EU has been central to Northern Ireland and Brexit may light a fuse that brings the demons of open conflict out of their sealed box.

Firstly, by being a member of the European Community and then the EU the Irish government found itself for the first time in history on an equal footing with Britain. Though not equal in terms of size, economic power or geo-political reach, when the British Prime Minister sat with the Irish Taoiseach in a European Council Ireland's vote weighed the same as the vote of the UK.

London and Dublin got used to regular contacts and cooperation in the EU. Britain, for example, continually defended Ireland's low corporate tax rates against criticism from some continental EU member states. The question of the border between Northern Ireland and the Irish Republic has always been contentious. There was always widespread smuggling whenever duties or tariffs imposed by Dublin and London varied sufficiently to give a price advantage to petrol or cattle or alcohol that were more expensive under one jurisdiction than another. Irish nationalists were bitter about how the frontier was drawn in the 1920s, with the predominately Catholic city of Derry placed under Protestant supremacist rule. The discrimination against Northern Irish Catholics who were denied all access to better-paid industrial jobs or public-sector jobs was continuous from 1920 until the 1980s.

A favourite target for the IRA from the 1930s to the 1990s were border posts. Bombs blew them up and British soldiers or police officers were shot. The abolition of the frontier as part of a broader EU integration process removed these targets of choice. A Brexit-induced return of a guarded frontier will provide tempting targets for any republican or nationalist extremist.

John Hume, the former Social Democratic and Labour Party (SDLP) leader and relentless opponent of the fascistic terrorism of the IRA and Sinn Féin, saw at an early stage that Europe might be a partial melting-pot in which the historical hatreds of nationalism and unionism could be partly dissolved and so it turned out. Hume told me once how his father, an educated, cultivated book-keeper could find no work in the Unionist-dominated Northern Ireland of the 1920s and 1930s. 'Then when war came and the shipyards boomed they needed every man to work as so many went off to fight in the war', he said. 'So for the first time my father had regular work and pay. But in 1945 at the war's end and the return of the Protestant soldiers he was fired as there was no chance of an Irish Catholic being treated with respect by the men who run Ulster for the English.'

As an MEP and British MP Hume worked tirelessly to secure EU funding for bridge-building between the two communities and a gradual relaxation of the once fiercely patrolled, mined and watch-towered frontier. Since 1995, the EU has contributed €1.3 billion to various pro-peace community projects or for building roads and bridges to lessen the importance of the frontier. Today you drive from the United Kingdom into Ireland much as you drive from England into Wales. There are no border posts, no obligation to show passports, no queues to search cars or vans to clear customs. The only difference is that road signs show distances in kilometres, not miles.

Now, thanks to the victory for the anti-Europeans in the Brexit plebiscite, all this coming together and slow dissolution of what was once a very hard frontier, nearly 500 km in length and traversing rough country including lakes (loughs), as well as the financial support for community development aimed at ensuring Northern Ireland never reverts to its terrible twentieth-century history of conflict and violence, may end or at least be put under considerable pressure.

In theory, an EU member state must have a clearly demarcated frontier with a non-EU member state, even if it is not vigorously enforced. Thus while there are no frontier posts if you cross the Rhine from Germany to France there are some on the main crossings from Switzerland into the EU, even if frontier guards on both sides usually wave through cars without even checking passports or identity cards. When huge waves of refugees surged into Europe fleeing violence in Iraq, Syria and Libya governments reintroduced border-crossing controls as a temporary measure to try and channel the flows.

In addition, all Irish citizens benefit from what is called the Common Travel Area (CTA) set up after Ireland separated from Britain in the 1920s. This means that every Irish citizen can live on mainland Britain with all the rights of British citizenship. Irish citizens can live, work or stand for election to local councils or even parliament without requiring any permit or visa. Altogether about 10 per cent of the UK population has at least one grandparent born in Ireland (this author included), and after 1945 up to a million Irish immigrants came to find work in Britain. The CTA could be seen as a prototype of EU free-movement principles. Even at the height of the IRA bombing campaigns on mainland England, no one suggested that free movement between Ireland and Britain should be suspended.

Both Dublin and London have made clear since Brexit that neither government is searching deliberately to create difficulties, but if Britain, for example, does withdraw from the Customs Union or bring in agricultural subsidies for UK farmers significantly different from those of the Common Agricultural Policy then it is hard to see how a soft, non-policed and unguarded frontier between the UK and Ireland can be maintained. The share of agriculture in the Northern Irish economy is two and half times that of the UK as a whole. Since the end of the three decades of violence, 1968–98, Northern Ireland has attracted considerable foreign direct investment. Food, drink and other agricultural produce make up 35 per cent of Northern Ireland's exports to the EU, compared to 10 per cent of the UK as a whole. So losing automatic tariff- and duty-free access to the EU, as well as possibly facing customs clearance checks regimes, will be a big blow to Northern Ireland. Any food scares affecting livestock would immediately lead to a shut-down of export markets for Northern Ireland's farmers. And this time there would be no British ministers and officials sitting as of right in all the EU decision-making bodies to defend Northern Irish interests, as was the case during the 'mad cow' episode.

This may explain why there was a 55 per cent vote against Brexit in the referendum, though one should never underestimate the pleasure of the Irish in voting against what rightwing and anti-European figures like Nigel Farage, Boris Johnson or Chris Grayling recommend. But politics in Northern Ireland is still frozen in an alternating power-sharing between hardline unionists in the DUP and Sinn Féin so there is no effective voice from Northern Ireland that finds any echo in the wider UK national debate on Brexit. The pro-Brexit DUP lost votes in the election in March 2017 to the Northern Ireland Assembly, while pro-European parties increased their share of the vote. This appears to confirm the trend in other elections in the UK, where there is a turn away from politicians perceived as being anti-European. Nonetheless Northern Ireland remains a sadly, badly divided community, and the impact of Brexit and heightened difficulties for the Irish government will lead to new tensions and even worse.

The fear is that Brexit and the return of an English supremacist political culture disdainful of Europeans – and the Irish see themselves as full-right Europeans, not second-class cousins of those on the superior British mainland – could reawaken old demons. There are many in Ireland who believe that the Good Friday agreement has not settled the eternal Irish question. There also many in Northern Ireland who think that Sinn Féin and its leader, Gerry Adams, is now more interested in an Irish political future. In the 2016 elections to the Irish parliament, the Dáil Éireann, Sinn Féin overtook the Labour Party to be the third biggest party in terms of votes cast.

Thus while Sinn Féin and Adams focus on Dublin, a vacuum is created in republican circles in Belfast and elsewhere in Northern Ireland. The new Northern Irish nationalists yearning for an end to being British subjects and who reject Sinn Féin's participation in a UK devolved government set up a new party three months after the Brexit vote. Called 'Saoradh', which means 'Liberation' in English, the party has opened an office in Belfast and is actively recruiting amongst former Irish republican prisoners and their supporters. They describe themselves as dissidents and reject a return to violence and the armed struggle. Another much smaller group of disaffected Northern Irish nationalists are called dissenters and they still proclaim the virtue of armed resistance to what they see as an occupying colonial state.

Elements of similar political organisation can be found in the Basque country and Corsica and they are very difficult for the established state apparatus to handle. Both London and Dublin are united in detestation of Sinn Féin and its murderous armed wing, the IRA. Working together in the EU from 1973 until 1998 allowed the democratic forces in Britain and Ireland to use the EU almost as a relationship counsellor. It opened doors to find ways out of violence and towards a new status that allowed Irish nationalists to feel they were not giving in to British domination and equally allowed the Ulster unionists to know that in accepting broader EU citizenship they could still maintain a link with Britain, hold British passports and not be seen as accepting rule from Dublin, even as they lived under the laws of the EU, which Ireland, like every other EU member state, had voted.

Dr Kevin Bean of Liverpool University follows these debates in the Northern Irish dissident and dissenter movements and argues that Brexit has raised the temperature.

> Every time we get a debate about Brexit, we get a debate about the border because it is a very immediate presence in the life of many republicans who live close to it. The overall Brexit debate is about self-determination and of where the nation is in regard to other nations. It brings back into play the idea of what is the nation. Is there a national interest in all of Ireland staying in the EU?
>
> We used to say that people who were talking about national sovereignty were living in the past. […] But this is back on the table again. Use whatever cliché you like, but the genie is out of the bottle.

Although a majority in Northern Ireland voted against Brexit, unionist Protestants formed the bulk of Leave voters and almost all the Catholic nationalists voted Remain. But neither side, at least in their public declarations, want to see a hard UK–EU border installed and most Catholic nationalists agree with the statement of Bertie Ahern, then Irish prime minister, responsible for the Dublin end of the 1998 peace agreement, that the issue of a united Ireland should not be on the agenda.

But this well-meaning and sensible conclusion ignores the fact that the peace created between the two communities in Northern Ireland was based on a loosening of twentieth-century national identification with either the British or Irish nation. The existence of a European dimension, including the concept of European citizenship, lessened the binary either Irish or British divide that had obtained throughout most of the twentieth century.

Almost every aspect of Brexit, from the border to the right of all EU citizens to travel freely to Ireland and thence onto Britain, the impact on investment and Northern Irish exports, loss of the Single Market and leaving the Customs Union, the disappearance of the European Court of Justice as a tribunal whose rulings London would accept even if the complaint was initiated by the Irish government, is now under challenge.

The senior Irish politician Phil Hogan, now Ireland's EU Commissioner, warned early in 2017 that Ireland's relationship with Britain would change.

> It would be a fundamental error on our part to place an exces-
> sive reliance on our bilateral relationship with the UK as the
> best means of ensuring that Ireland's strategic interests are best
> protected in the Brexit discussions. We have the opportunity
> to redefine and reassert Ireland's position as both committed
> Europeans and good next-door neighbours.

Hogan's cautious words reflect how far he can go as an EU offi-cial, but they also reflect the concern in Irish political circles that the Tory–UKIP axis that won Brexit has torn up the idea of power-sharing or joint sovereignty inherent in European construction. Brexit will not only require a redefinition of Anglo-Irish relations but can call into question the peace in the six counties of the Irish province of Ulster as Brexit changes the atmosphere in Ireland, north and south.

In itself, finding a satisfactory solution to Northern Ireland outside the EU and Ireland remaining a proud EU member could take years of negotiation and search for compromise. That time is not available under the short period of the Article 50 negotiations. In December 2016 Michel Barnier said: 'The UK's decision to leave the European Union will have consequences. In particular, perhaps, for what are the EU's external borders today. All I can say at this moment in time is that I am personally extremely aware of the importance of this particular topic.'

Barnier was the EU commissioner for regional development when the Northern Ireland peace agreement was ratified and he supported it generously with EU funds from his budget, so he was being sincere when he stated: 'We will, throughout these negotiations with the UK and of course with Ireland, do our utmost to find a way in order to preserve the success of the Good Friday process and, of course, retain the dialogue there.'

After 1997 there were only two key players at government level to bring about the peace settlement that ended 30 years of murder, torture and terrorist bombings arising from the Northern Ireland dispute over the meaning of nationhood. They were the prime ministers of Britain and Ireland, Tony Blair and Bertie Ahern. They had two teams of experienced, thoughtful, politically sensitive negotiators and the watchful involvement of the United States.

In the greater scheme of Brexit, Northern Ireland is a sideshow. Today there are 27 other EU heads of government who seem determined that the vote against Europe, won by 20-year campaign against EU membership waged by nationalist forces in England, will not weaken or undermine the European Union they wish to preserve and strengthen. Barnier may want a reasonable solution, but can the Conservative government constituted under its leading Brexit hardliners and a prime minister who needs to keep her anti-European party happy be able to offer any compromise? Dublin's low tax regime for US multinationals that make a fortune selling services and products in Europe but locate head offices in Dublin so as to avoid paying much tax has not endeared the Irish government to its European colleagues.

Apple, for example paid an effective tax-rate of 0.5 per cent to the Irish government and the European Commission required Apple to pay US$14.5 billion in back taxes to the Irish government since the tax-breaks Dublin offered Apple were a form of state aid. The Irish government has said it will join with Apple to appeal this ruling to the European Court of Justice. All this will be happening at the same time as the UK Brexit negotiations get under way. It not likely that there will much sympathy for the Irish government if it seeks some deal over the border with Northern Ireland that allows something like the status quo to be maintained. That would mean a special treatment of the UK which other EU governments are unlikely easily to concede, especially as they feel Dublin has connived with some of the richest economic actors on the planet to stop other European governments at least getting some tax from the profits made from sales across the EU.

Nigel Farage and some pro-Brexit Tory MPs have suggested that Ireland should also quit the EU and perhaps join the Commonwealth so that in place of the president of the European Council the Irish could live under the British monarch. Laughable? Yes. But the question of Ireland never featured much in the Brexit debates and it is doubtful if many who voted for or against Brexit paused for a moment to reflect on what the vote might mean for peace in Northern Ireland. But amongst the many, many questions Brexit has thrown up once again, as in the history of all the British Isles throughout the ages, a strident vote for English nationalist supremacy may have untold consequences.

Scotland has also been changed by Brexit. Many Scots see a Conservative–UKIP axis of English nationalists confiscating Scotland's right to be able to live freely as a European nation enjoying all the rights of other Europeans while remaining part of the UK. Theresa May has been wagging her southern English finger at the Scots, lecturing them on being better off in a Union with England while at the same time siding with those in her party desirous of the full destruction of the Union with other European countries.

In effect, the Brexit vote was a godsend to Scottish separatist politicians like Nicola Sturgeon and Alex Salmond in the Scottish National Party (SNP). They had been exercising sole power in Scotland for some years while presiding over an under-performing economy, an NHS inferior to the health service south of the border and seeing Scottish education results sink in the annual PISA ranking of school performance carried out each year by the OECD.

After 23 June 2016, Mrs Sturgeon could ignore the unimpressive performance of her party as the government of Scotland and instead return to the favourite music of Scottish nationalism – blaming England for all of Scotland's problems. She kept brandishing the menace of a new independence referendum. Mrs Sturgeon knows the risk. As in Quebec, separatists can lose one referendum (as the SNP did in 2014) but if two are lost the question of independence is lost for a long time.

Opinion polls in Scotland remained divided 50–50, but if, for example, Scotland starts to lose foreign investment when the UK as a whole loses access to the Single Market and there are other economic negatives following a full amputation Brexit, then the Scots may decide their future is as a small independent nation in the EU rather than as a junior partner of an isolated England.

When dismissing the idea of Britain taking part in the very first stages of European cooperation and integration in the 1950s, the Labour foreign secretary, Ernest Bevin, said: 'If we open that Pandora's Box, all sorts of Trojan horses will jump out.' The Brexit vote and the insistence that it must be a hard Brexit has indeed opened Pandora's Box as far as Northern Ireland and Scotland are concerned.

PART FOUR

WHY BREXIT WILL CHANGE EUROPE

19

HOW EUROPE CAN SURVIVE BREXIT

Europe and the European Union now enter a new era. Following Brexit, many intelligent and clear-sighted supporters have written of the EU facing possible disintegration. The centrifugal forces in Europe have received a major boost from the British vote for Brexit.

The American historian Robert O. Paxton has written important studies of the origins of fascism. He lists, in *The Autonomy of Fascism*, as one of the sources of the rise of fascistic politics in Europe after 1920 the politics of an 'obsessive preoccupation with community decline, humiliation, or victimhood'. Europe is not reliving its inter-war years, though aspects of the economic crisis and the rise of nationalism have some parallels. But for today's anti-European political militants in Britain, France, Germany, Greece or the Nordic countries and the Netherlands, the rhetoric that Brussels has humiliated or victimised the nation and that the former national community has disappeared to the profit of a post-national economic and multicultural order which turns citizens into victims of the Brussels bureaucracy is vivid and strong.

The collapse of confidence in liberalism or Christian and social democracy based on partnership and co-determination has opened the door to a strident national identitarianism amplified by new forms of media communication which are post-truth and ignore facts as well as despising the give-and-take arguments of representative parliamentarianism.

It would be a foolish head of government who submitted a new EU treaty to a plebiscite, but the clamour for referendums on EU questions grows daily.

If Europe is to move forward, or move anywhere new, rules are needed. The EU is a legal construction shaped by international treaty law. Strip away the visionary oratory starting with Churchill's 'United States of Europe' appeal in September 1946 and what we have is the practical creation that has allowed European peoples to come together in a manner never known before in their history. Statesmen created the EU as a system of rules and regulations enshrined in international law.

Thanks to the Brexit vote a Conservative/UKIP mainly white majority in England has now said it does not care for reciprocal obligations and duties that are inherent in any international treaty organisation. Britain was encouraged by many of its elite politicians, business leaders and editors in taking that decision. But the decision has been made and cannot be wished away.

So all of Europe now has to decide how it reacts to the Brexit decision. There can be no Euexit. Europe cannot leave Europe. But equally it cannot be business as usual for the national heads of government or such EU institutions as the Commission, the Parliament, the European Court of Justice or the Central Bank, which decide Europe's policy and how to interpret, enforce or turn a blind eye to the EU's existing rules. Brexit will change Britain but also change Europe.

The Luxembourg politician Jean-Claude Juncker, president of the European Commission, put it well:

> There is an existential crisis in Europe. We must stop talking about the United States of Europe. The people of Europe don't want it. They like their land, their diversity. If they think Europe is on the way to becoming a state they reject it. Europe cannot be

built against the will of nations. Nations will last. Europe must be a complement to nations.

Juncker is fond of the 'last-chance saloon' metaphor for the EU. As he told a seminar in Paris in October 2016: 'It's the last chance we have to get Europe going again. We need to modernise the economy and make it a digital economy. We need a Europe with a real energy policy. Public finances have to return to health.'

Back in Brussels, officials in the EU Commission's finance and regional directorates circulated a paper which stated 'More and more citizens are losing faith in the Union's project – as it fails to provide them with confidence and hope for a better future.'

Who can disagree with that? But before we get to a workable solution for the European malaise of which Brexit is the most dramatic symptom, we have to ask more basic questions.

Firstly, what is Europe? A leading Eurosceptic over the years in Britain is the former governor of the Bank of England, Mervyn King. He had to keep his view under wraps when he was the UK's central banker, but no one who saw him at seminars or had private talks with him could doubt his hostility. Like many in the monolingual London establishment there was never any sense that King understood how other countries in Europe worked and saw themselves. He incarnates the 1980s Thatcher generation that lives in the world of the London wealthy and believes in the innate superiority of anything England does. Six months after Brexit he insisted that 'being out of what is a pretty unsuccessful European Union [...] gives us opportunities'.

Yet are countries like Germany, Austria, the Netherlands, large regions in France or northern Italy, or the Nordic nations really so unsuccessful? If Lord King visited many regions of Britain he would see levels of poverty, unsuccessful firms, poor public services and many, many smaller businesses only able to survive because of taxpayer-subsidised employment using low-pay European citizens. It is all too easy to set up the straw man of the EU, which has undertaken and is still undertaking the herculean task of bringing the backward, impoverished, ex-dictatorship nations of Europe up to the level of modern economic functioning all would wish to achieve.

Britain's productivity, indebtedness, deficit, education standards for poorer members of the community, much of its public transport, old-age care, balance of trade deficits, failure to collect taxes, its bloated prison population are not hallmarks of a highly advanced nation. Martin Wolf, chief economics commentator at the *Financial Times*, lists the UK's

> longstanding supply-side failings. The list includes: low investment, particularly in infrastructure; inadequate basic education of much of the population and the innumeracy of its elite; a grossly distorted housing market; over-centralisation of government; and a corporate sector whose leaders are motivated more by the share price than by the long-term health of the business.

Boris Johnson put it equally sharply in a *Daily Telegraph* column in May 2013 when he wrote: 'If we left the EU […] we would have to recognise that most of our problems are not caused by Brussels but by chronic British short-termism, inadequate management, sloth, low skills, a culture of easy gratification and under-investment in both human and physical capital and infrastructure.' Of course Johnson has performed more U-turns than a stock-car racer and may yet turn and find favour with Europe if that is where public opinion heads over the next years and is his best chance of entering 10 Downing Street.

If that happens he will discover that the UK is a nation state and is responsible for its failings. Europe or the EU is not a nation, still less a state, and it is foolish to blame failures by nation states within the EU on the EU's existence.

The EU is not a state, even if it has many presidents – of the Commission, of the Council, of the Parliament, of the Central Bank, to name the most prominent. It makes and enforces rules. But so do scores of other international treaty organisations. William Gladstone, Britain's Liberal prime minister for four terms in the nineteenth century, declared that for Britain the 'arbitrament of the court is preferable to the arbitrament of the sword'. Each international organisation, from the World Health Organization to the IATA or the International Labour Organization, issues rules – laws, directives, conventions – which are binding on member states. They help guarantee – one hopes – a healthier world, safe air transportation and decent conditions at work.

The EU also makes rules – called directives in Eurospeak – to help ensure – that at least is the intention – full access to a market of 500 million consumers for anything made in Britain or any service that British creative or professional sectors like publishing or architecture may wish to market across the Channel. There are still many barriers to commerce across frontiers within the EU. Try and buy a house in France, for example, and one hits a mish-mash of French laws and customs about buying a property that require using a notary, a local lawyer, who takes his cut from the transaction.

National rules on professional qualifications or protection of citizens' money when placed with pension or insurance funds still exist. Judges and lawyers who plead in court tend to be under national control, but legal advice, the drawing up of contracts and other legal work not involving court appearances may now take place across European borders.

Universities are bastions of protection, as many across Europe insist that the diplomas and degrees awarded in other countries have no validity when it comes to offering full, tenured posts to foreigners. Indeed if there is one area of Europe crying out for reform it is the university sector. Take out British universities, which are full of foreign professors, lecturers and above all students, and there is not a single EU institution in the world top 25 universities. Dutch universities now do their undergraduate teaching in English, as the clever Dutch realise they have to adapt to the world's *lingua franca* if Dutch higher education is to flourish and serve the national interests of the Netherlands. By contrast British universities will be crippled if the Brexit ministers get their way and slow down the arrival of foreign students and teachers as part of curbing immigration. Universities in North America and Asia have helped source important breakthroughs in new economic added-value activities. Continental European university protectionism has been one of the biggest areas of failure in EU integration, failing also to develop Europe's universities towards world-beating excellence, teaching students from all over the world and attracting the best minds to work and help grow the EU.

The example of second-class universities shows that the national traditions and the historical culture and emphasis on the nation state continues to permeate the EU. It was not meant to be thus. From day one of European integration it was agreed it would be based on the pooling of national sovereignty. In the middle of the last century the key source of energy was coal and the most important national product was steel. In order to bind together the nations of Europe it was agreed the coal and steel industries of Germany, France, Italy, the Netherlands, Belgium and Luxembourg would be placed under a supranational body, the European Coal and Steel Community.

At the time, this was seen as a fundamental break with Europe's previous focus on the nation state as the only or highest form of political and economic organisation. Twice in the previous 40 years the nation states of Europe had gone to war. Now it was time to try something different. The European Coal and Steel Community was governed by a High Authority, whose members were nominated by governments. They were accountable to a parliamentary assembly – consisting of MPs from the six participating countries, who thus got to know each other and work cooperatively, both to defend their own national needs and also to do so in a wider context of European cooperation. There was a court, so that differences between, say, German approaches to its privately owned steel firms and the nationalised French steel industry could be settled and judgements enforced. It was agreed that hiring in these industries could not be done on the basis of national discrimination. This is the origin of the concept of free movement of workers.

To be sure, at any stage, one of the six countries could have walked out. They retained full sovereignty if they decided that what was being agreed at a supranational level was so unacceptable it justified leaving the treaty organisation – much as Britain has done with the Brexit plebiscite.

The British stayed out. Labour ministers in 1950 were unable to see that sharing a little sovereignty would do no harm to Britain. Once the Conservatives were returned to power from 1951 to 1964 they rejected the supranational authority of the ECSC. When the six continental nations decided to move forward to a broader common market Britain again kept its distance.

Hapless Tory prime minister Anthony Eden refused to participate in the Messina conference in 1956 which negotiated the Treaty of Rome. Eden is more famous in history for the disaster of his Suez invasion fiasco, when President Eisenhower called him and said: 'Anthony. Are you mad?!' His Old Etonian successor, David Cameron, had managed to achieve both the disaster of his intervention in Libya (jointly with Nicolas Sarkozy) and Brexit, and future historians will struggle to find a British prime minister with a record of such spectacular failure as Cameron's plebiscite.

In 1956, Eden despatched a minor Whitehall civil servant to Messina with Britain's message to Europe's prime ministers: 'Gentlemen, you are trying to negotiate something you will never be able to negotiate. But if negotiated it will not be ratified. And if ratified it will not work!' The Treaty of Rome celebrated its sixtieth birthday in 2017.

Yet it was not a happy birthday. Britain removing its significant net contribution to the EU budget means a major recalibration of the money the EU can spend, especially in poorer EU countries that have got used to significant transfer payments from Brussels. The loss of the UK net contribution to the EU budget will be offset, assuming full Brexit occurs, by EU revenue arising from levying duties on imports from the UK into Europe, but whatever the final balance, there is no doubt that the UK no longer paying its share into the common EU budget will be damaging.

No one has any clear idea of where Europe and the EU should now go. Almost every week there is a learned or perhaps a polemical book from an academic, a politician, an intellectual or a journalist seeking to describe the EU's malaise and then suggesting ways of reinvigorating the tired, sagging body. In a sense Brexit is almost a welcome experiment, as we shall see if a country that decides to leave the EU can not only survive but flourish.

The Brexit vote was part of the unfolding process of the failure of globalised capitalism to win new generations of political support. Post-national capitalism is confronted with a trilemma. It has been unable to deliver or get into alignment shared economic prosperity, social investment and progress, and a stable programme of development for poorer countries, including those who have joined the EU in the twenty-first century.

Post-national capitalism wants workers to be available at a moment's notice, especially to generate wealth in the new people-intensive industries of cafés, bars, cleaning, caring and transport. Modern capitalism long ago gave up on any sense of a national social contract to train young men and women and give them skills in the non-graduate labour market.

Despite the grandiose claims of 'Social Europe', and despite the undoubted protection that EU law does provide for employees, the swift and uncontrolled movement of people across frontiers and arriving as immigrants in local labour markets has caused tension and stress that the EU has not found an answer to.

In general, increases in trade and in commercial exchanges have motored ahead of growth since the era of globalisation began at the end of the 1970s. Trade increased 6 per cent each year in the 1990s while world growth overall increased by an annual 3 per cent. Between 1950 and 1990 trade was the magnet that pulled along economic growth. This era is over. Global growth in 2016 is a little over 3 per cent (according to the IMF, it would have been higher but Brexit has introduced massive uncertainty into economic and investment decision making). Trade flows increased in 2016 by just 1.7 per cent. Protectionism led to all the candidates who ran for US president in 2016 saying they would ditch the US–Pacific trade deal. German and French political leaders have flatly rejected the proposed trade deal between the US and the EU – TTIP, the Transatlantic Trade and Investment Partnership.

This rise of neo-protectionism can be seen in the increase of individual protectionist measures by national governments. There were 50 in 2008, 1,200 today. Brexit was part of this slow rise of protectionism. The advocates of Brexit promised to protect the British people against the arrival of unwanted foreigners. They said they would protect British workers by claiming that wages would increase if no more non-British workers were allowed to take jobs in the UK. They claimed they would protect British firms from the EU external tariffs or paperwork.

The natural reaction of any citizen is to want to be protected from negative pressures and claimed threats from outside the nation. The troika of protectionism, nationalism and xenophobia constitutes a powerful political battering-ram at any time. But as trade, growth and fair distribution all quietly decline, the appeal of populist-nationalism, economic protectionism and foreigner blame-games is hard to resist. The parallels with the political language of the 1930s is clear in the denunciation of cosmopolitan internationalism from Brexit politicians.

There are also worrying parallels with the rejection of the trans-pacific and transatlantic trade deals. They are not quite at the level of the Smoot–Hawley tariffs on 20,000 goods imported into America in 1930, which ushered in the collapse of world economic growth and depressed trade. Nor has anti-trade ideology reached the level of the London conference of 68 nations in 1933, when the US refused any debt relief to European nations, much as today Germany refuses to consider debt relief for Greece. Nonetheless, history at least suggests that when barriers and frontiers are put up to the exchange of goods, ideas, people and money-making services then the outcome is bad for economic growth and bad for democratic politics.

Will Brexit be the catalyst for European renewal? Or will it further expose the fault-lines in the EU as anti-Europeans devoutly hope, so that following Brexit the EU slowly sinks under the weight of its contradiction and begins to disintegrate?

Dick Pels is a Dutch political writer and university lecturer who recently published *A Heart for Europe: The Case for Europatriotism*. He argues that:

> European civilisation is the never-ending quest for a more gentle, more relaxed, less dangerous society. But Europe currently faces a 'perfect storm' of populist nationalism, Russian revanchism, neoliberal financial havoc, religious terrorism and refugee chaos. Given these challenges, we urgently need to rethink our ideals of peace, freedom, democracy and sustainability, in order to reinvent the idea of a civilised European patriotism.

Wow! The EU must sort out peace, freedom, democracy and sustainability! Altogether or one after another? I may be in tune with Mr Pels, but these are huge demands to make of an imperfect institution that needs to be made to work better, not turn the world into a paradise on Earth.

Pierre Moscovici, the veteran French social democratic politician, who has held senior ministerial positions in France and then became the EU Commissioner for Financial Affairs, has argued for greater European integration based on the members of the eurozone. At first sight that makes sense. Yet the eurozone is far more heterogeneous than its apparent unity may lead one to believe. Annual per capita incomes range from US$11,000 in Slovakia to US$110,000 in Luxembourg. One eurozone nation, Cyprus, remains partly occupied by a foreign power, Turkey, which has now been repudiated as a possible EU member state by the European Parliament. Another eurozone nation, Ireland, is inextricably bound in with the United Kingdom economic space. In fact, London and British taxpayers bailed out Ireland after the 2007/9 financial crash and subsequent collapse of Irish and British banks even as the UK government haughtily rejected any involvement in the wider rescue financing of Europe.

Some eurozone nations run big deficits – they borrow more than they receive in tax and other income – while others like Germany have significant surpluses which they are loath to share out with eurozone economies that refuse to balance their books or take the kind of painful economic reform decisions that Germany did as a result of unification, not to mention the need to recapitalise and make competitive German manufacturing industry, as happened under the Gerhard Schröder government at the beginning of the century. Sandro Gozi, Italy's Europe minister and one of the most thoughtful and forceful of the next generation of European politicians, complains that in the second five-year term of the European Commission president José Manuel Barroso between 2009 and 2014, 'the European Commission gave up its role and became a secretariat for national heads of government ever anxious not to oppose them. Berlaymont [the home of the European Commission] was reduced to a pointless building full of offices.'

Yet whenever the European Commission pleaded with the Italian government of Matteo Renzi in which Sandro Gozi served to obey core

EU rules on debt and deficit and to reform the economy, especially its banks, along lines agreed at EU level, the Commission was told to go away and stop telling sovereign Italy what to do. The idea of a unified Europe based on the eurozone is easy to declare as an ambition. Yet unless national governments of Europe post-Brexit are as willing to share sovereignty like the generation of, say, Kohl, Thatcher and Mitterrand in the 1980s, the stubborn reality of national priorities and preferences will come to replace the integrated cooperation and accepting a common rule book that is essential to make the EU function.

Pierre Moscovici also insists:

> We need to strengthen the European Parliament. How can we do that? By proceeding with the 'Europeanization' of European elections. This implies continuing to elect the *Spitzenkandidaten* – the lead candidates chosen by the different political families to run for the presidency of the Commission. It also implies creating transnational lists and strengthening its role of supervisor and democratic monitor, including when it comes to economic governance of the euro area.

Has this got the process the wrong way round? It is not the European Parliament that needs strengthening but the role of national parliaments representing the populations of Europe in the democratic supervision of EU decisions. At every European Parliament election since MEPs were first directly elected in 1979 participation has gone down – from 62 per cent in 1979 to 42 per cent 35 years later in 2014. Curiously the exception is the UK, where participation has risen from 32 per cent in 1979 to 35.6 per cent in 2014. But with two-thirds of British voters not bothering to vote for MEPs the latter lack credibility, especially when the European Parliament vote is used to express prejudice and emotion that borders on old-fashioned xenophobic nationalism. Some countries have shockingly low participation in European

Parliament elections. In 2014 just 23.8 per cent of Poles voted to send representatives to the European Parliament and the figures were lower in the Czech Republic (18.2 per cent) and Slovakia (13.05 per cent).

So it is hard to see an institution that commands ever-decreasing support in terms of electing its members by the wider European population as the beating heart of European democracy.

Indeed there may be a case for arguing that if a nation cannot mobilise more than a quarter or a third of its electorate to vote for representation in the Strasbourg Parliament it should simply not be permitted to have MEPs and instead nominate national MPs, as is the case in the parliamentary assembly of the Council of Europe. This may be harsh but would oblige some political education in Europe about the importance of democratic control and surveillance of EU decisions.

As it is, too many political parties use the European Parliament as a kind of rest home for former ministers or party officials who need an income. In Britain, the European Parliament was used in the past as a kind of holding pen for ambitious young politicians like the former Liberal Democratic leader Nick Clegg, until they won seats in the Commons. It therefore does not have a continuity or permanent *esprit de corps*. Over the years there have been numerous scandals over pay and expenses. Nigel Farage boasted in the 2009 election that he had claimed £2 million in expenses and allowances from the European Parliament, which puts in the shade the moneys MPs helped themselves to in the House of Commons expenses scandal. Thanks to pay, staffing and allowances for offices back home, the European Parliament has been an important financial source for the promotion of anti-European populist and identity politics of both the right and left.

Few MEPs are held accountable by the national or local media for what they do in Strasbourg and Brussels, and as long as they turn up for a few moments and sign an attendance register they can be very well remunerated. And some from nationalist-populist identitarian parties like UKIP or the Front National in France use the European Parliament mainly as a propaganda platform to attack the EU and obtain funds for anti-EU propaganda back home. On both the hard left and right there are parties that make populist appeals that win seats in the low-turnout elections to the European Parliament and then make no constructive parliamentary contribution to the often detailed and boring oversight work of committees.

There are many diligent, thoughtful and hardworking MEPs, and the signals they send via their collective decisions – such as calling for an end to EU negotiations on Turkey's membership – are important. But whereas there are 750 MEPs, there are also around 10,000 members of lower and upper houses of national parliaments and many more elected representatives in countries like Germany or Scotland where regional parliaments are important. These elected parliamentarians are the real core of representative democracy. It would be useful to associate national parliaments with the work of the European Parliament. One mechanism would be to create a second chamber – a kind of European Senate – consisting of national parliamentarians. Another would be to build joint committees covering all the main directorates of the European Commission so that national MPs were directly involved in overseeing the work of the Commission.

A third would be for more joint committees of inquiry to produce special reports relating to EU-wide policy. Much more oversight over EU policy can already be undertaken by national parliaments, including the House of Commons, on their own initiative. One of David Cameron's first acts when he became prime minister in 2010 was to abolish the regular House of Commons debate that preceded each EU Council meeting and which obliged ministers to come to the floor of the Commons to explain the UK government's approach to EU decisions. This was part of Cameron's disdain for and dislike of the EU as an institution. The losers were the British people, who have no idea of how little interest their MPs take in European policy and directives.

The Danish parliament has set up a committee that requires all Danish government decisions on Europe or proposals for changes in EU policy to be first debated and agreed before ministers are allowed to speak or vote in Brussels. Something similar could be set up in all national parliaments so that elected national representatives would have oversight of EU politics and policy.

Unfortunately the House of Commons, which sees itself as a very superior body, especially in relationship to the European Parliament, refuses to alter its practices to allow MPs to become involved in EU affairs. MPs who take a serious interest in EU policy are mocked as Europhiles, and getting reimbursement for any travel in Europe to link with other parliamentarians or MEPs is difficult, with accusations of 'junketeering' thrown at any MP who thinks finding out on the spot what is going on in Europe is part of his or her job.

There could also be term-limits on MEPs so that no one who had lost a national seat or job as a minister could be instantly parachuted into Strasbourg, with a maximum of two or three five-year terms, meaning that MEPs were regularly renewed and the European Parliament rejuvenated.

Politics cannot be wished away. Any half-awake journalist covering the EU can draw up a list of desirable reforms or make pertinent criticisms without having to write one of the long books that intellectuals and professors opining on the EU love to produce.

But somehow most elected politicians in Europe feel left out of the business of the EU. A major priority post-Brexit should be to downscale the grandiose buildings and declarations in Brussels and reconnect the EU to democratic politics at the level of the nation state, sub-nation and region.

20

WHAT IS TO BE DONE?

I patrol bookshops in the main EU capitals and I cannot think of a single book about Europe that I have seen produced in more than at best two languages. This remains one of the fundamental problems of European discussion. There is no common EU history, philosophy, intellectual opinion-shaper, journalist or media that fully transcends borders.

Worthy efforts are made but most flounder on the problem of language. Occasionally a pan-European historian like the late Tony Judt or political commentators like Timothy Garton Ash or Josef Joffé will get a book or commentaries published in newspapers outside England or Germany. At an elite level papers like the *Financial Times* or *The Economist* have a pan-European readership but appeal only to English-reading very important people. *Politico* is an excellent weekly with sprightly daily web bulletins but only for Brussels insiders and EU obsessives. The German, Spanish, Italian, Polish or Dutch newspapers are not read outside the respective countries. Even *Le Monde* has a limited readership outside Francophone Europe. *Euronews* cannot match *Russia Today* for pace and vividness of TV news presentation and is not routinely available. I have never come across a British minister, for example, who as a matter of routine read a continental newspaper or political weekly.

Democratic politics depends on public opinion, which is influenced by history, today's political leaders and the media. But how can the EU fashion a democratic politics and shape public opinion when it has no history in the sense of war, conquest, culture or sense of meaning? It has no common media and many elected politicians in EU states find it easier to condemn and blame the EU rather than support it.

In 2017 the EU celebrated the sixtieth anniversary of the founding Treaty of Rome (1957). Compared to many European states, the EU is a toddler, barely out of nappies. While the EU is young, Europe is getting older and has stopped having babies. Thanks to its open borders to immigration from Asia, Britain is one of the few EU nations with a growing population. But even in Britain the share of the active employed population has fallen below the inactive population (those without work, the young, retired people and others) and the UK needs more healthy, young, tax-paying workers if it is to survive, let alone thrive. Elsewhere Europe is ceasing to reproduce itself and one reason for maintaining free movement of workers is to have enough younger low-pay workers to look after ageing Europeans who are in need of care from younger people to wash, clean and feed them.

The figures are alarming. In Italy more than 50 per cent of voters are over 50. There are only six professors out of 13,000 in Italy under 40. In Britain, over the next seven years, an estimated 12.5 million jobs will be opened up through people leaving the workforce and an additional 2 million new jobs will be created, yet only 7 million younger people will be newly available to enter the workforce to fill these jobs. For the first time in British history we have fewer people at work than the rest of the population. Is it really so dreadful to have a few hundred thousand Poles or Italians coming to live and work in Britain, and gradually integrating into our population the way my father and grandmother did? Europeans have stopped making love or at least stopped making love in a way that makes babies.

Europeans retire far too early to eke out a third of their life on a pension and become increasingly dependent on supplementary social assistance paid for by taxpayers. The pension age of 65 was dreamt up by Bismarck when the nineteenth-century German leader introduced Europe's first national pension system. Average male life expectancy in Germany in the 1870s was 49 so many more paid into the pension insurance scheme than were paid from it. Today there should be every encouragement for older people to work. The Nordic countries have shown how to keep the over-sixties in work, whereas half of citizens of other EU countries have stopped working by the age of 55. The Duke of Edinburgh, a Greek-Danish immigrant, only retired when he was 95 – a model for others in Europe?

The current EU population of just over half a billion is expected to shrink to 450 million by 2050. Nor is Europe overcrowded. You can drive for miles in most European nations and see mainly open land. In the 1930s those campaigning against Jews coming to Britain from Nazi Germany said the island was 'overcrowded'. Then the population of the UK was 30 million, less than half of what it is today. Only 7 per cent of the UK is built-up urban dwelling, office and factory space.

Should Europe take more responsibility for its own defence? Winston Churchill, speaking in August 1950 at the Council of Europe, urged the 'immediate creation of a unified European army'. Europe is still waiting. Curiously, one of the first acts of European leaders post-Brexit was to call for the creation of structures that could give rise to a European army. There were proposals to set up an EU-based head-quarters for coordination of Europe's different military forces. The Czech prime minister supported the idea, as did Italy's Europe minister, Sandro Gozi, who said he would like to see a European army created 'yesterday'.

The Czech Republic spends just 1 per cent of GDP on defence and Italy spends 1.3 per cent – both well below the 2 per cent of GDP which is the standard NATO expects of its members. In both countries defence expenditure has gone down despite the threat of Russian aggressive posturing, the continuing neighbourhood crises that Europe faces and the constant urging from the United States that Europe accepts more responsibility for defence. The eastern and southern Mediterranean is a mixture of conflict zone and a region where people-smuggling and - trafficking, the transportation of illegal immigrants, occasionally of jihadists, into Europe, is rife.

This is Europe's most important external frontier but it is without defence, regular patrols or aggressive naval action against criminals. Instead of allocating more of their national budgets to control Europe's external borders and send messages about readiness to defend European interests, Prague and Rome want someone else to do the job. In fact, the EU minus Britain, post-Brexit, will lose a major defence capability. EU nations produce 37 different types of tank or armoured vehicle, 18 different types of warplane and 7 different types of naval frigate. The duplication and refusal to copy Airbus and have a single or just a few military products reveal how backward and protectionist EU nations are.

Angela Merkel blocked any efforts to merge German with French tank manufacturers or the proposed merger of the French defence firm, Thales, and the German led EADS consortium. As a result the EU is incoherent on defence, but no less incoherent than the US under President Obama, who all but gave up its global responsibility for the defence of the democratic world – a posture likely to be aggravated by President Trump with his neo-isolationist rhetoric about countries paying more for their defence if they wanted to count on American support and partnership.

In fact, Europe spends nearly four times as much on defence as Russia, and just four countries – Britain, France, Germany and Italy – spend US$188.6 billion on defence compared to Russia's $65 billion defence budget. Russia gets more bang for its buck in the sense that it can use its military to intervene in Georgia and Ukraine and menace

Baltic states with overflight and cyber-interference. But the West also used its military to invade Iraq and overturn the state in Libya, and used its money to support efforts to topple Assad in Syria.

There is uncertainty on the US military profile in Europe following President Trump's election. However, the powerful US military-industrial complex is unlikely to turn its back on European engagement and all-important arms sales within a single presidential term. Trump's appointment of a range of generals to key posts in his administration suggests that the Pentagon, with its acute sense of America's geo-political role and responsibilities, will trump, as it were, the capricious isolationist utterances of the 2016 election campaign.

As on the economic front, the weakness of Europe lies with its southern member states, which have seen a much sharper decline in defence spending this century compared to northern Europe. Greece feels permanently threatened by Turkey, whose NATO warplanes regularly invade Greek airspace by flying over islands in the eastern Mediterranean that are indisputably Greek.

Indeed, such threat against Europe comes from the south not the north, despite the impossibility of persuading Vladimir Putin to stop willy-waving with his military arsenal. But he's Russian, and until some major change in how the Kremlin sees the world occurs we must assume that Russian posturing will continue as normal.

Of greater concern is the threat from the southern and eastern shorelines of Europe – namely Arab Africa and the Middle East. This is the source of the ideological Islamism which justifies and extols the killing of non-Muslims and indeed Muslims on any number of grounds. In 1994, then King Hassan of Morocco met the European Commission president, Jacques Delors, in Rabat. The King told Delors that he had 5 million peasants or small farmers who would like to export their tomatoes to the EU. Delors, well aware of the fears of EU peasant-farmers of imports that would threaten their livelihoods, temporised. The King smiled and said, 'Monsieur le president, don't worry.

I understand your problems. But if today Morocco cannot export its tomatoes in ten years' time we shall be exporting terrorists.'

And so it came to pass. A decade later in 2004, Moroccan Islamist killers planted bombs at Madrid's main railway station. Over 200 people were killed and the government was defeated at the election held shortly afterwards, as the then rightwing prime minister tried to blame the Basque separatist ETA terror organisation. That was political stupidity on his part.

Nor is it the case that poverty or lack of democracy is the main driver of European terrorism, as the attacks in rich countries like France, Germany and Britain suggest. Islamist terrorism is driven by an ideological project rooted in rejection of democracy, women's rights and above all hatred of Jews and the existence of Israel. Tackling this is a long-term project but one the EU should engage in if it wants to defend it values.

The Mediterranean needs a strong presence of European naval, coastguard and police vessels able to intercept people-trafficking boats and return them to the African coastline. A simple arms build-up against Russia is not the priority. Investing in defeating cyber-attacks on democracy coming from Russia is. Indeed, as with the Cold War era broadcasts by the democratic world's BBC World Service, Deutsche Welle, Radio France Internationale and Radio Free Europe, amongst others, which sent accurate news and messages of hope to the peoples of Eastern Europe under Soviet occupation, the EU should invest in modern media messaging to give the Russians, the Iranians and the Arab world accurate information and the chance to discuss issues that are not possible without conditions of freedom of expression.

The key question however is: how can Europe start growing again? Jean Monnet is reported to have said: 'If I was starting all over again, I would begin with culture.' Historians cannot find an actual source for this widely attributed remark, which those in the culture and creative sectors love to cite, for obvious reasons. In fact, Monnet and all the serious builders of Europe, including Margaret Thatcher, have understood in a deep Gramscian sense that the material base of Europe – the economic relations between European citizens – is by far the most important source of legitimacy for European integration. A Europe that cannot be shown to be adding value to people's lives via the common currency, the open-border trading system and the movement of workers or the adoption of enforced directives on CO_2 emissions will start losing the support of a majority of its citizens, or the elected politicians of its member states.

In that sense, even given the uniquely poisonous cocktail of lies, weak leadership by David Cameron and Jeremy Corbyn and rank xenophobia that produced the Brexit vote, it would be foolish to deny that the lack of growth, economic energy, job creation and some distributive fairness evident in too many sectors of the EU's collective economy since 2000 laid the foundations for Brexit and indeed for all the other referendum rejections of Europe in plebiscites this century.

So what are the ways forward? A first measure would be to understand that change is constant. In 1980, the world was seen as overwhelmed by 'waves of change, colliding and overlapping. [...] In this bewildering context, businessmen swim against highly erratic economic currents; politicians see their ratings bob up and down [...] value systems splinter and crash' as the world lived with 'the deepest social upheaval and creative restructuring of all time.' This over-excited hyperbole was from the best-selling book *The Third Wave* by the futurologist Alvin Toffler, written four decades ago. Today there are plenty of commentators and writers to tell us that we are living in equally challenging and fast-changing times. Just so, but by any definition Europeans, even with all their problems, live a far better life than they did in 1980 and intelligent political choices can help.

As the British economic historian Harold James shows in his book written with Markus Brunnermeier and Jean-Pierre Landau, *The Euro and the Battle of Ideas* (2016), there are no immutable truths about how nations approach economic decision making. There have been times when France was excessively liberal and Germany keen on state intervention and deficit spending, even if more recently the opposite economic theories and practice appear more in evidence. Germany began from *Stunde nul* (zero hour) in 1945 and invented its own social market economy. The 1947 programme of Germany's Christian Democratic Party began by stating 'The capitalist era is over', and Germany was built on the basis of a weak, almost non-existent central state, the presence of trade union representatives on the boards of all companies, a devotion to rule of law (*Rechtsstaat*) and a belief in compromise, conciliation and consensus in a manner almost Swiss in its obsession with avoiding dominant leadership by the state or its political leadership. Every German government since the war has been a coalition, just as Europe's richest country, Switzerland, has been run since 1959 by a federal cabinet which has equal balance between liberals, socialists and conservatives. Perhaps coalition rather than single-party government is one way forward for better government in Europe?

Germany has been the first major state to adopt Green ideas as state policy, culminating in Angela Merkel's decision to pull out of nuclear power. In 1990, Germany took on the burden of financing the incorporation of the bankrupt, almost third-world state of East Germany and bringing it up to West German standards. West Germans were heavily taxed to pay for this remarkable achievement. It was a far bigger transfer in financial terms than the support the US provided via the Marshall Plan. German workers accepted a pay freeze in order to recapitalise German industry at the end of the 1990s, and Germany has provided capital and market access as well as open frontiers to workers from its Eastern European neighbours in a giant project of stabilising the ex-communist world after the collapse of the Soviet Russian imperium. By any standards the solidarity the German people as defined by responsible political parties and labour unions offered first to the

Germans from East Germany and then more broadly to the impoverished new democracies trying to find their feet after communism was
quite remarkable.

No one has ever gone from London or Brussels or Paris and publicly
thanked the Germans for not retreating into nationalism after 1990
but instead paying extra taxes and forgoing increases in income to turn
the peaceful liberation of Europe from Soviet tyranny into a win-win
moment of history. By the time the financial crash imported from
Greenspan's America hit Europe Germans were suffering from what
they call 'solidarity fatigue'. The appeals from Greek, Italian or Iberian
politicians for extra help to make good their own failure to deal with
endemic corruption and remediable inefficiencies did not find much
echo in the German public or political class. In his book on the EU
crisis, Yanis Varoufakis casts Germany as number one villain. Narcissus
at least had the grace to look at his own face.

Contrast this with France over the same postwar period: a cen-
tralised state which used technocratic planning decided by a small
elite in Paris to rebuild France after 1945. Trade unions that refused
all social partnership and erupted into strikes, including violent ones
like derailing trains bringing Marshall Aid supplies in the 1940s or
torching police cars in protests in October 2016 against some modest
labour market reforms. Wars of decolonisation in the 1940s and 1950s
that involved torture and murder of civilians. A confrontational political system with the populist French Communist Party and today the
populist Front National attacking political opponents in extravagant
terms as establishment lackeys. A palsied parliament and overwhelming
concentration of power in Paris, especially with the arrival of General
de Gaulle as a directly elected president-monarch chosen by plebiscite.

France had a world role as a nuclear power and permanent member
of the UN Security Council. By contrast, Germany was tucked away in
NATO and emphasised its rejection of *Machtpolitk* and a world leadership role.

What allowed the two countries to come together and grow in parallel and in a relatively harmonious fashion was the process of European integration and the acceptance of a common rule book and finally European citizenship and a common currency in the 1990s. Will Brexit be the beginning of the unwinding of the great coming together of Europe since 1945? The 2020s will answer that question. Even if Britain no longer has MEPs or a European Commissioner the nation's prosperity and security depend in large measure on Europe.

21

WHY THE EURO WILL SURVIVE

There have been endless books and memoirs on the steps towards European unity after 1992. Britain looked on from afar. The pound sterling was ejected from the forerunner of the euro, the European Exchange Rate Mechanism, and the then prime minister, John Major, rejected the Social Charter. His successor, Tony Blair, refused to enter the passport-free Schengen zone and promised in 1997 a referendum on the UK joining the euro – knowing full well that such a plebiscite would be lost and therefore would never be held.

The 1980s and 1990s had seen endless currency problems, with speculators, notably in the City of London, cashing in. There was permanent tension between Paris and Berlin over the exchange-rate value of the French franc and Deutschmark, all well told in David Marsh's books on European central banking and the problems of the euro. In the 1980s inflation was still strong – running at about 10 per cent in France (13.6 per cent in 1980). Today there is price stability in France at around 1.5 per cent, though some economists believe that to be too low. Low interest rates mean France saves between €30 and €60 billion a year in debt payment. Between 1986 and 1992 the difference in borrowing costs – the spread, in technical jargon – between Germany and

Italy was 5.1 per cent. In 2016 it was 1.4 per cent. The spread between German and French borrowing costs was 1.9 per cent between 1986 and 1992. In 2016 it was 0.3 per cent.

There are of course tensions as the common currency has to cover economies that are run differently according to national political priorities. Above all, national politicians have refused so far to accept a common economic governance as a corollary to the common currency. In the manifesto which took him to the Elysée, Emmanuel Macron promised a 'common budget' for the eurozone. It remains to be seen if he can work with the German government to establish such a system. But a major contribution to his victory was the suggestion from his rightwing anti-EU, pro-Brexit rival Marine Le Pen that France should walk out of the euro and revert to the French franc of the 1970s and 1980s. Most French savers, including older people who might have been attracted to other aspects of her nationalist programme, were horrified at the loss of value to their savings and wealth that leaving the euro would entail.

Margaret Thatcher's insistence on abolishing national sovereignty and vetoes over trade rules to force through the Single Market raised the question how could a truly single market coexist with component nations of the EU changing the price of every good or service by devaluing or revaluing more than a dozen different currencies?

A nationally controlled currency can, in theory, be one of the best protectionist devices there is. There were political reasons as well. With the end of communism and the unification of Germany, the new European nation with its capital in Berlin was overwhelmingly the biggest in terms of population and economic weight. Moreover it was clear that Germany would be – if not hegemonic – at the least the hub and turntable for investment and economic development in the new Europe. Creating a common currency with Germany tied France and Germany together in a manner that would prevent any of the old rivalries and tensions that had bedevilled relations across the Rhine ever resurfacing.

In exchange, Germany accepted French ideas of enlarging the European union of nations to take in the southern and much poorer states of Spain, Portugal and Greece, though none of those weak economies had a developed, mature, modern economy such as had been established further north in Europe. Austria and Nordic states joined the EU in the 1990s and then eight former communist states came in as EU members in 2004. Bulgaria, Romania, Slovenia and Croatia followed in due course. Norway never signed the EU treaty but accepted most rules of EU membership, including the four freedoms of movement of capital, goods, services and people, and made contribution to the EU budget as if a member state. Switzerland also stayed aloof, but in a series of bilateral treaties accepted EU rules and contributed to the common EU budget. The Swiss voted in 2014 to stop immigration from within Europe, much as the Brexit vote did in 2016. By February 2017, the Swiss parliament had quietly turned the referendum vote into a system of internal management of people movement which allowed European workers into Switzerland and was acceptable to the European Commission in Brussels.

Many were aghast at this rapid expansion of the EU from a grouping of states with roughly similar levels of development based broadly on the system of responsible, open-trade liberal capitalism with a social face that put down roots after 1950, despite widely varied political and government systems.

Greece was perhaps the most egregious example, though southern Italy would run it a close second. The creation of the euro was meant to have a double effect. It would allow the Single Market to expand, as every economic actor would now stop worrying about currency wars or need to hedge against the uncertainty of what a franc, peseta, lira or drachma would be worth. It would of course symbolise the union of European states, even if it was clear that the two major treaties of the Single European Act (1985) and Maastricht (1992) represented the high-water mark of European integration. But it was also hoped that the transparency of all national and private accounts using the same measure of value and worth would have a kind of osmotic effect as good money drove out bad national budgetary practices.

It did not work out like that. The year 2000 opened with unreformed states and economies in Greece, Spain, Portugal and Ireland suddenly being deluged with cheap euros, as going into debt – whether as a state, a private business or consumer buying a house or car – became cheap and cheerful. Politicians of all parties were delighted that they had access to cheap money over which they exercised influence and control via their presence in the government bodies of regional or local banks or savings institutions.

The EU was gearing up for the absorption of eight new member states from bankrupt ex-communist Europe and embarked on a forlorn search for a constitution to produce what Joschka Fischer called a European *Finalität*. This desire for a final definition of Europe is understandable, but not realistic or realisable. The idea that Europe was marble architecture, not a messy garden in need of constant weeding and replanting, was wishful thinking. The Greeks under both their centre-left Pasok and centre-right New Democracy governments took the cheap euros offered to them by banks in northern Europe, notably in Germany and France. They were used to buy votes, as the Greek state refused the most elementary reforms to restructure labour markets, modernise trade unions or reform corrupt clientalist practices. The Greek parties made no effort to get rich shipowners or the Orthodox Church with its massive land and property portfolios to pay a modicum of tax. The Athens journalist Yannis Palaiologos narrates the unbelievable corruption and clientalism of Greek politics in his book *The 13th Labour of Hercules: Inside the Greek Crisis* (2014).

If the Greeks were hooked on the drug of cheap money, the smooth bankers of Berlin and Paris were the drug dealers who encouraged their addiction. But as usual it is the addict, not his dealer, who got punished. The saga of the Greek disaster is well told by the economist Vicky Pryce, who came to study at the London School of Economics as a 17-year-old from Athens and has been an adornment of the UK economics profession, including a stint as the government's joint chief economist. Her book *Greekonomics: The Euro Crisis and Why Politicians Don't Get It* (2013) explains the unfolding drama that has done her country so much damage. Between 2010 and 2016, Greece has seen its economy shrink by a quarter, unemployment stands at 24 per cent, pensions have been slashed, wood-burning stoves and barter have returned in Athens as Greece felt the full force of a global financial crisis and the refusal of its creditors in Berlin, Paris and elsewhere in the national capitals of Europe, as well as the IMF, to take appropriate action. Greece was like a sick patient on an eighteenth-century surgeon's operating table. The only remedy was to bleed the patient and in the finance ministries of Berlin and The Hague were elected politicians who were happy to see Greece bleed to death rather than tell their own electorate that such policy was utterly counter-productive.

Equally the political class in Greece blamed everyone further north in Europe but never looked in a mirror. In a rare moment of honesty, the veteran Greek Pasok politician Theo Pangalos, deputy prime minister in 2011, said 'We ate it all together' as a way of describing how all Greek politicians shared responsibility for the disastrous way the nation was governed.

Instead of uniting when the crisis broke, the viciously adversarial and personalised nature of Greek politics, its endless demagogy exemplified by any speech made by one of the transient ministers, Yanis Varoufakis, meant that it was more important for New Democracy and Pasok and then Syriza politicians to score points against their opponents than unite on a programme to save Greece. The one exception was George Papandreou, who had grown up in Sweden and the US and sounded, indeed looked, more like a tall, sensitive Nordic social democrat professor of economics than a loudmouth Hellenic know-all politician. In November 2011, under mounting pressure from the left in his Pasok party, who had always refused the social democratic compromise reformist politics of their north European comrades and who believed that if they said 'Socialism' loudly enough socialism would happen, Papandreou told Angela Merkel and Nicolas Sarkozy that he wanted to hold a referendum to put the Greeks fully in front on their responsibilities.

Either they voted to stay in the euro and the EU, or they rejected the single currency and possibly, in consequence, membership of the EU. The implication was clear. If the Greeks wanted the euro, which opinion polls consistently said they did, then Papandreou was asking them to decide to accept the consequences of a major reform of the way Greek politics, economics and society was organised.

As Arnaud Leparmentier, the EU chronicler of *Le Monde*, recounts in his book *Ces Français, fossoyeurs de l'euro* ('Those French, the grave-diggers of the euro', 2013), Nicolas Sarkozy and Angela Merkel ordered Papandreou to come to a G20 meeting in Nice in November 2011 to be told that under no circumstances should he hold a referendum. Jean-Claude Juncker, president of the Eurogroup at the time, told the Greek socialist that referendums on any aspect of the EU were bound to be lost.

Papandreou resisted. He understood that the crisis had to be confronted by the Greek people and their political leaders, who could not hide behind party animosities and risk Greece being relegated to the status of a failed Balkan state as it returned to the drachma and possibly left the EU. But Sarkozy, soon himself to lose power and then face judicial investigation over corrupt financing of his election campaign, was adamant, as was Merkel. For Greece to hold a referendum that risked the country leaving the eurozone would be very expensive for German banks and other German businesses which had lent Greece money in the most irresponsible way after the Greeks joined the eurozone.

As Vicky Pryce wrote in 2012:

Greece has to learn to live by the injunction of the Delphi
Oracle: 'Know Thyself'. Greece, or rather the Greek elites, have
refused to know themselves, to accept responsibility for the many
failings in the stewardship of the nation. Politicians, professionals, prelates and power interest groups like parties, employers and
unions have all been in denial for too long.

Papandreou's referendum was the moment Greeks could have been
obliged to step out of their denial and accept responsibility. It was not
the EU in the sense of the Brussels institutions that prevented this
happening, but raw national politics and party political self-interest
in Berlin, Paris, Finland, the Netherlands and other European nation
states. Sarkozy was fresh from his disastrous intervention in Libya,
which destroyed the Libyan state and has destabilised the southern
Mediterranean littoral ever since, with profound consequences for
Europe as hundreds of thousands of asylum-seekers, economic migrants
and a handful of terrorists head to Europe.

Papandreou had made his name as one of the most innovative foreign ministers in Europe when he turned around relations with Turkey.
Papandreou opened a window of opportunity for the Turks to reorien-
tate their policy in favour of a European future – a policy now repudiated by Turkey's president Erdoğan, who has turned to an Islamic
authoritarianism to crush press freedom, democratic opposition and
end the search for a *modus vivendi* with the Kurds in Turkey.

At the same G20 meeting, President Obama lectured Merkel and
Sarkozy on their poor handling of the euro crisis. 'What you have failed
to do is put enough money on the table so that the speculators are
chased away like we did after the Lehmann Brother collapse in 2008.'
Indeed, the Greek crisis was made far worse by the poor handling of
it by Germany, which brushed to one side the European Commission

under José Manuel Barroso. German politicians were under pressure themselves, as the German political class denounced any idea that Greek debt might be written off or that financial help be extended to Greece as an unacceptable transfer of German taxpayers' money to corrupt, wasteful Greeks. Similar views could be heard in Finland, the Netherlands and London.

Nationalist Greeks of the right, centre and hard left responded by painting a Hitler moustache on Angela Merkel's upper lip. Suddenly arcane details of EU financing became tabloid headlines in Athens, Berlin and elsewhere. The European Commission looked on helplessly. The power and passion of national politics rose like demons from the deep to overwhelm a rational and balanced response. Greece had lost much sympathy in Europe, as it refused to work constructively at finding a solution to the break-up of Yugoslavia as a result of Serb-initiated wars. Unlike Berlin, Paris, London and Washington, Athens lined up with the Kremlin in refusing to recognise Kosovo, the small new nation that had claimed its independence after suffering quasi-genocidal attacks by Serb warlords and Slobodan Milošević. This was an arcane, intra-EU foreign policy question, but as with the refusal to allow Macedonia to exist as a state under its own name, the sheer pettiness of Greek nationalist politicians left them without friends when the crisis struck.

The European Central Bank was in the hands of the French central banker, Jean-Claude Trichet. Contrary to the arguments advanced by Harold James and his co-authors that the euro crisis is, in part, the result of a kind of genetic national disposition in France and Germany to see and then handle economic decision making as a result of immutable national cultures and history, Trichet was more German than the Germans and had been an inflexible governor of the Banque de France, running an austere, 'strong franc' policy, which he believed was the only basis for economic growth and stability. As the second governor of the European Central Bank he raised interest rates twice in the space of three months in 2011, thus deepening the eurozone's lack of growth. At a time in the economic cycle when Greece, Italy, Spain, Portugal and many other poorer regions in eurozone states needed investment to help restore confidence and growth after the 2007/9 crash, Trichet behaved like a parody of a German inflation hawk and did lasting damage to the European economy by raising interest rates at precisely the wrong moment in the economic cycle. His policy was reversed by his successor, Mario Draghi, an Italian central banker, who had a better feeling for the politics of economics. In July 2012, once Trichet had gone, Draghi promised to 'do whatever it takes' to promote growth.

But the Trichet years and the overwhelming dominance of German austerity ideology had already done their damage. For the British, with a much more flexible approach to monetary policy, including the Keynesian policy of so-called 'quantitative easing' – in effect printing money, launched in 2009 under Gordon Brown, a politician who understood economics – the refusal of dominant national capitals in Europe to promote pro-growth policies allowed pro-Brexit politicians to denounce the eurozone as a promoter of policies that stopped growth, increased unemployment, especially youth unemployment, and imposed public spending or pension cuts.

The accusations were accurate, but the fault lay with national capitals and national political classes. It was not anyone in Brussels who refused all debt relief for the beleaguered Greek economy, but hardline ideologues in Berlin, and to a lesser extent in some other northern European nation states.

There was no evidence that reverting to drachmas in Greece or lira in Italy would have eased their problems faced by Greeks and Italians. If anything, such a move would have led to massive capital flight, a devaluation of savings of ordinary people and a collapse in economic confidence. Smashing up the eurozone, as many of those who supported Brexit called for, would have done nothing to create a single job.

Despite claims by anti-Europeans that the EU is a super-state interfering to destroy national economies, the long history of the crisis since
the US caused world financial crisis of 2007/9 has shown up the lack of
power and authority in the European Commission and the European
Parliament. The two presidents of the European Council, Herman van
Rompuy and Donald Tusk, were bystanders in the crisis as all decisions
reverted to national states.

In a speech at the Davos World Economic Forum in January 2007,
Jean-Claude Trichet, then president of the ECB, had alerted European
policy makers to the coming turbulence. 'The recent explosion of
financial products based on derivatives makes it increasingly difficult
for regulators and investors to evaluate risks. [...] Investors have to
get ready for a significant reduction in value of certain shares.' But
Trichet was not ready to campaign against the existing model of global economic relations. The dominant figure was Alan Greenspan. He
was worshipped by London, and awarded an honorary knighthood on
Gordon Brown's nomination. But London was completely unprepared
for the financial storm that broke as the deregulated Greenspan model
opened the door to endless criminal and corrupt banking practices.
The neo-conservative right in Wall Street and their fellow-travellers in
Britain, in the City and in the British Treasury, doted on him and took
no notice of a French banker, even if Trichet was head of the ECB, who
dared to point out that Emperor Greenspan was less than fully clothed.

In the 800-page award-winning biography of Alan Greenspan by
the British financial journalist Sebastian Mallaby there is no index
entry for Trichet, let alone his warning at Davos in January 2007 that
a financial crash caused by Greenspan's ideology lay round the corner. In their book *The Euro and the Battle of Ideas*, Harold James of
Princeton University and his co-authors observe that 'A great deal of
the interpretation of the course of the euro crisis was shaped by the
British and American press – the *Financial Times*, the *Economist*, the
New York Times and the *Wall Street Journal* – and that outside vision

has filtered through a sort of condescension about Europeans not really getting it.' Blaming the poor quality of the monolingual messenger is an insufficient explanation for the absence of a European political leadership able to rise to the challenges of the twenty-first century. If the EU is not simply to survive but start becoming confident again a new political era must open.

22

NEW POLITICS ARE NEEDED IN EUROPE

A partial explanation of Brexit and the crisis of Europe's future lies in the end of the historic political compromise that sustained European construction during the second half of the twentieth century. The centre-right grouped around Christian democratic and liberal parties shared power in a rough-and-ready way with their social democratic colleagues. They kept at bay populist-nationalist communists and the weak revivals of the far right. The Socialist François Mitterrand worked with the Conservative Margaret Thatcher to bring in the Single Market. The liberal rightist Valéry Giscard d'Estaing cooperated closely with the Social Democratic Helmut Schmidt to create the European Exchange Rate Mechanism, the forerunner of the euro.

Today, European social democracy is weak and unable to offer convincing leaders or policies. The federation of centre-right parties, the European People's Party (EPP) group, dominates in Brussels. It has held the presidency of the Commission and the Council and Central Bank for more than a decade. It has now appropriated the presidency of the European Parliament. This total takeover of all top EU leadership positions (save the foreign policy High Representative who is the former international secretary of the centre-left *Partido Democratica* in Italy) is unhealthy and leaves the EU lop-sided.

The European democratic left has declined to the point of semi-irrelevance since the start of the twentieth century when leaders like Tony Blair (Britain), Gerhard Schröder (Germany), Lionel Jospin (France), Massimo D'Alema (Italy), Göran Persson (Sweden), Poul Nyrup Rasmussen (Denmark), Aleksandr Kwasniewksi (Poland), António Guterres (Portugal), Victor Klima (Austria), Miloš Zeman (Czech Republic) or Costas Simitis (Greece) held office at a time when more social democratic, socialist or labour parties were in government than at any time in history. The failure to convert that coinciding democratic left hegemony into a coherent project for governance across Europe will go down in history as the European democratic left's greatest failure. In each case, the primacy of national political needs and egoisms trumped any chance of effective European cooperation. As ever, far from there existing a European federalist project so often denounced by the anti-European ideologues, the parties of the left in government could agree on very little and Europe remained firmly under the control of nation-first centre-left leaders.

Today, the socialist presidency in France (2012–17) has not been a success, François Hollande not daring to stand again to defend his record. Matteo Renzi had to resign. The once-mighty German Social Democratic Party has not been able to find a way so far to overcome Christian Democratic hegemony, and the years when a Spanish socialist prime minister dominated the Iberian peninsula are long gone. Social democratic parties in eastern and central Europe fail to attract voters. In this vacuum, voters who feel left behind by modern European capitalism turn to populist demagogues of the right or left who blame Brussels for all the problems that different communities face. One unintended consequence of Brexit may indeed be to answer the question whether leaving the EU is the magic solution to the lack of fair-pay jobs, social investment and support for poorer communities and health services that were promised by those campaigning for Brexit in 2016. Britain is now the guinea pig in a unique experiment to test the thesis that amputation from the EU is the best way to national growth and wealth.

Politics must return to Europe. The Polish political scientist Leszek Kołakowski, exiled in All Souls, Oxford, once defined social democratic politics as 'an obstinate will to erode by inches the conditions which produce avoidable suffering, oppression, hunger, wars, racial and national hatred, insatiable greed and vindictive envy'. Social democratic or centre-left politics somehow have lost sight of those aims as they seek to locate political action in culture, gender and ecological issues. It was commonplace to describe 2016 and the Brexit–Trump vote as uniquely connected to populism, as if politicians had never sought to be popular or use easy-to-grasp slogans. The Soviet Union intervened with much greater success in the politics of other countries than Putinbots. The US also granted itself the right to intervene in the internal politics of sovereign nation states, sometimes to the point of overthrowing democratically elected politicians.

What 2016 may also have been about was not the populism but the sheer novelty of a Donald Trump or a Brexit plebiscite. It was the newness of a political process which allowed voters to buy a shiny new toy – Brexit or Trump – which had never before been on political offer. But gleaming toys lose their shine and often stop working. We should not give up on adult politics. According to the Swiss Liberal politician Christa Markwalder, former speaker of the Swiss parliament, 'It is time for democratically accountable and elected politicians to take back control from the populists.' As Hans Kundnani has written, 'The European Union itself often takes a rather technocratic approach that seeks to insulate economic policy making from politics.' Until Europe's political parties devote serious resources to forging an effective set of policies that can bring together competing national visions, priorities and cultures, or at least decide on a set of key priorities, the crisis will continue and Brexit will be the first sign of the Balkanisation of Europe.

No one can magic up a new twenty-first-century social democracy, but the imbalance of power – with nearly all key decisions taken by centre-right politicians in today's Europe – leaves the EU like a stork balancing on one political leg. A further problem is the failure of trade unions to modernise themselves. In the 1930s trade unions in Sweden and Switzerland looked at the twin threats to democracy posed by fascism and communism. In 1938 they concluded historic compromise agreements with employers. In broad terms, the unions left the political struggle to politicians and in exchange for recognition as social partners by the bosses and owners of capital they agreed to push back the strike weapon to one of the ultimate last resort. The unions agreed that the constant renewal and investment in national firms and support for free trade, including inward and outward investment, was essential to national success and the ambitions of trade union members to get more pay, more leisure and investment in the social state of pensions, affordable housing, health care and education.

After 1945, unions in Germany, Austria, the Netherland and Nordic nations followed within their own national traditions the Swedish–Swiss model developed in the 1930s. Strikes were rare. There was full support for firms investing overseas and opening markets to competition. Contrast this to Britain, where a leading trade union general secretary, Ken Gill, denounced the arrival of Japanese automobile companies in the north of England in the 1980s as leading to the coming of 'alien practices'. Unemployed workers in the North East liked such alien practices as jobs and decent pay. In France in 2016, militant trade unions all but destroyed the French socialist government with a series of militant, sometimes violent strikes and protests in opposition to minor labour market reforms that had been accepted by trade unions across the Rhine or further north decades before.

In Italy, Spain, France or Portugal trade unions were off-shoots of political parties or the Catholic Church and obeyed the line of the communist party leaders or cardinals. Trade union membership slumped as deindustrialisation in the 1980s and 1990s eliminated the majority of jobs in the metal industries, where archetypal working-class trade union organisation was strongest. Women and immigrant workers were more difficult to organise and had different priorities from the classic twentieth-century white male proletariat. Unions gave up the difficult task of organising the new post-industrial proletariat and instead focused on public-sector workers – teachers, civil servants, hospital workers, public transport workers, employees of state agencies. These workers needed trade unions, but if ever they took strike or other action the victims were members of the public who could not leave their children at school or use strike-hit public transport to get to work. Trade unions were no longer confronting capital to get a fairer share of the wealth their labour created, but the wider public, who resented having to pay ever-higher taxes for the pay and other entitlements public-sector employees felt were their due.

As economies and societies have reformatted themselves and with the arrival of so-called AI (Artificial Intelligence), even more jobs may disappear, to be done by computers. Trade unions have remained imprisoned in their early or mid-twentieth-century structures and rhetoric. If the nations of Europe were in the driving-seat of EU policy in the twenty-first century, especially under weak European Commission presidents, the trade unions of Europe were even more marked by their national heritage and provenance. In the 1980s, the Australian trade union movement sent a fact-finding commission to Europe and North America to look at the best models of trade union organisation. Not all suggestions were adopted, but the Australian trade union movement reformed and renovated itself and was able to play a key partnership role in rebooting the Australian economy to adapt to globalisation and invest in policies to help all Australian citizens, not just manual white-working class union members.

The European Trade Union Confederation and European Trade Union Institute are both smart, professionally run organisations. But

like the European Commission they have no power over national affili-
ates and can only do what their bigger members allow them to do.
If Europe is to get going again it needs a historic new compromise
between capital and labour along the lines of the 1930s agreements in
Sweden and Switzerland. Europe should seek to be a strike-free region
in the world, not because unions are broken, but because they realise
that keeping the wheels turning makes sense for all. Unions should
lose links with political parties, while continuing to support those that
champion in broad terms social justice. Unions should be centres of
information about the world of work and support open society economics, not beggar-my-neighbour protectionism, which is one of the
underlying drivers of support for Brexit.

To be sure, these are big ambitions, but if the broad mass of
employed people do not believe they want to join a union or enter-
tain the idea of trade unionism as a force to help achieve what Hobbes
called 'commodious living', then they are more easily seduced by the
populist appeals of the far right and hard left against cooperation and
sharing power in Europe.

More and more of the evangelists of the deregulated, society-
destroying, 'greed-is-good' and survival-of-the-fittest economic model
are now running around telling us there are real problems with unequal
distribution, poverty and the revolt of voters who have lost confidence
in traditional parties of government. But moving to a new paradigm
demands new forms of political and labour movement organisation.

Anatole Kaletsky, former *Times* and *Financial Times* columnist and
author of *Capitalism 4.0: The Birth of a New Economy* (2010), argues:

> That is what happened after 2008. Once the failure of free trade,
> deregulation, and monetarism came to be seen as leading to a
> 'new normal' of permanent austerity and diminished expecta-
> tions, rather than just to a temporary banking crisis, the inequal-
> ities, job losses, and cultural dislocations of the pre-crisis period

could no longer be legitimised – just as the extortionate taxes of the 1950s and 1960s lost their legitimacy in the stagflation of the 1970s.

Kaletsky believes that

> governments can redistribute the benefits of growth by supporting employment and incomes with regional and industrial subsidies and minimum-wage laws. Among the most effective interventions of this type, demonstrated in Germany and Scandinavia, is to spend money on high-quality vocational education and retraining for workers and students outside universities, creating non-academic routes to a middle-class standard of living.

But so far in European nations like France, Italy, Spain or Greece and above all in Britain, politicians, business leaders and trade unions prefer to camp on their old positions. Brexit has not produced any such rethink, only more shrill partisan denunciations or boasting from the old parties.

Europe needs to shift taxation away from labour and onto capital gains and wealth, as Ånders Aslund and Simeon Djankov argue in *Europe's Growth Challenge* (2017). VAT as a tax provides a solid base for national government income, as well as EU revenue. But it is regressive – that is, those on lower incomes pay a higher share of their income in VAT taxes than those who are better off. High rates of tax for lower-paid workers discourage young people from entering the labour market if unemployment and other benefits plus bits and pieces of work in the unofficial labour market or help from parents allow a lifestyle that is not based on regular work. Schooling must be more rigorous. Entry to high-level state functionary posts should require a working knowledge of two European languages and one in two posts should be for those who have university-level mathematics, computer science or hard sciences diplomas.

One of the saddest aspects of Brexit will be the elimination for British students of the opportunities provided by the Erasmus programme. Some 200,000 young British men and women have used EU Erasmus grants in the two decades since the programme was launched to go and study in a university in another EU member state. Erasmus students from the rest of Europe coming to Britain are an important part of university income. In fact, if anything, Erasmus should be expanded so that it can help non-university students to get vocational and language skills. In the early twentieth century it was common for apprentices who had completed the years of study and training in order to become skilled workers to take a kind of gap year to work in Germany or France to improve their skills and employability when they came home to start earning a living. Jacques Lafitte, a former senior EU Commission official who now advises firms and governments on EU policy, has suggested that a major relaunch of a second generation of Erasmus programmes for non-university training and education should be a major priority for the new EU Commission after 2019. He is right.

Reforming European universities so that they become world-class universities and Europe becomes a university teaching centre for the planet should be a priority. Unpalatable as it seems to be for many European university elites, depending solely on state provision cannot deliver the resources to lift European universities to a high level. French intellectuals spend the morning writing denunciations of any suggestion that their students should make a financial contribution to their education and the afternoon applying for posts at North American universities where this is the norm, as it is in Britain. It seems unfair that workers and others who do not get the chance of university education have to pay from their taxes so that the children of the wealthy and the middle classes, who benefit most from university education, can go there for free.

Indeed, the principle of contributory solidarity should become the European norm. Forms of collective insurance in which all are required to pay on their own account for their future health or old-age care needs would encourage public health campaigns. Instead of relying passively on centrally controlled government provision of health care, the focus should be on prevention of avoidable illness by aggressive promotion of healthy living and diet.

23

THE EU AFTER 2019 MUST BE DIFFERENT OR IT WILL DIE

The European Commission needs to be braver and harder in telling national governments when their policies are failing or to highlight examples of successful policies at national level, such as the Dutch pensions system. The European Commission also needs renewal. Contrary to the myth of a crushing European officialdom, the Eurocrats of lore, the 30,000 officials of the European Commission are dwarfed by New York's 460,700 city government employees. But no one should work as an EU Commission official for more than 10–15 years and the norm should be to return to national government service in order to inject know-how into national administrations on how the EU actually works.

The same should be true of members of the European Parliament. Indeed, there is a case for national delegations for the European Parliament to be chosen at the same time as national parliamentary elections so that the composition of the European Parliament more faithfully reflects the will of the people in the member states. It is not a question of the nation versus Europe but of the nation *and* Europe and of finding a new balance that generates more national support for what the EU can do better at its level.

The proposals from Viktor Orbán and Jarosław Kaczyński to reform Europe – returning it to veto-wielding nation states that can protect national interests and frontiers *über Alles* – is an instant way of destroying Europe. In the eighteenth-century Polish parliament there existed the concept of *liberum veto* – the right of any member of the parliament of notables to veto any proposition he didn't like. As a result this nationalist veto-based governance of Poland left the nation backward, undeveloped and an easy prey to Russia, Prussia and Austria, who promptly dismembered the country.

On the contrary, if the nations of Europe want growth, reform and a re-energising of their own nations based on open markets and social cohesion, the answer they have to accept is that they must learn to share, not hoard power. A commonplace demand in the wish-list of EU reforms is that various internal markets should be completed – the internal market in services and the energy market are the two most frequently mentioned, as is the idea of a capital markets union. Yes, but. All imply a transfer of power, control, sovereignty, authority – call it what you will – to the European Union, principally the European Commission.

A paradox of Brexit is that with the UK outside the EU, it may be possible to have one official language in Europe which, of course, would be English! Today neither France nor Germany (and Spain and Italy) can accept English as the main EU language because to do so is seen as granting primacy to one major EU member state – the United Kingdom (with Ireland tagging along.) With the linkage between the language – English – and the EU member state – the UK – broken, once political Brexit occurs it should be possible for English to be an agreed common language for the EU. In effect, all EU Commission and Council officials speak English, particularly following the enlargement to take in the Nordic states and Austria in the 1990s and the former communist bloc states a decade later.

One of the worst aspects of Britain's involvement in EU affairs has been the precipitous decline in British MPs, MEPs and officials speaking and reading a European language fluently. The Labour education minister Estelle Morris did the nation a great disservice when she abolished compulsory foreign-language teaching in England's secondary schools. It should be obligatory for any official anywhere in Whitehall seeking promotion to the highest ranks of state service that they speak at least one other language so they can pick up a newspaper from a European country and read it to get a feel of what's going on. The space Britain's monolingual editors give to coverage of European politics is now so low as to be a scandal. It is all but impossible to gain a thorough understanding of the flow of political decisions in other EU nations without reading some foreign-language media.

At the same time, the EU's level of communication is lamentable. Despite statements from the current president Jean-Claude Juncker that the idea of a federal United States of Europe is not on anyone's agenda, the easiest line of attack by anti-Europeans is to state and keep repeating that a European super-state is poised to absorb all the European nation states and abolish their separate existence.

There is nothing ignoble about wishing for and writing in support of a more federal Europe, but it is not going to happen in any conceivable future. The EU massively supplements what its member states do, but with a tiny budget, as most EU money goes straight back to nation states for agricultural, regional, research and other national-level spending. The idea that a giant super-state can be built on such a minuscule revenue base is laughable.

Yet somehow no EU official or national EU head of government seems to change the discourse. The Ozymandian buildings in Brussels and the proliferation of presidents and commissioners does not help. At a minimum, the Commission should be halved in size. Much EU work can be off-shored to national cities within the EU. Trickier is the rule that allows each nation a commissioner. The UK has had four commissioners in ten years, as British prime ministers attach little importance to whoever holds the post. Might it be possible to have a commissioner from each nation every second term – five years on and five years off, as it were? With modern communication systems there is no need for each nation to have its man or woman in the EU Commission.

The Council of Ministers meeting could easily be televised so that European citizens see that far from being a secret Eurocracy cooking up deals, the governance of Europe is in the hands of national ministers and heads of government. The Brexit negotiations, either those on Article 50 or later ones between the EU and the UK, could be a good place to make more transparent what is discussed. The press conference after each Council meeting could involve all heads of government and journalists from all countries, who could thus learn how their national leaders defended or promoted different positions. Europe moves at the speed of the political will of its nation states and they should not be allowed to hide their own decisions by blaming Brussels.

There are calls for a more political union based on the eurozone, which could theoretically take place once Britain leaves. But will it? There remain fundamental differences between France and Germany. The crises of the eurozone this century are caused by too little Europe, not too much. If the EU had been more involved in overseeing the tax and budget policies of countries like Greece or Portugal or Spain, for example, then perhaps the disaster of easy access to euros without any accompanying reforms might have been avoided.

But as with the demand that the scope of the ECB should include a commitment to supporting employment in the manner of the US Federal Reserve rather than only focusing on inflation, such suggestions have to win support in national political systems, which is not likely. Perhaps following Brexit there can be moves to harmonise corporate tax levels, but nominal tax rates do not necessarily equate with real taxes paid to government, as firms find loopholes or ways of offsetting expenditure on research or in other fields to set against tax.

Of course, there should be a common energy policy, a common capital market union and a common defence procurement policy. The

EU should take control of universities from governments and above all from the sclerotic, inward-looking, self-referencing, ageing university professoriat that has reduced continental European universities to a low provincial status. But politicians love national champions. Germany is committed to fully renewable energy and to abandoning nuclear power. France believes passionately in nuclear power and Poland believes equally passionately in burning brown coal (lignite), the most polluting, CO_2-emitting source of energy. These profound differences cannot be wished away. More effort might be spent highlighting how all European nations lose out when they defend national economic interests. More work and more publicity is needed to highlight the costs of non-Europe. A report by the European Parliament showed that the absence of a single digital market cost €990 billion to the EU-wide economy as each nation tinkered with its own digital market economy rules.

But again and again this comes back to the main question: more not less Europe in the sense of common decision making and application of rules is needed but there is no one willing to spell out that self-evident truth. When Margaret Thatcher and her successor John Major were promoting the Single Market, the UK government public affairs budget for its 'Are EU Ready' campaign involved films, television spot advertisements, major newspaper advertising and other publications and events that are the norm when a government wants to explain a major new policy to its citizens. When I was Europe minister a decade later my budget for promoting a greater understanding of Europe was cut by £150,000. Compare that to the massive budget for public relations for the armed services.

If the British and other governments cannot invest in explaining Europe, they should not be surprised if voters start to believe the propaganda and lies of the anti-Europeans. If there is an effective spokesperson for the EU – the sort of super-spin doctor who is an indispensable part of any serious political or business organisation – his or her name escapes me. Commissioners do produce worthy speeches or even short books trying to defend the work of the Commission, but the key word is 'defend'. There is no confident, stylish, communications policy by the Commission, Council or agencies like the EU foreign policy unit, the European External Action Service (EEAS).

Indeed, foreign policy outreach is one area where the EU could seek to speak with one voice, but again we hit the buffers of national political positions. Most of Europe was horrified at the Iraq intervention in 2003 supported by Tony Blair, Silvio Berlusconi and then Portuguese prime minister, later the Commission president, José Manuel Barroso and Eastern European leaders. But no one knew how to stop the folly, just as eight years later, Berlin and Warsaw looked on aghast as David Cameron and Nicolas Sarkozy rushed to topple Colonel Gaddafi and destroy the Libyan state. Then France joined with the US and Britain to support the rebels in the Syrian civil war – again leading to years of chaos and mass movement of Arab Muslims to Europe.

National foreign policy is usually driven by national public opinion and it is a rare leader who knows how to think long term and not worry about the day's headlines from a warzone. There is no European public opinion. Some have chided the Hungarian, Slovak or Polish governments for not accepting their quota of MENA (Middle East and North African) refugees, but the decision to open the doors of Europe was a unilateral one taken by Angela Merkel without any consultation with her neighbours. That Germany is big and powerful and thus could get such a unilateral decision validated by the European Council does not mean it had the support of all EU nations, even if most kept their heads down and muttered and moaned behind closed doors – save in Britain, where the arrival of so many incomers from the Middle East and North Africa played into the hands of the Brexit campaigners.

The EU has its embassies in every capital of the world, and for smaller countries that cannot easily afford a fully staffed diplomatic presence in every corner of the world an EU embassy makes sense and

can defend the consular interests of European citizens who find themselves in trouble far from home. However, the focus of a meaningful
EEAS should be on Europe's Near Abroad – Russia, Belarus, Ukraine,
indeed all the nations that are members of the 47-strong Council of
Europe, including Turkey, Georgia, Azerbaijan and Armenia as well as
all the MENA nations along the southern and eastern Mediterranean
shoreline.

A concentration of EU political, economic and diplomatic resources
and investment on the Near Abroad, with the aim of creating a stable
community of nations whose citizens believe they have a future at home
rather than emigrating *en masse* to Europe would be a noble ambition.

At different times there have been efforts to create a Union of the
Mediterranean, but these have become talking shops undermined by
intra-European rivalries. Both France and Spain, for example, take
different lines on how to handle their former colonial possessions
in North Africa. As long as Islamist ideology dominates the Israel–
Palestinian problem there is little point in wasting time on finding a
solution, which will come about when the US decides to impose one.

European development aid, which is frittered away wastefully all
over the world, especially on nations like India which spends billions
on nuclear weapons and wants to send people into space but will not
invest in basic literacy and running water for all its citizens, could be
focused on Europe's Near Abroad.

It would indeed be agreeable to hope that Brexit would be a spur
to serious new thinking about what Europe should be or do. On the
surface the 19 members of the eurozone are those nations which have
taken the biggest step towards integration. But the evidence is that the
differences between different nations and regions within the zone are
as great if not greater than between euro and non-euro members of the
EU. In the coming years will Germany and France agree on economic
and fiscal reforms for Europe? Spain's government is shaky, and the
problem of Catalonia has not been solved. Italy lost one prime minister

at the end of 2016 and his replacement went into hospital for heart surgery. In fact, the Brexit crisis has coincided with one of the most fallow periods of political leadership in post-1945 Europe. It is not just politicians. There seem to be no editors or intellectuals, no business leaders, no writers who can articulate any vision that commands support. Putin, Trump and Erdoğan represent all that is worst in the idea of political leadership, but without leadership, followers cannot follow.

One man who saw what Europe could and should be was Friedrich Hayek. His short book *The Road to Serfdom* (published in 1944) is often hailed as the founding charter of postwar economic liberalism. It was seen as an assault on the collectivist, statist, social democratic and socialist ideas that were emerging as the response to both Nazism and communism. Margaret Thatcher venerated the Austrian-born economist and gave him one of Britain's top honours in 1984. The Mont Pélerin Society was founded in Switzerland to give voice to his ideas. Hayek became an icon for the right, especially the anti-European right. Yet a study of the book shows a man who seems to be promoting the very federalist ideas, as well as endorsing a strong political Europe, that his disciples on the British right find anathema.

Hayek quotes approvingly Lord Acton, the greatest of England's nineteenth-century historians.

> Of all the checks on democracy, federation has been the most efficacious and the most congenial. […] The federal system limits and restrains the sovereign. It is the only method of curbing not only the majority but the power of the whole people.

As he contemplated the organisation of the postwar world, the nation was for Hayek the source of problems. 'There is little hope of lasting peace so long as every country is free to employ whatever measures it thinks desirable in its own immediate interest', Hayek wrote. The individual citizen or firm, not the nation, must be at the heart of the post-Nazi, non-communist world order. 'If international economic relations, instead of being relations between individuals become increasingly relations between whole nations organised as trading bodies, they inevitably become the source of friction and envy between whole nations.'

These insights are contained in the last chapter of Hayek's book. It is probable that Mrs Thatcher and all the other Hayekians did not bother to examine closely the arguments advanced in the final pages of *The Road to Serfdom*. Hayek, however, makes a better case for the European Union as it has developed than many a more overt Europhile. As he wrote: 'We cannot hope for order or lasting peace after this war if states, large and small, regain unfettered sovereignty in the economic sphere.' Contrary to the belief that the EU should simply be a free-trade economic sphere, Hayek argued that:

> Far from its being true that, as is now widely believed, we need an international economic authority while the states can at the same time retain their unrestricted political sovereignty, almost exactly the opposite is the case. What we need is […] a superior political power which can hold the economic interests in check and in the conflict between them can truly hold the scales.

Hayek advocates 'the form of international government under which certain strictly defined powers are transferred to an international authority, while in all other respects the individual countries remain responsible for their internal affairs' and concludes that the name of this form of governance is 'federation', which should be 'neither an omnipotent super-state, not a loose association of "free nations" but a community of nations'.

Did Hayek, already in 1944, have premonitions of the shape of European construction to come? It is uncanny to think of this Austrian intellectual, later a Nobel economic laureate, sitting in cold, dark, rationed wartime London and describing much of what became first the EEC and then the EU. He dismisses the dreamers who called for global federation, those like the nineteenth-century poet Tennyson, who wrote in 'Locksley Hall':

> When I dipt into the future, far as human eye could see,
> Saw the Vision of the world, and all the wonder that would be;
> [...]
> Heard the heavens fill with shouting, and there rain'd a
>   ghastly dew
> From the nations' airy navies grappling in the central blue;
> [...]
> Till the war-drum throbb'd no longer, and the battle flags
>   were furl'd
> In the Parliament of Man, the Federation of the world.

Hayek was more modest and precise in his geography. 'The comparatively close association which a Federal Union represents will not at first be practicable beyond perhaps even as narrow a region as part of Western Europe, though it may be possible gradually to extend it', he wrote.

But today the opposition from within the nations of Europe to sharing, in the model of Hayek, more sovereignty and allowing the EU via its institutions to take initiatives in the interests of the EU's 500 million citizens as a whole remains. The EU is thus in the position outlined in 'Stiff Upper Lip', a song by the Gershwin brothers in the appropriately named 1937 movie *Damsel in Distress*:

> When you're in a stew!
> Sober or blotto,
> This is your motto,
> Keep muddling through!

The EU is in some distress, indeed in a stew. But it has to keep muddling through. Its only hope will be that accountable politics somehow recovers its confidence and can relegate the nationalist-populism that has blocked all but minimal progress in re-energising European economic activity. As Brecht wrote in another troubled era for Europe, 'Erst kommt das Fressen, dann kommt die Moral', roughly translated as 'Grub first, politics later'. The EU must revert to being a material project that brings a better standard of living to its people. If it cannot achieve this, its future is bleak and Brexit is the first major symptom of that worrying future for a Europe that can celebrate its past but not shape a future.

AFTERWORD

24

HOW THE UK STAYS IN EUROPE

In 1992 there was a narrow majority in a Danish referendum to reject the Maastricht Treaty. The Danes, like the British, are a proud, longstanding European democracy. Their election system is based on proportional representation, unlike Britain's first-past-the post system. There has been no majority one-party government in Denmark since 1909. The government insisted that while it accepted the clear expression of the will of the Danish people in the plebiscite, it invited the nation to reflect on whether that was the final and only word, following which Denmark's future lay in being isolated from its European partners.

But they were careful not to rush forward simply to reject the result and insist on a second referendum. The chief Danish government official for Europe at the time was Joergen Oerstroem Moeller, the state secretary for European affairs. He argues that the immediate calls after the Brexit vote in Britain for a second referendum were misplaced and too early. Instead he maintains that, 'In two or three years, circumstances may be so messy that a referendum could be the most democratic response to a number of unpalatable scenarios.' Moeller makes an important point when he states that:

> The main justification for the referendum would need to be clear and transparent: to enable a decision on known withdrawal

terms, which was not the case in June 2016. It would be legitim-
ate and reasonable to ask voters whether they wished to confirm
or reverse their earlier decision. The poll would not be a 'second
referendum' or a plea to repent, but a new consultation of the
people on an eminently democratic basis.

His point is reinforced by the writer Hugo Dixon, who argued in a letter
to the *Financial Times* (September 2016):

When businesses realise [the damage full Brexit entails], they
may sound the alarm. When voters see they were lied to, they
may change their minds. Pro-Remain politicians who have run
for the hills since the vote may then agree that British people
should be asked whether they really want to leave once we know
what Brexit means. This is democratically the right thing to do
and the way to fight hard Brexit.

A referendum is just another vote. Its authority must be respected, just
as we respect the result of a vote to change a government. But the whole
point of democracy is that everyone has the right to challenge a vote,
especially when won as the Brexit vote was won – on a campaign of demonstrable lies without parallel in British electoral history. In the winter of
2016/17 there was much concern in the country about the state of the
NHS, with reports of patients lying for hours in corridors before being
admitted or being discharged while still unwell and unable to cope at
home. In the referendum campaign all voters were promised there would
be an additional £350 million a week for the NHS if they voted Leave. It
was as grotesque a lie as ever was told in any British political campaign.

Of course, everything depends on events, especially in the economic sphere. Britain was still fully in the EU in the first period
after the Brexit vote and will remain so until the presumed withdrawal treaty before the next five-year term of a new EU Parliament,

Commission and Council begins in May 2019. Before then the markets are likely to take some economic decisions, especially on investment and the value of sterling, which may change minds. It may well be that the UK economy will boom and flourish and that inward investment will flow in to create jobs and sustain wealth. If this is the case, the British people will judge the Brexit vote validated, even if Britain no longer plays a part in making the rules of the EU or shaping jointly with the other 27 EU member states the response to issues like climate change, Russian aggression, the threat of Islamist terrorism and Europe's geo-political role in the twenty-first century as power shifts to rising Asian states and away from North America and Europe.

Mrs May lost her election in June 2017 even if the Tories had nearly 60 more seats than Labour. Other polls, including parliamentary by-elections, will take place over the next period. Will pro-European and anti-Brexit candidates perform well, which suggests support for Brexit is weakening amongst voters? To be sure, the further one moves from 23 June 2016 the less sacred and incontestable the vote won by a campaign of lies will seem.

There is an interesting parallel with the Swiss referendum of February 2014. Voters were asked to vote against 'mass immigration' and amend the constitution accordingly. The speaker or chair of the Swiss parliament in 2016 was Christa Markwalder, a young member of the centrist Swiss Liberal Party, who rose fast to national prominence.

Talking in January 2017 to British Tory and Swiss MPs at their annual New Year ski-race meeting in Switzerland, Ms Markwalder said:

> Like you we also had an important referendum three years ago about 'taking back control' of immigration to Switzerland. A tight majority of the voters accepted it. [...]

As the dust settled and excitement died away we began to see that the emotion of saying 'Managing immigration ourselves' may answer a question on a ballot paper. But it does not answer the question of what should be done.

It should be clear that we cannot shut borders and hope to survive, let alone prosper. So in the three years since the referendum of February 2014 we Parliamentarians and the economic actors of Switzerland had to decide whether emotion against foreigners should have greater weight than the economic interests of our country.

We had many talks with the EU and the message was firm and clear. Brussels respected the Swiss referendum but could not change the rules and treaty obligations that the 28 EU member states had agreed to live under.

And so in the end we produced a compromise based on strengthening internal controls of our labour market instead of preventing European citizens getting access to jobs in Switzerland.

This compromise based on internal rather than external controls has the backing of the nationalist rightwing Swiss People's Party (SVP), which has two members in the seven-strong Swiss governing Federal Council. Jürg Stahl is the SVP speaker of the Berne parliament and says: 'I am reasonably confident that the compromise proposal of the Swiss government, based on internal controls of the Swiss labour market not external barriers, will be accepted.'

The Swiss compromise, which allows access to the Single Market rather in the way that Norway and Lichtenstein enjoy, is imperfect. It may be subject to new pressures, including a fresh populist anti-European referendum. It reflects the position of a neutral nation that only voted to join the UN in 2002, after a referendum in 1986 saw 75 per cent of the Swiss voting against membership. But those who had higher ambitions for Switzerland bided their time, patiently made a new set of arguments and in due course won. Referendums are not a sacrosanct last word in democracy.

Another country offering an example of referendums being subject to rethinks is Sweden, where voters decided to reject a government decision in the 1950s to move Sweden from driving on the left, as in Britain, to driving on the right, as did all of Sweden's neighbours. As postwar car and lorry usage intensified it was clearly difficult to maintain the age-old Swedish tradition of driving on the left, as the Nordic nations have always been open one to the others and in effect constituted a mini Euro-Nordic union open to trade and commerce and tourist visits. But in a referendum nostalgia trumped modernity and the Swedes in an 8–1 vote said 'No' to switching their driving lanes. The government just bided its time until it became clear it made sense to drive on the same side of the road as Norway, Denmark and Finland (and the rest of Sweden's economic partners in Europe) and a new vote in the Riksdag, the Swedish parliament, settled the matter eight years later.

The same thing happened in 1980, when Sweden was caught up in one of the periodic waves of anti-nuclear emotion which sweeps the world after a nuclear power station accident. In 1979, there was an accident at Three Mile Island, at the site of a US nuclear power station, and the Swedes held a referendum which voted for a phasing out of nuclear power. Today there are still ten nuclear power stations delivering reliable carbon-emission-free nuclear energy in Sweden and the Riksdag dropped the phase-out policy in 2009.

Again we are talking about one of the strongest democracies in the world. However, the Swedes refuse to make a fetish of one plebiscite, preferring to locate that important consultation in a broader framework of democratic decision making. In both cases, there was no immediate rush to implement any decision one way or another arising from a referendum. Time was given to let the implications of continuing to drive on the opposite side of the road from Sweden's neighbours sink in, and then, two decades later, the same process was

repeated after the nuclear power referendums to allow Swedes to realise that wind power could not deliver the right to press a switch and
have light and warmth and that coal was dreadfully polluting and a
major global warmer.

Britain has far more time to reflect than Denmark had in 1992–3,
but not as long as Sweden did in the 1950s and 1960s. Nor can any
British government turn a Nelsonian blind eye to the Brexit vote in the
way Swedish politicians did after the nuclear phase-out vote of 1980.
In fact, it is unclear what the UK's time line is. In theory, Article 50
negotiations can last longer than the two years stipulated in the treaty
if both London and a majority of EU capitals agree. Britain can also
suspend its Article 50 procedure if the government decides the conditions have changed to the extent that pressing strongly ahead with a
full withdrawal from Europe would be too damaging to the national
interest.

Equally, even if political Brexit is achieved by May 2019 all the
other forms of Brexit covering trade, the Customs Union, defence
procurement, many European institutions in which Britain plays a
part, the rights of workers, the European Arrest Warrant, participation in university programmes or regulating insurance, banking and
investment funds will take a considerable length of time, stretching well into the 2020s, to unravel and new arrangements negotiated. Millions of British people who have got used to travelling in
Europe as if travelling in Britain, or working, living, renting or buying a home or retiring there will wait and see if their politicians can
guarantee these rights while simultaneously imposing discriminatory
measures on European citizens. Solutions will have to be found as
well as for the EU citizens who have made a life in Britain. Many will
lose rights they have taken for granted and many families in Britain
who have to deal with relatives who return as a result of Brexit and
loss of EU citizenship rights may question if the 23 June 2016 vote is
indeed the last word.

But this is for the future and was not uppermost in voters' minds in the aftermath of the victory for the anti-European zealots in the summer of 2016. In 1649 the zealots who hated the idea of monarchy won a vote by MPs to execute the first King Charles. England lived under the rule of an increasingly incompetent Cromwell who organised wars and massacres in Ireland and Scotland but did little to improve the material well-being of ordinary people. When he died the people decided to reverse what had seemed an irreversible decision and again live under a monarchy. There was an 11-year wait between one parliamentary vote and a new vote to restore the monarchy. Now we live in the twenty-first not the seventeenth century, just as Britain is not Switzerland, Sweden or any of the countries that have looked a second time at an initial referendum decision on Europe.

That the government was unprepared for Brexit and had no plans is not disputed. It would be helpful to write an updated Domesday Book for Brexit – a national audit of every town, city or district and what the implications of different types of Brexit might mean – the full, hard amputation of losing all Single Market access and leaving the Customs Union. Or variations of the above. Bringing in internal controls to change the UK labour market in favour of local employment might be given priority over bringing in Cold War-era visas, residence and work permits, schemes for seasonal workers or quotas which will ignite anger against Britain if such discriminatory measures are enacted against European citizens. This also buys time to find a solution to the problem of British citizens living under EU treaty provisions on the continent. If the UK economy does indeed decline as more and more investors refuse to place their money in Britain until the final outcome of Brexit is known, that will certainly slow down arrivals from Europe as they only came because there was a paid job waiting. Britain could also look at the level of immigration from non-European, non-English-speaking people, though many British BAME families would see that as racist.

De-demonising the European Court of Justice and describing it for what it mainly is – a commercial disputes court and an administrative tribunal interpreting EU law – would help change perceptions.

The Brexit majority exists. Thirty-seven per cent of the electorate did indisputably vote to leave the EU as they believed the lies and promises they were told. Yet as David Davis points out, 'If a democracy cannot change its mind, it ceases to be a democracy.' Might Britain change its mind? All these are decisions that would need parliamentary approval. If restoring British parliamentary sovereignty means anything, then both the Commons and the Lords should have a full role in the unfolding Brexit discussions. Indeed, if following the end of the Article 50 talks Britain did cease to be an EU member and there then followed negotiations on trade and economic status and access to the Single Market, as well as discussion on the rights of EU citizens to live and work in Britain and equivalent rights for 2 million British citizens established on the continent, these talks could last some years.

In that process, both Britain and the EU will have changed, and so the EU that Britain voted to leave after the campaign of lies in the summer of 2016 will no longer be the same institution and British business may finally have decided to campaign seriously against the potential damage that leaving Europe may cause.

In that context, parliament should come back into play. Much depends on the Labour Party. Jeremy Corbyn certainly did well in June 2017 but Labour remains uncertain on Brexit. The Labour election manifesto suggested imposing immigration controls. This is regarded in the EU as 'cherry-picking' and all EU leaders have said the four freedoms of movement (of capital, goods, services and people) are indivisible. As it stands the official Labour policy thus means leaving the Single Market. Can this line change to one promoted by pro-European London Labour MPs insisting that Labour must stay in the Single Market and Customs

Union and develop internal controls on immigration by means of a better managed labour market policy?

In the Article 50 vote in the Commons, Labour decided to be in the same lobby as Conservative and UKIP MPs. The argument advanced by Labour MPs in private and in public was that Labour must not stand against the 37 per cent of the electorate who voted for Brexit. Thus the 63 per cent of the population who did not vote for Brexit and the 48 per cent who actively voted against isolationism found that their only voice in parliament came from Scottish National MPs who have their own separatist agenda, a tiny number of Liberal Democrat MPs and a handful of brave Labour MPs who honoured their political commitment to oppose amputation from Europe and to stand with their own constituents in all the districts which voted against Brexit. Labour's trimming and U-turn support for Brexit and leaving the Single Market did not save a single seat in the general election, rather the reverse.

Labour leadership MPs from London constituencies where there was a majority against Brexit now ignored the views of their voters. When Tony Blair politely pointed out that the Labour Party had 'debilitated' itself with its incoherent contradictions since the Brexit campaign and vote he was attacked by Labour MPs on the BBC and in the press. As in the early 1980s, Labour had decided to make itself irrelevant on the issue of Europe. Labour ministers failed to join in the early stage of European construction in the 1950s, and now seven decades later the party was as lost as ever as it struggled to make sense of Europe.

When Labour's John McDonnell enthuses about the opportunities of Brexit it is not clear which particular Brexit he has in mind. British politics has been here before, as Labour tried to trip up the Conservatives in the early 1970s and early 1990s over Europe and the Tories reciprocated by always attacking the EU policy and positions of Tony Blair and Gordon Brown.

Jeremy Corbyn is close in age to Theresa May and from a time when Britain was a very different country from what it is today – as indeed was the world. Neither has a strong record on EU affairs and both left it to other politicians in their respective parties to make the running from a pro- or anti- point of view on EU questions. But they viscerally dislike each other's politics and parties and neither has a history of placing a broader national interest above party or ideological considerations. If parliament is to assert its ancient constitutional authority, the leaders of the two main parties are not, at first sight, the woman and the man to rise to the challenge.

MPs should assert the right to vote on whatever is being negotiated in the nation's name by ministers who have long been committed to visceral hostility to Europe. While there needs to be a decent interval between the June 2016 plebiscite and any future referendum or indeed election sometime in the 2020s, when the full impact of Brexit can be measured, which is not the case today, it surely cannot be right that the British people are denied a voice and a vote on the country's twenty-first-century future as part of Europe.

In the next decade, Brexit would have to have been seen beyond any doubt to have made or to be making Britain poorer, with a visible loss of inward investment and money-making for sectors like finance, rising unemployment, a reduction in the rights of British citizens across a range of issues – residence in Europe, access to funding – new tensions in Northern Ireland before there is a big enough shift in public opinion to warrant parliament taking back control of the nation's destiny from the financiers, off-shore media magnates and xenophobes who won the vote in the summer of 2016.

The SNP obsession with shattering the union of the British Isles while claiming to support the union of European nations leaves it in a weak place, with no purchase on public opinion on the Brexit question elsewhere in the United Kingdom. The Liberal Democrats were the cutting edge of pro-European politics up to 2010. The decision to become bag-carriers for pro-austerity Tory ministers and allow David Cameron to proceed with his plebiscite for internal Tory party political reasons has sent the party back to where the Liberal Party was between 1951 and the 1980s – a great history but no MPs. Above all, it will be the internal workings of the Conservative Party in the first years of Brexit Britain that will decide whether isolation from Europe becomes permanent or whether, as with the US after 1920, the Tory love-in with anti-Europeanism dies away.

The idea that the referendum was the final, only, definitive decision on Britain's relationship with Europe makes little sense. It was an advisory referendum and, as has been noted, had none of the normal qualifications on a major national constitutional decision, such as requiring a minimum threshold for participation, requiring a clear majority or permitting all citizens to vote.

Calling for a second referendum was premature. We simply do not know what will be on offer between today and the arrival of the new European Commission and Parliament in 2019 or between then and the British general election in 2022. Europe does need reform, does need new leadership, does need to refocus on its nation states cooperating and integrating but not being subsumed into a single new federal state. So before long the European Union that Britain voted to leave in 2016 may no longer exist. The chances of a hard or train-crash Brexit cannot be excluded. Much depends on the inner workings of Prime Minister Theresa May's mind. How fanatical is she in her hostility to Europe? Is she too close to her party activists, many of whom approve of much of what UKIP and Nigel Farage say?

Can she stand back and look at the wider national interest? Can she find time for reflection or must Brexit happen in a rush? Does Britain have to spend years isolated from Europe before deciding that partnership and cooperation and a common rule book may be preferable. Are there any politicians younger than the sexagenarian Mrs May and Mr Corbyn who can offer a perspective for the future? Rupert

Murdoch and the editor of the *Daily Mail* are not immortal. Bigger, faster changes have happened in British politics.

Can Britain limit Brexit to a political Brexit – leaving the EU treaties but coming to its own version of a Swiss or Norwegian or EEA relationship with the EU? Once UKIP is dead – when it no longer has MEPs or offices and staff paid for by taxpayers via the European Parliament – can the Conservative Party quietly ditch its UKIP fellow-travellers and centre itself as the party of traditional economic common sense and bottom?

At this point one leaves what has happened and what is happening and enters into what will or may happen. I predicted in January 2015 that Brexit would happen. I now believe that my country will not allow an isolationist ideology to triumph completely and Britain will stay in Europe. For nearly two decades in parliament I had good personal relations with David Davis, the Brexit minister. It is worth repeating his 2012 declaration that 'If a democracy cannot change its mind, it ceases to be a democracy.' Sadly, David Davis today does not believe that British democracy may be able to change its mind about a plebiscite won on the basis of lies after a 20-year political project of mendacity orchestrated by a rich and powerful if shadowy elite and using new populist and xenophobic, sometimes openly racist, political groupings.

In January 2015 when I published my book asserting Brexit would happen I was confident I was right even if no one would listen. Today I remain no less confident that once confronted with the truth about what full amputation from Europe entails, the British people will draw back and a majority of MPs will decide that losing all the rights we have gained as British Europeans is not how they see their nation's twenty-first-century future. My generation took us into Europe, but did not know how to tell the underlying truths about Europe that Winston Churchill and Margaret Thatcher seized intuitively. Lies about Europe penetrated every corner of Britain before truth could get its trainers on.

If we base the future of our great nation on lies then that future will be sad and bad. So my appeal is to the young of Britain. Sir Henry Tizard, the postwar chief scientific adviser to the government, declared in 1947: 'We are a *great nation*, but if we continue to behave like a Great Power we shall soon cease to be a *great nation*.' Britain, my country that I love dearly, is a great nation. If we cut ourselves out of Europe we will become small, petty, no longer a leader and shaper of our part of the world – Europe. We are better than that. The full and complete Brexit desired by the liars who won their populist plebiscite shortly after the seventieth anniversary of my father's generation fighting, being wounded, dying to liberate our Europe from the nationalist-populist, post-truth leaders who ran continental Europe in the 1920s and 1930s will not happen.

'Never, never, never give in', said Churchill. Many will appease and accommodate themselves to the Brexit Liars. But I am confident the British people will not. To adapt and add to the words of Albert Camus: 'Each generation doubtless feels called upon to reform his or her country. Mine knows that it will not reform Britain, but its task is perhaps even greater. It consists in preventing Britain from destroying itself by leaving Europe and the European Union.'

INDEX

Acton, Lord 277
Adams, Gerry 219
ageing population 242
Agency Workers
    Directive 32, 138
Ahern, Bertie 222
AI (Artificial
    Intelligence) 265
Albion perfide 95
Alternative für
    Deutschland 62
American Chamber of
    Commerce, UK 58
Andorra 172
Anglosphere 52
anti-Europeanism
    fashionable 104
    in the City 109
    in London salons 145
    political project 109
anti-Jewish attacks after
    Brexit 43
Apple 58, 223
Arendt, Hannah 2
Arrest Warrant,
    European 31
Article 50, 3, 8 ff, 21
Ashcroft, Lord
    Michael 113
Ashton, Lady Catherine
    (Cathy) 28
Aslund, Ånders 267

Baggini, Julian 45
Bailey, Rich 154
Barnier, Michel 19, 26,
    70, 78, 222
    explain negotiating
    priorities 83 ff
Barra, Mary 164
Barroso, José Manuel
    257, 275
BBC
    Eurosceptic
    presenters 148
    turns Nigel Farage
    into national
    hero 146–55
    World Service 244
Bean, Kevin 220
Beckett, Andy 115
Benn, Tony 93
Bennett, Catherine 154
Bertelsmann
    Foundation 112
Bevin, Ernest 224
bien-pensant
    establishment 103
'Big Bang' 158
Blair, Tony 102, 135,
    222, 262
Boleat, Mark 162
Booker, Christopher 15
Border EU–UK in
    Ireland 216 ff

Brazil 172
Brecht, Bertolt 280
Bretton Woods 157
Brexit, Single
    Market 15, 25
    Customs Union,
    4, 8, 26
    expats 30
    generation 98
    geo-political, 30
*Brexit: How Britain
    Will Leave Europe*
    (published
    2015) 88, 94
British Airways 10
British Bankers
    Association
    108, 161
British Chambers of
    Commerce (BCC)
    102, 199
British Election
    Survey 115
British Medical
    Association 36
British National Party
    (BNP) 99, 112
Brown, Gordon 103,
    131, 207, 258
Browne, Anthony 161
Bruegel think-tank 203
Butler, Robin (Lord) 57

Buy American legislation 182
by-elections 142

Calenda, Carlo 73
Cameron, David 92, 117, 178, 231, 238, 246
  alliance with anti-Jewish politicians, Poland 164
  campaigns against Jean-Claude Juncker 120
  liberal views 68
  Remain campaign 118 ff
Camus, Albert 291
Canada 167
Canada–EU Trade Agreement (CETA) 82, 168
Cash, William (Bill) 94
Centre for Economic and Business Research (CEBR) 50
Centre for European Reform 133, 152
Chassny Anne-Sylvaine 71
cheese, EU duties on 26
Churchill, Winston, 2
  'I am a European' speech 66
  'United States of Europe' speech 226
City (of London) 81, 108, 158
civil service, new Brexit hires 57
Clark, Greg 164
Clegg, Nick 143, 237
Clinton, Bill 215
Common Agricultural Policy 33, 201, 208
Commonwealth 223
Community Security Trust 43
Common Travel Area 175, 217
compositional amenities 195
Confederation of British Industry (CBI) 102
Congress, US 18
Conservative Party 6, 20, 64, 74, 82, 100, 120, 163, 181, 291

Constitutional Convention 157
constitutional treaty 86
Cooper, Andrew 91
Corbyn, Jeremy 133
  in referendum campaign 134–7
council houses 111
Council of Europe 48, 55
Cox, Jo 42
Craig, Oliver 92
Customs Union 19, 218 ff
Czech Republic 242

Daily Express 20, 90, 116
Daily Mail 20, 60, 116, 136, 194
Daily Telegraph 189, 193
Darling, Alistair 131
Davis, David 11, 12, 78, 161, 209, 292
Defoe, Daniel 194
de Gaulle, General 93
Deliveroo 121
Delors, Jacques 102
Democratic Unionist Party 215
Deutsche Welle 245
Dijsselbloem, Jeroen 75
Dixon, Hugo 282
Djankov, Simeon 267
Donne, John 14
Donoughue, Bernard 101
Dorling, Danny 95
Duncan Smith, Iain 39, 77, 94, 117
Dunt, Ian 96
Dyson, Sir James 153

Easyjet 37, 83
Eden, Anthony 231
EIOPA (European Insurance and Occupational Pensions Authority) 34
Electoral Reform Society 127
Electronic System for Travel Administration (ESTA) 201
Elliot, Matthew 119
Emerson, Michael 186
empadronados 30

English mindset 95
English, use of in EU Institutions 271
Equality and Human Rights Commission 44
Erasmus 268
Euratom (European Atomic Energy Community) 34
Euro, future of 250 ff
Euro-Atlantic Project 2
European agencies 39
European Banking Authority 40
European Central Bank 257
European Civil Aviation Safety Agency 40
European Coal and Steel Community 93, 188, 230
European Council of Foreign Relations 98
European Court of Human Rights (ECtHR) 32, 55, 66
European Court of Justice (ECJ) 26, 66 ff, 69
European Defence Community 97
European Economic Area (EEA) 211
European External Action Service (EEAS) 275
European Free Trade Association (EFTA)
European Medicines Agency 40
European Parliament 236 ff, 261
  2004 election 137
European People's Party (EPP) 261
European Securities and Markets Authority (ESMA) 35
European Trade Union Confederation 265
European Works Councils 32, 210 ff
Europol 31
Eurozone 146

Falklands 172
Fallon, Michael 80
Farage, Nigel 100–101,
    121–22, 126, 127, 155
    and BBC 146–55
    and xenophobia 43
farming 129
fascism 225
fellow travellers 170
Field, Frank 142
Fischer, Joschka 253
Fitch 35
flag, European 13
Fletcher, Martin 151
Foot, Michael 93
Fox, Liam 94
*Frankfurter Allgemeine
    Zeitung* 73
Fraser, Giles 103
Freedland, Jonathan 4
Free Democratic Party 62
free trade, agriculture 82
Front National 31
Führerprinzip 53
Fukuyama, Francis 96

Gaber, Ivor 153
Gabriel, Sigmar 208
Gaitskell, Hugh 93
Garton Ash, Timothy 240
General Motors 164
Geneva 172
Germanophobia 99, 101
German Social Democrats
    208, 262
Germany 247
gerrymandering, Tory 118
Gershwin brothers, 279
Ghose, Katie 127
Ghosen, Carlos 164
Gibbon, Gary 92
Gibraltar, 5, 12, 37, 79, 85
    threat of war over 78 ff
Gill, A.A. 130
Giscard d'Estaing, Valéry
    205, 261
Gimson, Andrew 92
Gladstone, William 229
Goldman Sachs 133
Goldsmith, Oliver 139
Good Friday agreement 214,
    219, 222

Goodhart, David 195
Goldman Sachs 133
Goldsmith, Oliver 139
Gove, Michael 117
Gozi, Sandro 235, 242
Grainger, Andrew 177
Grant, Charles 133, 151
Grayling, Chris 218
Greece 244, 252 ff
Greenspan, Alan 259
Griffin, Nick 99
Guardian 103

Hague, William 99, 100,
    104, 119, 136
Hall, Tony (Lord) 152
Hammond, Philip 163
Hannan, Daniel 21, 33,
    105, 117
Hassan, King of
    Morocco 244
hate crimes after Brexit
    5, 42 ff
Hayek, Friedrich 277 ff
Healey, Denis 93, 117
Healey, John 93
Heath, Allister 21
Heseltine, Michael 132
Hilton, Steve 68
Hitachi 133
Hogan, Phil 221
Hollande, François 29, 69
Honda 81
Hong Kong 157
Howard, Michael 79, 113
Humphries, John 13

identitarianism 225
identity cards 197
immigration controls 198
India, 36
    tariff on Scotch
    whisky, 25
International Labour
    Organization 229
Ireland, impact of
    Brexit 85
Irish citizens in UK 190
Irish Republican Army 208
Isaac, Davis 44
Islamists, Morocco 245
Italy 241

Japan
    reaction to Brexit 57
Japanese firms in UK 6
Jarvis, Dan 142
Javid, Sajid 120
Jenkin, Bernard 94
Jenkins, Simon 103
Joffé, Joseph 290
Johnson, Boris 55, 61,
    83, 113
    compares EU to
    Nazis 123
Johnson, Alan 134, 137
Jones, Owen 103
Joseph Rowntree
    Foundation 111
Jospin, Lionel 262
Jóźwik, Arkadius 44
Juncker, Jean-Claude
    69, 70, 71, 74,
    226–27, 255,

Kaczyński, Jarosław 53, 271
Kaletsky, Anatole 266
Kant, Immanuel 96
Katwala, Sunder 90
Kaufman, Eric 114
Kennedy, Charles 133, 150
Kenny, Enda 7, 73
KernEuropa 204
Kettle, Martin 143
Khan, Sadiq 31, 165, 169
King, Mervyn (Lord) 227
Kinnock, Neil 132
kite-mark 180
Kołakowski, Leszek 263
Kosovo undermines EU
    foreign policy 137, 257
Kundnani, Hans 263

Labour MPs
    ordered to vote with
    Tory-UKIP MPs on
    Brexit 142
Labour Party 3, 82, 93, 149
Lafitte, Jacques 268
Lamont, Norman 94,
    100, 117
Lamy, Pascal 71
Lanchester, John 44
Landau, Jean-Pierre 246
Langrish, Jason 168

Laughland, John
Lawson, Nigel 100, 117
Leach, Rodney 102
Leadsom, Andrea 122, 125, 126, 152
League of Nations 96
Leave campaign 117 ff
  Leave lies 122 ff
  Leave vote 101 ff
Le Monde 239
Leonard, Mark 98
Leparmentier, Arnaud 255
Liberal Democrats 82, 98, 111, 143, 150, 290–1
Libya 275
Lichtenstein 204, 284
Low, Adrian 115

Maastricht Treaty 86, 188, 281
Maclay, Michael 205
Macmillan, Harold 68
Macron, Emmanuel 28, 251
mad cow disease 168
Major, John 102, 130
Malmström, Cecilia 169
Mandelson, Peter 167
Marchais, Georges 196
Markwalder, Christa 263, 283
Marshall Plan 2
Mason, Paul 103
May, Theresa
  anti-immigrant hostility 233, 195
  arrives in Downing Street 92
  'citizen of nowhere' jibe 65
  Lancaster House speech, January 2017 77
  pro-EU speech April 2016 120
  pro-EU speech May 2016 64
  referendum campaign 122
  'Shop an Immigrant' vans 63
McDonnell, John 289
McKinsey Global Institute 140
Medef 181

Menon Anand 91
Merkel, Angela 3, 69, 247
Messina conference 231
Michel, Charles 73
Miliband, Ed 136
Miller, Gina 43
Milošević, Slobodan 257
Mitterrand, François 86, 261
Monnet, Jean 245
Moody's 35
Mordaunt, Penny 122
Morgan Stanley 161
Moscovici, Pierre 61, 206 ff, 235 ff
Mosey, Roger 155
Muktupāvela, Laima 200
Multispeed Europe 204 ff
Murdoch, Rupert 101
Muslims, 5, 31, 137

National Health Service (NHS) 196
National Institute of Economic and Social Research (NIESR) 163, 171
naturalisation 189
Naughtie, Jim 89
'Nazi European Union' 123
New Statesman 134
Niblett, Robin 208
Nissan 81, 164, 184
Nixon, Simon 109
North Atlantic Free Trade Area (NAFTA) 3
North, Lord 1
Northern Ireland, six counties of, *see* Ireland
Northern Ireland Assembly 215
Norway 81, 252, 284
Nuttall, Paul 142

Obama, Barack 242
Office of National Statistics (ONS) 22
oligarch 159
Open Europe 102
Orbán, Viktor 271
Osborne, George 124
Owen, David 205

Palaiologos, Yannis 253
Pangalos, Theo 254
Papandreou, George 254 ff
passports, Single Market 9
Patel, Priti 113
Paxton, Robert O 225
peace process, Northern Ireland 212 ff
Pels, Dick 234
Persson, Goran 262
Piris Jean-Claude, 7
Poles,
  hate crime against 44 ff
  in UK since 1945 189
Politico 105
Portes, Jonathan 171
Posted Workers Directive 32
Powell, Enoch 99, 137
Powell, Jonathan 213
Pret A Manger 30, 121
Pryce, Vicky 254, 256
Putin, Vladmir 3

Quebec 113, 224

Radio France International 245
Rasmussen, Lars Løkke, 73
Rechtsgemeinschaft 13
Redwood, John 170
Reenan van, John 124
Rees-Mogg, Jacob 200
referendum
  Danish 281
  Hungarian 54, 107
  Scottish 107
  Swedish 285
  Welsh 107
Referendum Party 95
Remain campaign, 118 ff, 129–31
  complacency 105
Renzi, Matteo 235
residence rights in UK, 9, 11
Resolution Foundation 110
road haulage industry, UK 27
Road to Serfdom 277
Rogers, Sir Ivan 49
Rolet, Xavier 19
Rome, Treaty of 202, 204
Ross, Wilbur 51

Royal Institute for
    International
    Affairs, 208
Rudd, Amber 68
Russia Today 240
Ryanair, 37, 83
Roycroft-Davis, Chris 20

Saoradh (Liberation) 215
Sapin, Michel 74
Sarkozy, Nicolas 29
Sarson, Tim 177
Schmid, Thomas 61, 205
Schmidt, Helmut 261
Schröder, Gerhard 262
Schulz, Martin 209
Scotland 223 ff
Scottish Nationalist Party
    (SNP) 224, 290
Senate, European 238
Shipman, Tim 92
Shore, Peter 93
Sinn Féin 215, 219
Siglitz, Joseph 103
Singapore 157
Single European Sky 38
Smith, Ian 21
Smith, Joan 43
Smoot-Hawley tariffs 234
Social Europe 86, 102
Socrates 65
Spain 172
Starmer, Sir Keir 144
Stuart, Gisella 117
Sturgeon, Nicola 224
Süddeutsche Zeitung 67

Summers, Larry 140
Sun, The 115, 136
super-state 207
Swiss People's Party 50
Switzerland 49, 81
Syriza 168

tariffs 184
Taxpayers Alliance 119
Tawney, R.H. 48
Tea Party 100
Tennyson, Alfred Lord 279
Thatcher, Margaret 6, 100,
    102, 193, 251
Tizard, Sir Henry 293
Toffler, Alvin 246
Toyota 81, 185
trade 233
trade unions, reinvention
    of 264 ff
Transatlantic Trade and
    Investment Partnership
    (TTIP) 82, 178, 181
Trichet, Jean-Claude
    257, 259
Trump, Donald 1, 3, 7, 17,
    18, 31, 100
Turkey 206, 238, 244
Tusk, Donald 259
Tyrie, Andrew 169

Uber 121
Unified Patent Court 41
United Kingdom
    Independence Party
    (UKIP) 9, 16, 99, 102

and Leave campaign 121
UK citizens in
    Europe 188 ff
UK Investment
    Association 162
universities 33, 229
Uruguay Round 171

Valls, Manuel 70
Varoufakis, Yanis 103
Verhofstadt, Guy 74
Véron, Nicolas 160
Versailles, Treaty of 96
Villeroy de Galhau,
    François 72
votes for
    16–17-year-olds 118

wages, decline of in decade
    before Brexit 110
Warner, Jeremy 165
warplanes 244
Watson, Tom 134
Wheeler, Stuart 102
Wilders, Geert 135
Wilson, Harold 163
Windrush 189
Wolf, Martin 228
World Today 208
Working Time
    Directive 32
World Trade Organization
    (WTO) 14, 15, 171 ff

xenophobia 192